PAULA M. SINGER AND LAURA L. FRANCISCO

Developing a Compensation Plan for Your Library

SECOND EDITION

American Library Association

Chicago   2009

Paula M. Singer is the president and principal consultant of The Singer Group, Inc., a management-consulting firm she founded in 1983. She provides compensation consulting, strategic planning and alignment, organization design and development, performance management, leadership development, and other services to clients in the public, private, and nonprofit sectors. Libraries throughout the country have engaged The Singer Group to conduct a variety of studies and projects. She is the author of the first edition of this book and coauthor of *Winning with Library Leadership: Enhancing Services through Connection, Contribution, and Collaboration* (with Christi Olson) and *Human Resources for Results* (with Jeanne Goodrich), all published by the American Library Association. Paula is also a frequent speaker at ALA, PLA, and state library association conferences and events.

Laura L. Francisco is a senior consultant with The Singer Group, Inc. For nearly fifteen years, she has provided compensation, classification, performance management, and other consulting services to clients in the public, private, and nonprofit sectors. She has consulted with many library systems across the country to develop and implement compensation and classification systems designed to meet the particular needs of the library system. Francisco is a member of the American Library Association and has been certified as a Professional in Human Resources by the Society for Human Resource Management.

Library of Congress Cataloging-in-Publication Data
Singer, Paula M.
    Developing a compensation plan for your library / Paula M. Singer and Laura L. Francisco.
— 2nd ed.
        p.   cm.
    Includes bibliographical references and index.
    ISBN 978-0-8389-0985-0 (alk. paper)
    1. Library employees—Salaries, etc.—United States. 2. Library employees—Job
descriptions—United States. 3. Job evaluation—United States. 4. Job analysis.
    I. Francisco, Laura L. II. Title.
    Z682.3.S53 2009
    023'.9—dc22   2008045378

ISBN-13: 978-0-8389-0985-0

Printed in the United States of America

13 12 11 10 09   5 4 3 2 1

Contents

WEB   **Additional content can be found on the book's website, at www.ala.org/editions/extras/singer09850.**

Figures

Worksheets

WEB

Interactive worksheets can be downloaded from the book's website, at www.ala.org/editions/extras/singer09850.

Acknowledgments

We want to thank The Singer Group's library system clients, especially those in Maryland, where we first began working with libraries. In particular, our gratitude goes to Linda Mielke, Muffie Smith, and Gail Griffith of Carroll County (Maryland) Public Library, for their time, insights, and support.

A book is never a one-person effort. We continue to learn a great deal about libraries through working with Linda Saferite and Shauna McConnell of Tulsa City–County Library; Ginnie Cooper and Eric Coard of DCPL; Joan Airoldi of Whatcom County Public Library; Donna Lauffer and her team at Johnson County Library; Skip Auld in Durham; Arevik Dornan in Sacramento; John McGinty, who directs the Loyola Notre Dame Library; Jim Fish at Baltimore County Public Library (Paula's public library); and many, many others. Many examples in this book were taken from work done with the library systems they direct.

There are four others without whose contributions this book would not have been possible: my coauthor, colleague, and friend, Laura Francisco; Lorraine Kituri, who is always there to add value and provide support; pal and writing buddy Christi Olson; and most of all my husband, Dr. Michael Pearlman, who was supportive of my writing this book even when it took time away from him and added chores to his list. Thank you all.

—PMS

I am lucky to have such insightful and enthusiastic library clients and am particularly thankful for the always-fantastic help and support of Lorraine Kituri. Most important, I am thankful a thousand times per day for my beautiful family—my husband, Jody, and my son, Steven, both of whom are always good for a group hug when necessary.

—LLF

Introduction

Libraries that may not have the human and financial resources to commit to strategic planning or organizational development projects will fight for the resources to examine and update their compensation and pay plans. They realize that they *can't afford* not to attend to what they pay their staff, especially in a tightening economy where every dollar of funding received must be used as wisely as possible to recruit and retain qualified and productive employees.

Although pay is not the only factor that has an impact on the recruitment, motivation, and retention of staff, it is certainly an important one because turnover is very costly. In addition, because the library environment of today is one marked by competition and customer service, the members of your workforce can make or break your system's circulation and reputation. Libraries need to have pay policies that allow them to recruit and retain high-quality, motivated staff at every level and to ensure that employees are paid fairly and equitably. The challenge is to design an affordable, realistic compensation strategy that is appropriate for your culture, objectives, and strategy while being both internally equitable and competitive with the external market.

In our current economy, Wal-Mart and McDonald's are hiring entry-level staff at pay rates that exceed minimum wage and sometimes include benefits, incentives, profit sharing, or other bonus opportunities. Employees who may have previously had some loyalty to your library are leaving to work at another employer—perhaps the local public school system or county government—for 25 or 50 cents more per hour. For some positions a library's competition for hiring qualified staff does not come simply from the public or academic library in the next county. The competition for attracting new staff and keeping current staff expands to include other employers who, although they may not be in the same business, may offer a compensation package that influences people to change jobs or indeed careers.

PURPOSE OF THIS BOOK

A clear need remains for increased attention to compensation planning and administration in libraries. However, given the complexity and resource-intensive nature of compensation studies and structure design, how can libraries move forward in this arena without a significant infusion of budgetary resources for external consultants?

Some libraries have successfully established an internal compensation planning team rather than contracting out the complete project to consultants. The consultant's role has been to help these teams design a compensation process that best fits the organization, its resources, and its future. Based on personal experiences with these teams and their successes, *Developing a Compensation Plan for Your Library* was created to help libraries develop and support an internal team in the process of designing a compensation plan that

> supports the library's strategic and other long-range plans
>
> reflects the compensation philosophy of the library system
>
> is flexible and meets the needs of the library

This book is written to meet the following four goals:

1. Provide library staff with an overview of the planning steps necessary before a compensation study begins.

2. Educate the library's staff overseeing the work of consultants about the compensation process and help them maximize the benefit of this relationship, *or* provide libraries with tools to undertake the design of a compensation program if they choose to do it themselves.

3. Identify issues pertaining to compensation and link them to broader organizational and strategic issues.

4. Provide an overview of current issues in compensation and reward systems including a discussion of nonmonetary strategies and employee retention.

WHAT'S IN THIS BOOK FOR YOU?

You might be wondering, what is a compensation system? What does this have to do with me? We don't have a compensation plan—do we? You might think you don't have a compensation system, but if you are paying employees, you do. Every library system needs to determine what employees should be paid, and each system must decide how that payment decision will be made. It must also know what it can afford to pay and how to allocate its salary budget in a way that will effectively move the system toward meeting its goals.

A compensation program is a tool—that's all. It is a business tool that should be designed to help your library meet its goals and objectives. Although the cost of labor is critical to any organization, it is especially important in libraries where salaries and benefits are the largest expense.

Some say, "Money doesn't matter," especially in mission-driven organizations such as libraries and other service or nonprofit organizations. Others say, "We're in it for the public good," or "It's our contribution to society." Many say these should be the mantras of library personnel. However, now more than ever, library personnel do not work only for the love of the job: they need to pay bills and buy gas and groceries, too. Pay has a direct bearing on the standard of living enjoyed by most employees as well as on the status and recognition they are able to gain. It also serves as a measure of their relative worth in comparison with other employees. If there is an objective system for determining the value of each person's job and for making each person aware of this determination, employees are less likely to perceive themselves as being victims of inequity.

In recent years it has become fashionable among some theorists to minimize the importance of pay in comparison with other motivators. Although it is possible that pay does fail to motivate employees in some organizations to the extent that it should, this failure is most likely due to the way in which compensation plans are developed or administered rather than to employees' disinterest in money. The implementation of thoughtful and well-designed compensation programs can contribute effectively to meeting the objectives of your library system.

Compensation management plays a key role in human resources development within any organization. It has an impact on all facets of human resources:

Recruitment—Rates of pay can impede or aid recruitment, and the supply of applicants can affect wage rates.

Selection—Rates of pay can affect the degree of selectivity, and selection standards affect the rate of pay required.

Training and development—The rate of pay can motivate training efforts, and training and development can lead to higher rates of pay.

Performance evaluation—Performance evaluation can be a factor determining rates of pay, and wage rates can bias evaluation of performance.

Employee/labor relations—Employee perceptions of unfair pay administration practices or pay rates at an extreme variance with the market may contribute to employee-relations issues or encourage employees to pursue third-party representation (unionization).

Furthermore, the importance of paying attention to creating or updating your compensation program at this time is reinforced by national trends that are placing greater importance on

- high-performance workplace initiatives
- competitive employment practices
- strategic employee retention
- time off, flextime, telecommuting, and work and family relations
- new methods for training and development

WHAT'S NEW IN THIS EDITION?

If you read the first edition of this book, you might be asking, What could possibly be new in this area? The short answer is—*a lot!* Much has been added recounting the real-life experiences of library systems nationwide in conducting compensation studies. In the past several years, some of our own methods and preferences have changed, and we have included descriptions of these new approaches. Finally, new research has been added throughout. The new and updated topics include

- executive compensation
- pay equity
- salary compression
- educating employee committees
- updated trends in compensation and human resources
- updated sections on job evaluation and employee communications
- many new or updated forms and examples

WHO SHOULD READ THIS BOOK?

Developing a Compensation Plan for Your Library is a handbook for library professionals, staff members, and human resources personnel. It is also a resource for members of compensation review teams working in public, academic, and special libraries as well as in the nonprofit sector. Students learning about human resources and human resources consultants will find this book useful as well.

HOW TO USE THIS BOOK

This book will tell you how to conduct a salary survey, analyze the data, and use it to design a pay plan that fits your culture. It will lay out the steps of the process and show you how to analyze jobs, write job descriptions, and plan for communications. Figures and worksheets provide spreadsheets, letters, job descriptions, and PowerPoint presentations that you can adapt for your use (see www.ala.org/editions/extras/singer09850). Chapter 1 helps you think through your compensation program objectives and goals. It provides worksheets to help you get started with your compensation study. Chapter 2 focuses on the commitment you will need to obtain from the library director, board of trustees, employees, your staff association or labor union (if any), and elected or appointed officials. This chapter will help you plan your strategy for obtaining commitment from various stakeholders and provides a sample employee communications plan and examples of employee committee/task force charters. In this chapter you begin to focus on your own compensation program objectives.

Chapter 3 presents important issues regarding the library's compensation philosophy and pay policy for you to think through in the context of your library system. Your compensation philosophy will ultimately guide the many decisions you make as you conduct the study.

In chapters 4 and 5 you will learn how to obtain information about the work performed and accomplished by library system employees and how to write job descriptions using the data you collect. Job descriptions will help you identify the essential functions of each job and then use this information to assess the external value of each position.

Chapter 6 lays the groundwork for deciding whether to conduct an in-depth study of the internal equity of the library's position. If you choose this route, the chapter provides a detailed process for designing and applying a point factor plan.

Regardless of any other choices about how a hierarchical ordering of positions is made, we strongly recommend that you learn of the wage rates offered by those in your labor market. You can obtain salary and other data by conducting a custom survey or by purchasing published salary data. Procedures for doing so, along with a sample custom survey and tools for analysis, can be found in chapter 7.

Chapter 8 focuses on executive compensation, which may need to be approached differently than compensation for the organization as a whole. Information is provided to help you develop a separate compensation philosophy for the library's executive as well as tips on how best to collect data for this position.

Chapter 9 focuses on designing the salary structure. Putting together the information from the internal analysis and the external market review, you can custom-design a salary structure for your library.

Chapter 10 takes you away from "doing" to implementing and contains tips for "selling," communicating, and administering your system's new compensation plan. The salary administration section includes information on budgeting; tips on how to move employees through their salary ranges; best practices when facing and solving issues pertaining to salary compression; and policies for promotions, demotions, and acting-capacity pay. Finally, chapter 11 highlights trends in compensation and performance management.

This book is partly about human resources strategy, partly about compensation philosophy, and partly "how to." It offers something for those who like to plan cautiously as well as for those who want to jump right in. You can read the chapters that focus on your need—or better yet, read those that are the *opposite* of what you are inclined to read, and broaden your perspective.

The design and implementation of compensation and pay plans are as much art as science. Both will be referred to in this book. Although an effort was made to distinguish between the two, sometimes the lines blur and the distinction is difficult.

The examples offered are just that—examples. What works for one library may—or may not—work for yours. Custom-fit your review team and the project process to your culture, organizational structure, short- and long-term plans, and labor market. Also consider the readiness of your system to make changes as well as the budget available to support them. For example, if your library is part of a municipal or county system, or if your employees are members of a labor union or association, you may be constrained in certain areas or you may need to add steps or be more creative. The important thing to keep in mind is that the pay plans you develop must fit *your* library system.

one | Compensation Plan Objectives

Although you have your own goals for conducting a compensation study (which you can explore in this chapter), the bottom-line objectives of any compensation program are to support meeting the library's strategic objectives and to fit the program within the library's organizational structure. Compensation systems are not ends in themselves; they are a means to an end.

Compensation plans should be designed to reward the employee behaviors that the library system communicates to staff, trains them on, and promotes. For example, a library that encourages employees to return to school for a bachelor's or an MLS degree will have some pay policies and practices different from those of an academic library that mainly recruits candidates already holding an MLS degree. Similarly, a system that wants to reward employee longevity will have a different compensation plan than a system that places a high premium on goal achievement. Because of local and regional competition from other employers, a library system may have to focus far more heavily on market pay than on the internal hierarchy of positions. These conditions, too, will create a unique compensation plan. Finally, libraries that are planning to downsize, reorganize to use MLS positions only at the management level, or open branches in many new communities will have different goals and consequently different compensation plans.

YOUR COMPENSATION PROGRAM

Although you have some specific expectations for your compensation program, you also need to make some general assumptions. For example, your program should

- effectively support the attraction, motivation, and retention of the number and kinds of employees you need
- be externally competitive
- gain employee acceptance
- be seen as equitable and fair by employees, governing and funding authorities, and taxpayers/customers
- be in compliance with federal, state, and local laws
- play a positive role in motivating employees to perform to the best of their abilities
- provide employees with the opportunities to achieve reasonable aspirations within the framework of impartiality and equity
- provide employees with an incentive to improve their skills and abilities
- be flexible enough for future revision in response to changing internal and external factors

be accepted by and have the support of the library's director and its board of trustees

be reasonable and proportionate to the resources of the library and to the priority demands of other human resource functions in terms of its nature, scope, and cost

be consistent with the library's mission, culture, and budget

Although these expectations are fairly self-explanatory, the last one suggests that the compensation program cannot be "one size fits all." Even though the focus of this book is libraries, the compensation program that is developed must fit your system. One compensation plan does not fit all libraries. In fact, one compensation plan rarely fits two libraries! The compensation plan at your library should fit your

strategic and tactical plans

type of business (public, academic, or special library; central versus regional versus branch library)

demographics—both customers and employees

Regarding your strategies, you will need to think about the library's

Mission—What is your purpose? Why do you exist?

Culture—What are your beliefs, norms, values, and management style? How do employees work together?

External environment—What is your labor market; pool of qualified candidates; competition with other libraries, sellers of print and nonprint media, and the Internet; relationship with city/county/university; relationship with other funding sources?

Legal environment—What are your union agreements, human resources policies, and related legislation and legal mandates?

COMPENSATION AND THE HUMAN RESOURCES SYSTEM

Compensation is one component of your human resources system, which also includes recruitment, performance management systems, training and development, employee relations, and so forth. Each of these facets of human resources management/development has an impact on the others, and together they make up the whole. The same is true of compensation. Your library's compensation plan is part of a total compensation *system*, which includes both direct (pay) and indirect compensation (benefits and other intrinsic rewards). Figure 1.1 shows examples of items included in both of these categories.

TOTAL COMPENSATION

The components of a pay system go beyond the two major categories of direct and indirect compensation, or, simply, the financial aspects. That is, total compensation includes a *total rewards* strategy:

Compensation—wages and bonuses

Benefits—paid time off and insurance

Figure 1.1
Components of Direct and Indirect Compensation

Direct Compensation

Base pay

Differential pay (evenings, weekends, holidays)

Short- and long-term incentive pay

Supplemental (i.e., bilingual skills, commercial driver's license)

Pay-for-performance

Cash recognition, bonuses, and achievement awards

Longevity increments

Out-of-class or temporary pay

Indirect Compensation

Legally required benefits

■ Worker's compensation

■ Social Security

■ Unemployment insurance

Other benefits

■ Health insurance (including dental, vision, and prescription coverage)

■ Short- and long-term disability insurance

■ Deferred pay

■ Pension and other retirement plans

■ Paid time off (holidays and sick, vacation, family, and personal leave)

■ Tuition reimbursement

■ Unpaid leave

■ Noncash recognition and achievement awards

Perquisites, including free parking, transit passes, discounts on materials, fitness club dues

Life insurance

Long-term care insurance

Accidental death and dismemberment insurance

■ Personal/career development (conference fees, ALA membership dues, etc.)

Social interaction—friendly workplace

Status/recognition—respect and prominence due to work

Task variety—opportunities to experience different assignments

Workload—right amount of work

Work importance—society's value of work

Authority/control/autonomy—ability to influence others and control destiny

Advancement—opportunities to get ahead

Feedback—constructive help for development

Work conditions—hazard-free workplaces and pleasant work environment

Development opportunities—formal and informal training to learn new knowledge/skills/abilities[1]

The focus of this book is primarily on *direct* compensation: how employees are paid in relation to one another and in relation to the market. However, consideration of a total rewards strategy is consistent with some of the current trends in compensation in both the private and public sectors. (Trends, alternative compensation strategies, recruitment and retention strategies, and some ideas on total compensation are in chapter 11.) These trends include

moving from a culture that values internal equity and longevity to one that focuses on performance (individual or team) and paying in accordance with the relevant market organizationally shifting from bureaucratic, hierarchical, "command and control" structures to those that value empowerment, reduced management layers, and a broadening of job scope

Many libraries are seeing a need for reward systems that support these trends. Some libraries are not yet ready to implement new pay programs such as incentives or pay-for-performance because "the change is too big," "there are too many changes right now," "the board of trustees will not accept it," "it will never work," "we have to do what our county/city does or they won't fund us," or "employees won't accept it." Even if you agree with those reasons, keep an open mind and think of some of these new ways of conceiving compensation as something you might want to plan for in the future.

YOUR REASONS FOR UNDERTAKING A COMPENSATION STUDY

If you are reading this book, you are probably contemplating updating your pay plan and conducting a compensation study for one or more of a variety of reasons. The reasons often mentioned by libraries for undertaking this process are to

pay employees the going rate

be able to compete with the local public schools, county government, community college, and so on

decrease turnover

improve morale

control labor costs

be fair and equitable

learn of the pay and other practices of competitor organizations

position the library system to attract and retain the best and most qualified employees

reward employees for long service

reward employees for doing a great job

provide a career ladder

be able to "pirate" outstanding employees from other libraries and competitor organizations

keep up with increases in the cost of living

obtain valid data that will be helpful in labor negotiations in a union environment

seek a fair pay plan to discourage union organization

As you can see, there are as many reasons for conducting a study as there are types of libraries. Some of these reasons may be yours as well, or you might have totally different ones. Seeing a broad set of possibilities might even spark additional reasons for you to go ahead with the process.

Some of the unanticipated outcomes of putting in a new compensation program have resulted in a number of benefits for library systems. For example, the process of developing a compensation program may improve communications between employees and their supervisors. It also creates a framework and tools for managers and supervisors to use when making decisions about hiring rates and about salary increases for promotions and transfers. A compensation system may provide justification to funding sources for budget increases, including providing the data necessary to advocate for pay equity with local government and the local public schools. A new compensation system may improve employee morale by involving employees in a transparent process, helping them to understand how compensation is set in your library. Furthermore, it can promote flexibility when assigning employees with certain knowledge, skills, and abilities to the new structure, resulting in an effective use of the workforce for the library and in greater career growth, development, and cross training for library employees.

MULTIPURPOSE STUDIES

Nothing in the library stands alone—it's all part of a system. Consultants are often retained to work on an organization redesign, reengineering, or staffing and structure analysis simultaneously with a compensation study. But which should come first?

Without a doubt, studies involving strategic planning and process evaluation *should* come first. If the library system has a plan and knows where it is going based on new technologies, changes in funding patterns, demographic shifts, or new or fewer services to the community, that knowledge should be the guide to designing or redesigning your jobs. The jobs might also need to be priced differently in the marketplace to reflect new duties and responsibilities or changes to them. For this reason, it is best to proceed in the following sequence:

1. strategic planning
2. organization design (to support the plan)
3. staffing and structure analysis (including job design to support the organization design)
4. job descriptions (or summaries) of the new or revised positions
5. compensation system to attract and retain qualified staff
6. pay-for-performance and bonus or incentive and other recognition programs to reward excellent performance and goal achievement

However logical and reasonable it would seem that the planning process should take place using the model outlined, it doesn't always happen that way. Often the library system starts with the compensation plan—largely because that's where the pain is strongest. The library system might be experiencing high turnover, an inability to recruit at all levels, or a feeling that employees are not paid in line with their recruitment market. Having a strategic plan is critical for a variety of reasons, but none is more important than having the ability to map out the work that needs to be accomplished to achieve your goals. This, in turn, will help you identify the skills that will be required of staff. Learn as much as you can about your future—what services you'll be expected to provide and what your staff will need to learn to provide those services—and incorporate that knowledge into your study.

Assuming you know what tasks you need your future or current employees to perform, there should be no problem finding matching data in the market for your redesigned jobs even if the jobs are still evolving or don't yet exist. When the organization design project comes after the compensation study, it can ultimately cost your library more money. That is, the job descriptions you might have just approved will need to be redesigned and market-priced again, and adjustments to some employees' salaries might also be warranted. The key is to deal with the issues as quickly as possible and communicate revisions or updates to all employees so they know what is happening and why. One very large, inherent danger in this scenario is that the adjustments to some employees' salaries could potentially be *downward* adjustments, which are virtually impossible to make without serious morale repercussions down the road.

GETTING STARTED

Now, with insight into compensation and its role in the library system, it's time to get started. The following sections ask you to think about your goals for undertaking the process and the motivators for and potential ramifications of engaging in a compensation study at this time. You should also reflect on the library's strategic initiatives and how a new or revised compensation program can support their fulfillment.

Goals

As you contemplate what others have said about their reasons for conducting a pay study, think about what is motivating your library to undertake a compensation study at this time. Here are some compensation program goals from an academic library:

- a market plan designed for our needs
- a competitive pay-for-performance plan that recognizes developmental achievements, performance levels, and positions within a range
- librarian salaries matched to faculty salaries
- wide and deep ranges allowing for growth without having to achieve a higher pay level

What are your goals? It is important to know what you hope to achieve, and to gain consensus about it. Every library will have different goals and desired outcomes based on needs, strategic initiatives, labor market, budget, culture, and human resource philosophy. Furthermore, although the study will have to take place within parameters, it will be conducted within the context of your environment. That is, your goals may be enhanced or limited if you are required to adhere to certain local government or university policies. Goals, therefore, should be unique to your library and established within any parameters that exist. Do not, however, limit your creativity based on funding or other perceived barriers. Set goals and design the compensation plan to fit your library. Scaling back, or phasing implementation if necessary, can come later. Use worksheet 1 to write a list of your goals for a successful compensation study.

It is important to keep these goals in mind as you design and implement the study. It is very easy to get sidetracked and say, "Oh, let's look at that, too." If you know what your goals are, you will be able to keep your priorities in order and focus on them. Later, you will be able to evaluate the degree to which your goals were met and plan for changes in the future.

Potential Ramifications

In addition to the positive outcomes, you will want to be aware of the potential ramifications. That is, although there will be many positive outcomes resulting from the compensation study, you should also be aware of potential negative outcomes. This is not mentioned to deter you from undertaking a study but to raise your awareness and alert

WORKSHEET 1 ■ Goals for Your Compensation Study   WEB

Goal 1. _____

Goal 2. _____

Goal 3. _____

Goal 4. _____

Goal 5. _____

you to the possibility of problems—a rose-colored-glasses reality check, if you will. If alert to these, you will be able to plan ahead to avoid or minimize the impact of negative outcomes in addition to managing the expectations of everyone concerned—from top managers to your shelving staff. Here are some real-life experiences of libraries:

Staff members learned that their pay rates were below the market, but no funding was available to remedy the situation.

Management and employees learned that their pay rates were *above* market rates—and read about it in the newspaper, thus causing morale problems.

The board of trustees did not approve the recommended compensation plan.

Funds to implement the plan were not obtained during the annual budget planning and approval process.

The hierarchical ordering of positions did not reflect the current or proposed organizational structure and realities of work.

Streamlined jobs led to the ability to eliminate positions or to combine some into lower-graded jobs.

Morale issues developed among employees assigned a job title in a perceived lower-grade level.

Employees yearned to maintain the status quo and resisted updated, flexible job descriptions.

Employees who did not receive expected salary increases had decreased morale.

Management did not communicate any findings or recommendations from the study to employees.

Are these scenarios really possible? Yes. All have indeed happened—luckily not all to the same client. All these situations will be described in further detail later in the book in the appropriate section. You need to be prepared for these possibilities, though, just in case. On the bright side, some of these negatives turned out to be positive. Employees and managers just did not perceive them that way at the time.

WORKSHEET 2 ■ Plan to Combat Possible Negative Ramifications   `WEB`

Possible Negative Results	Ways to Minimize
(Example) Employees are frustrated, as we do not have the funds to implement recommendations.	Budget for, or ascertain where funds might be available for, the possible fiscal impact to implement; create a 1- to 3-year implementation plan.
(Example) Employees don't accept the changes and are skeptical of the process.	Involve employees as much as possible; seek their input via questionnaires, interviews, and focus groups during the project; create a cross-functional review committee; communicate; set realistic goals and expectations.
1.	
2.	
3.	
4.	

You should be aware of the possible unanticipated negative outcomes that might emerge during or as a result of *your* project. Think about what they might be and how they can be minimized. Worksheet 2 provides two examples of a plan to combat possible negative ramifications. Complete the worksheet with your own possibilities. As you read this book you will gain insights into ways to combat potential negatives. Use the second column of the worksheet to briefly jot down your ideas while reading the rest of this book.

Focusing on Your Library

Your library is unlike any other library. Having reviewed your goals for conducting a compensation study, it's time to reflect on who you are. Doing so will help identify some of your human resource planning needs as you head into the future. Once you have a clearer picture or have reviewed where you are and are aware of your staffing needs, you will be able to clarify your library's compensation needs.

Define your library system by answering the questions on worksheet 3. Your answers to these questions will tell you more about your library and your strategic objectives. If you've recently engaged in a planning process, undoubtedly you will have already answered these and many other questions.[2]

1. What is the role of your library?

    What is your mission? Why does your library system exist?

2. What do you do?

    Do you have a strong children's program and often need to recruit children's librarians? Is outreach or technology crucial?

3. What is your organization structure?

    Do you have a flat structure with few levels? Do employees work in teams? Is individual contribution highly valued?

4. Who is your competition?

    Is your competition limited to other local libraries, or must you be aware of what other nonprofit organizations are paying? What about academic institutions? The private sector? Local government? Do you compete with the local school board for librarians and media specialists?

5. What is your financial situation?

    Do you have the funds to implement even small adjustments if employee salaries fall below a minimum market rate? Can you afford not to? Can you afford to pay above-market rates to recruit and retain the highest performers?

6. What are your other relationships?

    With your community? With funding sources/political entities if yours is a public library? With the university if yours is an academic library? If you need additional funds for implementation, will you have support from the community, local government, foundations, or the university? Does this community perceive your service as critical? Is it perceived as high quality?

7. What are your goals and objectives?

    For the next year? For your three- to five-year strategic plan? Do the members of the library's staff have the skills to meet these objectives? If so, will they be rewarded for having them? If not, will you hire employees who have these skills? Will you train incumbents? Do employees know what the objectives are and how they can contribute to them in their individual positions?

8. How do your board and senior management view human resources?

    Are employees perceived as costs or investments? Are they to be cultivated or do you expect a high turnover? Are employees viewed as just another expense item or as human capital? Do you have a succession plan in place?

If yours is like many libraries, two things will be quickly evident from worksheet 3: First, unless you recently went through a planning process, you may not know the answers to many of these questions. Second, the library is probably already undergoing some type of change process or considering major changes beyond the realm of compensation.

A *changing environment*—Most organizations are not static; this is particularly true of libraries in recent years. Technology has changed tremendously in a very short time and continues to do so at an even more rapid pace. This is evident in changes needed in employee skill levels, which vary greatly: On one hand you might see sixteen-year-old pages in suburban branches designing web pages and teaching Internet search skills. On the other, you might see librarians who graduated from library school many years ago and long-term circulation assistants who think that if they wait long enough, the computers will go away—or who hope that they can just wait it out until they retire. Should these employees be paid alike? Indeed, what type of work should they be doing?

A *changing workforce*—There are now four generations commingling in the workforce, each with different needs and expectations. How do these different groups communicate? How do they view compensation? How do they expect feedback to be provided?

Retirees—Look around. How many employees do you anticipate will retire in the next three years? In the next five? Do you have a plan in place to replace staff in these positions? In fact, do all these positions *need* to be refilled? If so, with employees doing the same or a different type of work?

Budget issues—Many library systems are facing budget issues. Some are in crisis, and others are obtaining increasing support from their educational institutions, local governments, philanthropic and fund-raising efforts, or foundations.

Competition for employees—The competition for recent MLS graduates is increasing. Many new graduates decide to cash in on their information management skills in corporate America, where the opportunity to earn more money is greater, instead of applying for positions in public or academic libraries.

Role of your library—In this time of dynamic change, the role of library personnel in academic and public libraries is being examined. To what level of tasks and responsibilities should an MLS employee be assigned? What is the role of the paraprofessional? Can an employee with a BA in music and some library-specific training provide similar services to customers? What is a customer anyway? Didn't they used to be called patrons? Libraries around the country are looking at their roles for the first time. Should they be like Barnes and Noble? Why? Should they adopt the Wal-Mart model of customer service? The Nordstrom model?

These are important issues to think about as you design a compensation program. They determine the types of jobs that you need, the duties assigned to each, and the minimum amount of experience and education required of each incumbent.

If you believe that your system will be changing in the next few years, it is best to design a system that is flexible and responsive to frequent changes. Throughout this book you will find examples of both traditional and more flexible models of compensation management and salary administration.

NOTES

1. G. T. Mikovich and J. M. Newman, *Compensation*, 5th ed. (Homewood, IL: Irwin, 1996), 18.
2. See, for example, Sandra Nelson for the Public Library Association, *The New Planning for Results: A Streamlined Approach* (Chicago: American Library Association, 2001).

two | **Preliminary Planning**

This chapter discusses the steps to consider before beginning a compensation study: obtaining commitment, developing communications, and considering the pros and cons of using consultants and of chartering an employee committee. Also included is a sample letter that could be adapted for pre-project communications to employees.

COMMITMENT AND INVOLVEMENT

Obtaining commitment before the project begins is critical. You should not begin a project like this without obtaining the commitment of your library director, board of trustees, any union or staff association that may be involved, the city/county/university if your library is a department within one of these larger entities, and library employees. These stakeholders have a voice or a perspective that is important to consider and include in any planning for any compensation project.

Time

People are often surprised at the amount of time and effort that is required of the project manager (the in-house staff person assigned to manage the day-to-day activities of the project) and human resources staff. They are less surprised by the costs of engaging consultants to conduct the study than they are by the amount of their own time and effort that is required throughout the project, whether consultants are enlisted or not. Remember—even if consultants are used, they cannot (and definitely should not) work in a vacuum. They will need information, data, meeting time, background, and feedback from you and your staff throughout the project. You don't want consultants that work only off-site crunching numbers. They will not have a feel for your organization's needs or culture.

Money

In addition, the team conducting the study is likely to recommend changes that cost money and alter the status quo. *Do not* undertake a major review of your compensation or classification plans unless you have the budgeted funds or can obtain the resources to fund the recommendations of the study at least partially or through a phased-in implementation plan. Also, do not commit to an implementation plan if it cannot be at least partially funded in the first year.

There are several reasons for this; it is not fair to psychologically set up employees for change if there is no budget for implementation. Although it is important to clarify expectations with employees at the outset of the project (e.g., they should not expect raises), most have the expectation of fair treatment assuming that changes in salary grade or compensation are necessary and will be attempted and recommendations budgeted into the fiscal planning process. If this does not happen, morale will be adversely affected. We will discuss developing cost estimates and implementation plans later in the book; however, a good set-aside figure to work with for study implementation is 3 to 5 percent of payroll costs. This does not mean that each employee would receive 3 to 5 percent but does provide a workable number in many cases.

Feedback

Projects that do not include follow-up, communications, or feedback to employees at the completion of a study are likely to result in negative feelings toward administration and toward the process of the study in general. If your library has a history of not communicating this type of information to employees, you may face strong cynicism and skepticism when you are ready to proceed with your next study. Employees may be understandably apathetic. You may hear such comments as "Oh yeah, another compensation study. . . . Nothing happened with the last one, so nothing will happen with this one either," or "Last time they hid the findings from us because they didn't want to pay us more." It takes time to rebuild the trust and enthusiasm that are so critical for any compensation project. Employees are more reluctant to be involved in something that they believe is, for all intents and purposes, lip service. Understand that involvement leads to buy-in, and buy-in is necessary for acceptance, support, and implementation of recommendations. Therefore, it is important both to be clear about expectations at the outset and to communicate at the completion of the project.

Stakeholders

Buy-in and commitment from several stakeholders or stakeholder groups are critical to the success of any project. In addition to employees, the key stakeholders are the library director, board of trustees, and staff association or union. If the library is a department or unit of a city, county, or university, that organization's human resources department or even the city or county manager might be a key stakeholder as well. Although some of these stakeholders—the library director and board of trustees in particular—are key decision makers and others may not be, it is still important to gain all stakeholders' commitment to the project or, at the very least, inform them about it and allow them an opportunity to ask questions at the beginning of the project. Although we don't recommend involving the board at a micro level, we have found that presenting periodic progress reports (i.e., monthly) to even a subcommittee of the board (personnel or finance) can be very helpful in ensuring acceptance and, importantly, understanding of recommendations at project completion.

The Library Director

The director of the library must be a key supporter of the project because he or she has to commit to and support the use of the library's resources in terms of both staff time and funds. The library director should also approve the project's process and time line, including the use and selection of a project manager, an employee review committee, and/or consultants. The director should shape and advocate for the compensation philosophy (more on this in chapter 3), which will ultimately guide the design and implementation of a new compensation plan. With staff help, the library director must also make the case to go ahead with such a project to the library's board of directors or trustees as well as to any appropriate city/county or university authorities.

The Board

Often, a project budget is developed and funds set aside to conduct and implement a project with the concurrence of the board. Budgets are a concern at this preplanning stage if consultants are to be retained to conduct the project or if other resources are needed. The library's board is also usually involved if a budget allocation is necessary to fund implementation. That is, if findings indicate that salary adjustments are warranted to maintain internal or external equity, it is important to ensure that the budget funds are available. Many boards of trustees are interested in potential salary inequities and want to correct them if they exist. They also want to make sure that employees are fairly compensated and that salary ranges are designed to recruit and retain qualified staff.

The board should be included as important stakeholders in the preliminary planning and go/no-go decision phase of the compensation study and should receive planned periodic updates that will minimize end-of-project surprises when findings or recommendations are presented. There is no one best way to involve the board of directors. Each library system board is different and has different ways of working. It is important to respect these differences and communicate with members in the most appropriate way. Educating trustees about the compensation study is helpful in gaining that commitment. Education and involvement early in the process enhance approval and acceptance of the study.

You can work with boards of trustees in a variety of ways. For example, in a study for a small library system, a member of the board of trustees participated as a member of the compensation committee. Although he didn't attend every meeting, he was informed about the process. In this case, both the executive director and assistant director also served on the committee. This is more common in smaller library systems, where there is a very small or no human resources staff. A side benefit of this level of involvement was that the board member became more connected with the library and its staff. Staff also became more appreciative of the board and its role in library governance.

Another example comes from a medium-sized public library system that serves the library needs of both urban dwellers and suburbanites. During the course of this project the consultant met with and gave periodic reports to the board of trustees' human resources committee. When the time came to present findings to the library's board of trustees, the human resources committee members made an unequivocal endorsement because of their understanding of the system and process. This vote of confidence in the findings and recommendations helped to pave the way to approval and funding. Another way of connecting with board members occurred with a medium-sized public library in a suburban community of Baltimore. In this situation, the members of the board's human resources committee, the library's deputy director, and the human resources director and assistant composed the steering committee.

Finally, in another library system in a large midwestern metropolitan area, we were able to include a statement of the board's commitment to and support of the project in a letter to all employees from the library's CEO at the beginning of the project. What a great way to let employees know the project had full buy-in from the top down!

Staff Association or Union

Involve the staff association or union up front if you have one. Sometimes compensation studies are conducted as a result of a negotiation or meet-and-confer process, where both the union and management agree to collect valid salary data to determine pay rates. If your library system has a collective bargaining agreement or memorandum of understanding with a union or labor association, review it before taking action to ensure that no violations will occur. Some agreements or memorandums provide for the involvement of the labor union or association in a variety of ways, including the selection of consultants (if any), the design of the study process, participation in a compensation review committee that is created, and review of findings and recommendations before they are presented to the library board for approval. If you are a party to any such agreement, follow the stipulated process.

Even if there is no formal agreement for the participation of a labor union or staff association, it is a good practice to involve them. Once the library director and human resources staff have an idea of the direction in which they want to go, inform the president of the union or association and discuss his or her role. It is worthwhile and expedient to invite a union representative to serve on any committee that is created, keeping union members informed and updated. The union or association should be treated like any other stakeholder group in this process. At a minimum, members should become informed, and their opinions should be sought in the data-collection process by inviting them to be interviewed and to participate in a focus group.

At a large urban library, the president of the staff association, a branch manager, was viewed as an important stakeholder. She was interviewed early in the process for the staff association's perspective on compensation and classification issues, problems, and needs, and she served as a member of the review committee and job-evaluation team. In a school system, members of the negotiations team served on the review committee, and findings were presented to the entire team. In a community college, members of the union served on project committees and provided a valuable communications link between the committee and staff in general.

City, County, or University

Many library systems receive their funding from a city, county, or university. Some libraries have their own personnel and compensation processes and policies that are separate and distinct from these funding sources, while others are a part of the larger administrative structure and do not have as much flexibility.

If the library requires additional funds to minimize internal or external inequities identified during a study, you may need to go to the city or county administrator or the city or county council or the university for support. Therefore, it is important for several reasons to schedule a discussion with the appropriate human resources or finance director even before you get started in the process. First, the director might be able to provide you with resources such as support from the human resources staff, salary data, experiences performing similar studies, best practices, and so forth. Second, he or she will let you know if you should not undertake a study at this time. For example, there may be no extra funding available if it is needed for implementation, or there might be plans to conduct a similar study and the director may invite your participation. You should ascertain whether you have the flexibility to design your own system or to identify the parameters you must follow as part of the larger compensation system. In one local library system, the director knew from meeting with county management that the system would have a much better chance of being funded if it matched as closely as possible with the county's pay structure. In this situation, even though the library director was not a big proponent of pay grades divided into steps, she elected to follow this system to make it more understandable and familiar to the county commissioners charged with approving the structure and its funding. Her compromise was to make sure, following implementation, that the library's employees received step increases based on a successful performance review.

In another suburban library system, the library's human resources (HR) director was particularly concerned about competing for employees with the local county government. Even though a comprehensive compensation study had recently been conducted, the HR director wanted to ensure pay equity with this specific organization. A compensation specialist from the county's HR department met with the library's HR director and the consultant. Together they matched positions in the library and county government for pay equity, comparing levels of responsibility, education, and experience in each. The library then received funding to ensure that library positions were placed in equitable pay grades compared with county government positions.

Some library systems are a department of a local government, and the library director is also a county department head. In these cases, the library is usually not given the go-ahead to conduct an independent study of its classifications. However, exceptions have been made when recruitment or retention problems arise because of insufficient salaries. The same may hold true with colleges and universities.

In a recent campuswide study for a large East Coast university, the director of the library served as a member of the project's advisory committee. Because of her involvement, the study addressed library issues. Since this was a market-based study, extra efforts were made to designate as many library positions as possible as benchmark (surveyed) positions (see chapter 7). Therefore, salary information was collected for those positions. Issues of faculty appointments for librarians were addressed as an outcome of the study, as were concerns pertaining to the technology skills required.

Where the library system is a department (as opposed to an agency) of local government, it is most likely that library positions will be studied when all positions are reviewed as part of an organization-wide compensation study. When the library is a separate agency, the choice is more likely to be the library's. Whenever possible, if the library system has the option it should do its *own* study. The reasons relate to time, attention, and focus. If you are doing your own study, your consultants or your staff review committee are totally focused on library, and only library, positions. In this scenario, all library positions and issues can be studied. This is not the case when the library's positions are studied along with those in the departments of public works, planning and zoning, and social services in local government or, in a university system, along with student services, financial aid, academic affairs, and finance and administration.

Having said this, one way to enhance your position in a large-scale or organization-wide study is to *be involved.* Don't wait for the university or local government human resources director to come to you. As soon as you learn that a compensation study is being considered, *run, don't walk* to volunteer to participate in the process. If consultants will be retained, offer your services as a member of the selection or evaluation team. Ask the top three consultants who submit proposals if they have experience with library systems. Once the project begins, ask to be included on the list of stakeholders to be interviewed, and ask to be made a member of the compensation steering or review committee. Yes, it will take precious time that you and your staff probably do not have; however, it will be more than worth it as your presence enables you to bring your library system's issues to the table and ensure that they are kept there. An extra benefit to this level of participation for your library system is that you will learn a great deal and find yourself educated about the compensation systems and processes that govern the library.

Employees

The same philosophy of involvement is equally if not more true for employees. Frankly, no project will ever be completely successful without this involvement. Build employee commitment by creating a communications plan that educates and later updates them about the project, talk to them and ask for their input, and ask them about their jobs. Communicate before, during, and after the project. It's very frustrating for employees to hear a big introduction and buildup about a project and then hear absolutely nothing for the four months it may take to complete the work.

Complete worksheet 4 to help plan your strategy for obtaining commitment and getting a go-ahead for the library's compensation study. Taking the time to go through this worksheet will help you assess who your stakeholders are in this process as well as the level of involvement you will need from each. Although some information has been filled in for you, delete from or add to this plan as appropriate for your library's needs, culture, and organization.

In the first column, determine which stakeholders need to be informed about the compensation study. Next, plan what you need to tell or ask the members of each of these stakeholder groups and specify what you need their commitment for. In the third column, include some considerations for working with each of these groups. For example, when informing the board about the compensation project, you might give a presentation about the process and ask for board input in defining the library's compensation philosophy. Identify the date by which each task will be completed and specify the responsible individual. Finally, note issues that might arise or outcomes you can expect from gaining commitment from each of these stakeholders.

COMMUNICATIONS

The communications plan should continue throughout the process of the compensation study. Members of the review team or employee committee should be held accountable for providing updates to all stakeholders, including employees, on a regular basis. Equally important as gaining the commitment of all stakeholders is keeping each group informed about the project through its life. Continual and regular communication is key. Figure 2.1 shows the outline for a communications plan with the various stakeholders. Of course, the board and employees are critical stakeholders in this process. Therefore, the following sections specifically address communications with these two groups.

Board Communications

Depending on the nature and structure of the board, sometimes consultants meet with board members or members of the executive, finance, or human resources committee early in the project to present a communications session and ask for their input, expectations, and ideas. Consider discussing compensation philosophy with trustees as well because this may result in a changed policy direction.

Without ongoing updates, board members who are uninformed may say, "Why didn't you consider X Library when collecting data?" or, "I think we should pay our

WORKSHEET 4 ■ Plan to Engage Stakeholders

WEB

Stakeholder	Gain Commitment	Provide Information	Date and by Whom	Possible Issues and Expected Outcomes
Library director	Importance of project Process Who will be involved Time and financial commitment Importance of communications to employees	Presentation or conversation		
Library trustees/board of directors	Importance of project Financial commitment Process	Presentation about process Input about compensation philosophy		
Labor union/staff association	Process Role	Interviews Participation as committee member		
City/county/university finance director, human resources director	Relationship of compensation systems Funding issues Parameters	Human resources interviews Human resources participation on committee		
Employees	Process Role Expectations	Focus groups Interviews Project updates Representation on review committee Hotline Questionnaires Employee survey		

employees above the market to attract the best staff. Why are you setting midpoints just at the market?" or, "We can't afford to do anything this year. We're building a new branch, ordering self-check machines. . . . Why are you doing this anyway?" Early education pays off and helps ensure a smooth approval process when findings are presented to the board. A recent presentation to a library board of directors (our first interaction with this group) found us presenting findings at the end of the project. Though salary data had been collected from libraries throughout the metropolitan region—a very appropriate survey cohort—the board was interested only in the two neighboring county libraries and the local county/city governments. Had we been able to meet with this group at the project's start we may have been able to provide some education as to why a broader group was appropriate, particularly at the professional librarian level and above. At the least, we would have gotten clear direction from them if they were committed to their philosophy of surveying only a select group and would not have taken the time and money to survey a much larger group.

Figure 2.1
Sample Communications Plan

Purpose	To Whom	What	By Whom	How	Date
Introduce study	All stakeholders	Outline steps	Library director or project manager	Interlibrary mail	Week 1
		Manage expectations		Intranet	
		Introduce team and/ or consultants		Face-to-face group meetings	
		List questions and answers		Videoconference	
				Video of communications meetings on intranet	
Announce e-mail hotline	Employees	Explain hotline and confidentiality	Library director or project manager	All-staff e-mail	Week 1
Feedback	Employees	Findings from interviews and/ or focus groups and/or survey	Project manager	Intranet Letter Meetings	Weeks 4–5
Updates	Employees, managers, board, staff association or union	Findings and project status	Project manager or team member	Intranet E-mail newsletter	Ongoing (following team/staff meetings) or monthly
Findings and recommendations	Board and, upon board approval, all stakeholders	Summary of findings and recommendations	Project manager, committee members, or consultants	Letter	At the end of the project after board approval
		Changes and impact on employees		Newsletter Individualized letter Frequently asked questions Group communications meetings	

If board members are not part of the project team, they *must* be kept informed at key milestones during the project. For example, although a consultant working with a large, East Coast library never met with the library's board of trustees or any of its members, she prepared presentations for the library director to give to the board. In general, at a minimum, consultants and committee members are often asked to make a final presentation to the board of project findings, recommendations, and proposed pay and classification plans. Your project manager and committee should plan to do the same.

Employee Communications

The importance of open and clear communications to employees during a compensation project cannot be overstated. Projects in which employees have been informed throughout the process simply have a better chance of successful implementation, *even if* results are not what they expected (in other words, everyone does not receive a raise). To begin the communication process with employees, an introductory letter and/or a presentation by the project manager or library director is the recommended first step. Ideally, both will take place: a letter will be sent to all employees and presentations open to all employees will be offered. The letter usually states the what, why, who, when, and how of the compensation study. That is, it should clearly tell employees that the library system is about to undertake a compensation and classification study and why. If presentations are made, the library director should open the meetings, introduce the team, and generally show his or her support and leadership. The presentation or letter or both should provide the following information:

- the name of the project manager
- an outline of the steps involved in the project
- the names of the members of the review or steering committee and a description of their role
- the role of employees
- time frames of the project
- what employees should expect—as well as what they should not expect

Worksheet 5 is a sample form letter to employees. You will want to adapt it for your own situation.

Managing employee expectations is very important from the outset. Educating your employees about what to expect will help minimize concerns. Emphasizing the following two very important points may help alleviate some of the anxiety that often accompanies compensation studies:

No employee will lose a job as a result of the compensation study.

No employee will have his or her salary decreased as a result of the study.

However, employees should also know that they will not automatically receive a pay increase as a result of the study. We have encountered many employees over the years who are truly shocked at the end of a project when they do not receive a huge increase, based on the recognition they think they deserve. Employees of course often do deserve recognition, but it should be clearly and repeatedly stated that a compensation study focuses on the duties and responsibilities of the position, not on the individual performance or characteristics of the person in that position.

Dear Library Employees:

As you may know by now, we have retained a consultant to conduct a compensation and classification study for the library. Our project will officially kick off on August 22 and 23, when the consultant will meet with our management team, the human resources committee of our board, and the employee compensation committee formed for the study. This committee comprises a cross section of library staff and will provide feedback and insight to the consultant throughout the project. It will also operate as a critical communications link with employees throughout the duration of the study. Four meetings are scheduled with this group. Members of the compensation committee are

[List members' names, titles, and department/location]

While on-site, the consultants will also meet with three large groups of employees at open communications sessions held at the main library, the Novel branch, and the Biography branch. All employees are invited and encouraged to attend one of these sessions to learn more about the study and to participate in employee focus groups regarding your concerns and suggestions on compensation at the library.

You will also soon be receiving a Job Analysis Questionnaire from the consultant. These questionnaires will be used to evaluate each of the library's positions and to ensure positions are classified appropriately. After reviewing the completed questionnaires, the consultant will schedule a series of individual and small-group interviews with a percentage of our staff to obtain additional information about our jobs. This information is crucial not only for understanding how the library defines its positions but also for accurately comparing our positions to those in other organizations. These interviews will take place in October and November. If you are selected for an interview, I encourage you to take the opportunity to provide additional information and clarification about your job.

Additional project steps include a comprehensive salary study and the development of an appropriate pay plan. As the project progresses, I will keep you informed of activities and findings.

Finally, a project hotline has been established for all employees to have another avenue for communicating during this project. The e-mail address for the hotline is AnytownStudy@libraryconsultants.com. All e-mail sent to the hotline will go directly to the consultant and will receive a direct response from the consultant. All e-mails will remain entirely confidential. Please use the hotline to express any concerns or questions you may have or to present items that you may not feel comfortable expressing in an open setting.

I am looking forward to this comprehensive look into our compensation and classification systems. Your input and participation are critical for the success of this project, which is important for you and the library as a whole. Let me assure you that no one will lose pay or lose his or her job as a result of the study. No employee should expect an automatic increase as a result of the study, either. All recommendations will be made based on the data gathered during the study. We anticipate having findings and recommendations to review in December, with an implementation plan developed by January. It is important to note that the board of directors fully supports the performance of this work.

If you have any questions or would like more information about this project, please feel free to contact me or [insert name], our project manager. Thank you for your participation in this important project!

Sincerely,

Library Director

ENGAGE CONSULTANTS—OR NOT?

Early on you will have to decide whether to use consultants. Consider both the pros and cons of using consultants for your project. Your decision will also be based on the circumstances and culture in your library system. Some of the pros and cons of using external consultants are shown in figure 2.2.

If you choose to outsource the project, find a consultant who is willing to be your partner in the process. Make it a joint effort in which the consultant brings the compensation design and implementation expertise and you—and your employees—provide the library system know-how and internal perspective of background and processes. Employees will truly appreciate the opportunity to be interviewed, participate in a focus group, attend an informational session, or even just be able to correspond with the consultant by e-mail. They want to be able to share their concerns and opinions with an objective third party, not to "tell tales out of school" but to be *heard* by someone with no vested interest in the outcomes of the project in terms of how positions are classified or paid. Employees also take pride in showing their worksites, processes, and outputs during job interviews. In one local government, we heard a horror story about a consultant who had been on-site conducting a project several years before the current study. The consultant was doing employee interviews at various worksites and was visiting the county's sparkling new 911 call center. The employees being interviewed were excited and enthusiastic about showing off the center to the consultant and taking him on a tour. According to employees, when asked to take the tour the consultant responded, "No thanks, you see one 911 center, you've seen 'em all." As you can imagine, that remark went over like a lead balloon, and, most important, employees lost trust and confidence in the process immediately. The point is, if using a consultant, make sure to select a firm you believe will be able to relate and communicate effectively with employees at all levels.

Retain a consultant who will provide ongoing education during the project so there can be a transfer of learning. There is nothing worse than completing a project, even a successful one, and then realizing three months after the consultant has completed the study that you don't really have a clue about how to administer and maintain the system.

Figure 2.2
Pros and Cons of Using External Consultants

Pros	Cons
Tend to be perceived by employees as more objective than internal employees or management	Need to learn your system, processes, people, culture, and norms
Have past experience with compensation within libraries and other organizations	May be seen as outsiders
Know what works well and what doesn't	May be costly
Have expertise in designing and implementing compensation systems	May not have as much commitment to the process as would an internal team
Have no preconceived agenda	Not as invested in your library
Save staff time to focus on day-to-day operations and customers	Still need a committee
Can bring credibility and integrity to the process	Can be perceived as "using consultants for everything"

Do you know how to classify a new position? Do you know what surveys were used and what cuts, or categories, of data were in those surveys so you can check market data on your own? Make sure the consultant builds in ongoing training or even a formal training session at the end of the project so that you have all the tools you need to move forward. Your consultant should support your goals, learning, and independence. Whomever you choose should be willing to work collaboratively with you and should be someone with whom you feel comfortable and whom you can trust. Needless to say, the consultant should have experience working with libraries and be able to provide references.

If you choose to work with consultants, this book is still an invaluable resource. You will also want to use other resources that might be available. For example, the human resources director of your local government or college may have salary data or a process that could be helpful. Look for other books on compensation. Call your state or regional library association. Network with your colleagues who have recently completed studies.

Whether or not you retain consultants, your first important task will be to appoint a knowledgeable internal project manager with good group facilitation and project management skills. Second, appoint a staff member (perhaps a reference librarian) as a researcher to learn about program designs, data collection tools, and so forth.

COMMITTEE APPROACH—OR NOT?

Should there be an employee committee? Definitely! Some of our colleagues don't agree, but our experience has shown that the resulting buy-in is greater and learning is promoted when a committee approach is used.

Does it take longer? Yes. Couldn't the consultants do it faster and easier? Again, yes. So why bother? Experience gained over the years indicates that, except in very small library systems, employee acceptance and buy-in are never as good when working only with the human resources director or library director as they are when working with a committee. Without a committee the number of appeals or requests for a review of the grade to which a position is slotted may be greater. In one instance a staff member went to the newspaper and a member of the board of trustees and alleged unfairness regarding study results. A committee also provides a valuable link between all staff and library management and consultants. Our committee process typically involves starting *each* meeting with a check-in, asking committee members what concerns or questions they have been hearing from staff, and ending each meeting with a discussion of information that can be communicated to staff.

Why not take advantage of the opportunity for members of the library staff to

> learn about compensation and classification
>
> experience working as a member of a cross-functional team
>
> learn more about the library system
>
> meet fellow library employees and see them in a different light
>
> showcase their individual abilities
>
> provide important feedback and insight about project outcomes

Two stories of positive/favorable outcomes come to mind, both relating to committees. In one project, a committee was asked to do some pre-project work researching issues. At the beginning of the first meeting, after asking for a volunteer to report findings, there was silence. A senior circulation clerk finally spoke and gave a wonderful presentation of her research. Needless to say, the ice was broken. More important, throughout the process this individual continued to show initiative, creativity, and ability. She was soon promoted to circulation supervisor in a midsized branch.

Another story—one with both good and bad outcomes for the library—involves a self-taught computer technician in a small public library. While serving on the committee, she increased her knowledge of technology, the skills that were in demand in the marketplace, and the salaries paid to information technology professionals. At the final committee meeting, she announced that she had asked the director for and had been granted a leave of absence to return to college to pursue a degree in information technology. She has since returned part-time, with more skills to offer—and at a higher salary.

Committee Type

Many libraries use a design, steering, advisory, or review committee in the process of conducting a compensation study. The differences are more than semantic. Each type of committee calls for a different level of hands-on involvement and of approval and decision-making authority. In addition, different public libraries and universities convene some of these types of committees more commonly than others. Experience has taught that it is best to use the name *design committee* only when consultants are not used or where the members of the team will actually be designing and developing the new compensation philosophy, classification plan, and pay structure. In addition, use *steering committee* only when the members have decision-making authority. *Advisory committees* are most often used in university settings or when the members are not necessarily a cross section of staff or are board members of the library. When working with an advisory committee, seek information from the members at the beginning of the project, including their perspectives on compensation issues, difficulties with recruitment and retention, compensation philosophy, and so forth. The advisory committee may not meet again until near the project's completion. During this late-term meeting ask the advisory committee to look for what might have been missed, what might not make sense in this particular system, or other minefields that need to be avoided or addressed.

It is best to use the term that is normally assigned by the library for employee committees. Where that is not clear, use the term *review committee*. Members of a review committee generally review all findings, suggest options, discuss alternatives, and become more involved in the process as a whole than do their counterparts on advisory committees. For the remainder of this book, the committee assigned to the project is referred to as the review committee.

Committee Makeup

In our experience, a committee that includes employees from a cross section of grade levels and functions within the organization works best for a number of reasons. First, you involve staff who may not normally be involved in this type of undertaking. Second, compensation affects *all* employees. Why not hear from a representative group about their particular concerns and issues regarding the topic, instead of *only* librarians or *only* supervisors. Finally, forming a group representing a variety of voices ensures you will hear not only what you want or hope to hear from employees but some straight talk as well about what employees worry about, have concerns about, or just plain don't like about your current compensation plan.

There is no right way to form the employee review committee. Human resources staff can draft a list to be reviewed by the library director. Department heads could put forward staff they think would add value to the group. However you select the members of this group, keep the following in mind.

Make sure you have branch representation. One recent client formed a committee consisting entirely of central library staff. The first e-mail we received from the hotline set up for the project was a complaint that branches weren't being represented. The library director and HR manager immediately added some branch staff to the committee.

Include one or more "squeaky wheels." Don't stack the deck with only employees who have never complained about their pay or their classification. In fact, we often suggest that libraries include one or more employees who have consistently requested reclassifications in the past. Serving on the committee does not, of course, guarantee that the position will be reclassified, but it definitely increases the chances that the person will have a better understanding of *why* the position is classified as it is.

Include a good mix of supervisory and nonsupervisory staff. If you only include managers and supervisors, you may face skepticism down the road from employees who feel that they weren't represented or heard in the process. If you only include nonsupervisory staff, you may not get the important perspective of the managers on your staff.

Be sure to include a representative from the union or staff association if your library has one. The communications link such members can provide to their constituencies is invaluable.

Committee Charter

The committee or team can be called whatever makes sense in your environment, as long as its role is *clearly defined*. This step is critical. Whether or not you work with consultants, a charter should be drafted so that the expectations and purpose of the committee are clear at the outset. Figures 2.3 and 2.4 are examples of charters that you may modify and adopt for your own library system.

The advisory committee charter (figure 2.3) was adapted from a slide shown during the first committee meeting at a large public university with which we had contracted to design and implement a new exempt compensation program. Most of the members of this committee were department heads—assistant and associate vice presidents. The second charter (figure 2.4) was given to the members of a review committee representing a cross section of the staff of an urban library. No matter the construct of the group, have members carefully read the charter and come to consensus that it is the guiding document for the group's work. We have often had committee members suggest wording changes or bring up important points for inclusion or do both. This type of dialogue is great, as it shows members are taking their responsibilities seriously and are interested in the effective functioning of the committee. Encourage these types of conversations—don't just hand committee members the charter as a done deal.

Another important feature of a charter is that it should state the objectives of the committee. It should also establish boundaries on what the committee will and will not review and the extent to which it serves as a reviewing, recommending, or decision-making body. A discussion of confidentiality is also critical and should be included in the charter. Though this is sometimes a tough leap for library management to take, committee members should be trusted to keep preliminary findings, data, and recommenda-

Figure 2.3
Compensation Committee Charter for a Public University

The role of the advisory committee is to discuss and identify current issues dealing with the following systems:

- compensation
- classification
- salary administration

Each member of the group will contribute ideas and provide feedback. The committee will serve as a sounding board for project ideas and recommendations, and will provide a heads-up if any potential staff issues arise. Finally, committee members will react to and advise on project findings and recommendations, informing the group of any "sore thumbs" or considerations that may have been missed.

Each member will be expected to attend four meetings during the course of the project.

Figure 2.4
Compensation Committee Charter for an Urban Public Library Compensation Review Committee

Charge

The compensation review committee is composed of a cross section of library staff. The members of this committee provide input to the consultants over the life of this project. The review committee is not a steering committee or decision-making body, nor is it the only or final group providing input to and review of project outputs. It is created because the consultants and library management value the input of library staff into compensation issues.

Meetings with the review committee will be scheduled approximately every three weeks. It is currently understood and anticipated that the role of the review committee includes the following:

1. to provide input into and understanding about compensation issues currently facing the library
2. to serve as a communication link with members of the library staff
3. to provide input into or review the

work plan
position description questionnaire
list of benchmark positions

position descriptions for salary survey
preliminary project findings
draft recommendations

It is expected that members of the review committee will keep committee discussions and preliminary findings of the consultants confidential until the appropriate time.

tions confidential until the appropriate time, as discussed during committee meetings. Throughout the committee process, members should be educated about why confidentiality is so critical, and how damaging it can be to morale if findings or recommendations are leaked prior to final approval. Finally, the charter might also specify the frequency of meetings, who will facilitate them, and the role of the facilitator during meetings. Some charters outline norms or ground rules for working together. Some include all the committee roles, such as timekeeper, note taker, and process observer. Keep the charter simple and consistent with other committee charters in your library.

Committee Norms

One of the first exercises we undertake with employee committees is setting norms for the group. The norms will serve as a guide for committee members throughout the project, reminding them how the group will work together. We usually put the norms on a large flip-chart page and tape it up at each meeting. Have each member suggest a norm important to him or her—input from the group is crucial, as they will need to agree to the norms. Norms we've noted for various committees range from the serious to the lighthearted, including

- Maintain confidentiality.
- Respect all opinions.
- Don't interrupt. Don't engage in side discussions.
- Have food at each meeting.
- Bathroom breaks do not require permission.
- Elect a member at each meeting to keep notes.
- Have fun!

Once you've identified the norms, ensure that each committee member agrees with them. Having the sheet of norms visible at each meeting also allows members to suggest new norms as needed.

With your committee formed and chartered, you are ready to think about and develop your library's compensation philosophy.

three | **Context and Compensation Philosophy**

After developing a commitment to your compensation plan, planning the compensation study, making decisions about an employee committee, and developing a communications plan, you will want to think through some of the important issues regarding the library's compensation philosophy and pay policy. As discussed in chapter 2, you will have already gotten board input regarding the library's compensation philosophy. Now it is time to build on that input and create a fully developed compensation philosophy for your library. It is never a good idea to adopt another organization's compensation system, because there really is no one-size-fits-all library plan. Each library system must think through a number of issues, starting with "What do you want your pay plan to accomplish?" For example, an entirely different design recommendation is appropriate if the average tenure of your workforce is greater than fifteen years and your library is in a stable (internal and external) environment than if you are losing your top performers who are only averaging one to three years with the system.

Your consultant—or, if you are not using a consultant, the project manager—should ask senior management important questions that may include those listed in the next section. As previously mentioned, in some cases members of the library's board of trustees or the personnel committee should also be interviewed to ensure that you have their perspectives as you begin your design work. Including these stakeholders increases buy-in by the board. In turn, board members are usually more comfortable during a final presentation because they have made a connection with you or your consultant personally as well as with the topic and have had the opportunity to provide their perspective. Interviews with trustees can be face-to-face, by phone, or in groups as an agenda item of a regularly scheduled (or special) personnel committee or board meeting. You can identify the appropriate option based on the level of board involvement you seek as well as what is typically provided by your board in similar situations.

INTERVIEW QUESTIONS FOR SENIOR MANAGEMENT AND THE BOARD

The questions that follow are a compilation of questions that were asked in an early phase in several recent projects. Included are more questions than would normally be asked or that time would typically allow. They show how this time can be used productively to get additional data that may be important for the *context* of the design and the *outcome* of the project. Tailor this list to meet your needs for information gathering. After each question is a justification of why the response to the question is important or what to look for to understand the library's compensation philosophy.

Issues and Challenges

1. *What are the key issues and challenges (both short- and long-term) facing the library at this time? Facing your department?*

   It is important to know where the library is going. The future direction of the library may not be in writing and may only be in the heads of library leadership. However, if the system is going to go through a major transition, face budget increases or decreases by a public funding body, transition to a Nordstrom model of customer service, or replace most circulation clerks with self-check-out machines (to name but a few possibilities), these will be important to know as you plan for a compensation system that is durable beyond six months. Similarly, it is important to know if the library is in a very stable situation, employs a core group of competent and qualified employees, and plans to, for the most part, maintain the status quo.

   If your library faces many possible changes, it is likely that you will want to design a flexible plan that reflects the market and has wider, open salary ranges. That is, your library should consider pay-for-performance, and your job descriptions should be broad while building in opportunities for job growth and development. Libraries in a stable environment might want to design a plan that values internal equity and is less flexible (see question 5, following).

   If you have a current strategic plan, this is the first place to look to make sure the relevant key initiatives of the plan are reflected in your compensation plan design.

The Compensation Plan

2. *What should the library's compensation plan accomplish?*

   If you hear "maintain internal relationships" or "reward longevity or length of service," yours will be a very different plan than if the responses include "reward performance," "pay according to the market," or "retain high-performing employees." Of course, hearing many responses regarding "rewarding performance" does not necessarily mean that your library is ready for a pay-for-performance system, but that is a discussion for another chapter.

3. *How would you describe the current total compensation package (including pay, benefits, retirement, time off, etc.) at the library? How does it compare with that of other employers?*

   In addition to assessing compensation, it may be important to conduct a survey to learn about the benefits provided in your market because your benefits package can be a very important motivator—or de-motivator—for recruitment and retention. Benefits can be very expensive to the library, and employees rarely have a complete understanding of the value of their benefit plan in actual dollars paid by the system and how it compares with that of other local organizations. While this may begin to change, public, academic, and school libraries generally offer benefits that are worth more than the norm in their area—a fact neither known nor appreciated by most library employees. Nonetheless, even when the quality of benefits is outstanding, many employees still focus on the cash compensation. "What is my salary?" and "How am I being paid compared to others in X?" are the questions generally asked. Applicants rarely consider the value of benefits. This is especially true of Generation X and younger candidates for employment. Benefits have traditionally been more of a retention tool for long-term service and older employees, because they are concerned about health insurance and take seriously their vesting in the library's retirement system. However, doing some research and data-gathering and providing employees with annual benefits statements can go a long way to building employees' understanding of and appreciation for the value of their benefits packages. At a recent employee review committee meeting in a medium-sized library, employees told us that they had recently received benefits statements from the library's HR department. Their comments were truly amazing! One circulation team leader told us that he saw a "real difference" in his staff after reviewing their statements. Another committee member told us that employees were "really moved" by the value of the benefits package provided and paid for by the library. The downside, of course, is that libraries often employ many part-time staff, and part-time benefits are rarely as rich as those for full-time employees.

4. *What factors should drive pay at the library system—market, skills, performance, education, contribution, length of service, or other concerns? Are the factors different for different jobs? Should they be?*

The answers to these questions will tell you and the members of your review committee what the library and management value and want to reward. The design of your compensation system will need to reflect and support these values. It is not difficult to correlate what management values to the compensation program design. For example:

> If management wishes to pay in accordance with the market, the design will focus on obtaining, via custom-made and published surveys, salary data for employees in your marketplace (as you define it; see question 5) and developing pay ranges that reflect the market data.

> If a high value is placed on length of service, your design may include provisions to award long-term employees additional salary—perhaps in excess of market rates—as part of their base pay or as a bonus paid in a separate check.

> If your system values performance, your design may reflect open ranges rather than steps (by which all employees, regardless of the level of performance, are typically entitled to the same increase on completion of a year of service).

Competitive Market

5. *When employees leave your library system, where do they go? From where are your best new employees hired? Are there any positions, departments, or even grade levels where recruitment or retention is a problem?*

The answers to these questions will help you understand your market and thus target the sectors of the economy and specific public, private, and nonprofit organizations from which you will want to collect data.

> Employees in nonexempt positions, such as clerk, administrative assistant, financial assistant, and driver, usually leave for and are hired from all types of organizations, both private and public, in the local area.

> The market for non-library-specific professional employees, such as director of marketing, chief financial officer, accountant, and human resources representative, is both local and regional—with a focus on local—and often includes nonprofits as well.

Recruiting practices for professional librarian positions, especially department heads and directors, are often regional or national, depending on your library's needs and the market (see also chapter 8, "Executive Compensation").

It will be important to learn about jobs for which recruitment and retention are problems to

determine whether there are any patterns that may or may not relate to compensation causing the situation (i.e., employees may leave circulation clerk positions because they can get similar customer service work without having to work evenings or weekends)

ensure that these positions are thoroughly studied and sufficient data collected

consider extending the market studied for these positions from, for example, local and public to regional and private

Assessment

6. *From your perspective, what is working and not working with the current pay plan? What would you change? How? Why?*

Often management sees a problem emerge with a common thread in a compensation plan. An example is that management realizes that 80 percent of the library's employees are at or approaching the maximum of their pay grade. This might be a symptom of a number of things: It could be that employees, as a group, are long tenured and have been given step increases each year, thus placing them near the maximum of their pay grade and possibly over the market rate for the position. It could also indicate that the ranges for the jobs are too narrow from the minimum to the maximum of the pay grade and do not allow for sufficient growth unless the ranges are moved regularly to match the market.

A variety of root causes might be attributed to each problem. Before setting out to fix the problems, each needs to be analyzed for its cause. Once you understand the cause and suggest ways to rectify the problem, you will need to consider findings and alternatives for correction in light of

the library's compensation philosophy

what is financially feasible in the short term as well as over time

what is politically feasible in both the short and long term

7. *If a point factor system is in place, from your perspective, what's working and not working with it? How, if at all, should it be changed?*

These questions are asked when a library system uses a point factor system to evaluate and classify jobs (see chapter 6). A typical problem with internally focused job evaluation plans is that if you were to assign a salary grade to hot-spot jobs in a range that reflects the points assigned, you would not be able to fill those positions because market rates are generally higher than the point values. Therefore, to meet market demand, job evaluators ultimately make the points fit the market. This must be documented so that when classifying future positions, human resources (HR), library management, and/or the review committee can see how positions were classified in the first place. This question may not be appropriate for board members, as they would not typically be using the system themselves, but would certainly be appropriate for library management, HR, and others involved in the classification process.

8. *What is the appropriate balance between external market equity and internal job worth?*

   Here you are attempting to see what should drive pay rates when the results of the market study are inconsistent with the point factor or other internal job evaluation results. This response will also guide your work even when designing and implementing a market-based pay plan. Since you will not be surveying all library jobs (see chapter 7), you will need to slot non-benchmark jobs. Reviewing the internal value of the job in addition to what you know about the market will aid in this effort. (Note: Those of you who have experience with library compensation programs will be familiar with these concepts; other readers will learn about them in chapter 7.) Even without an emphasis on internal equity, you will need to be aware of the impacts of salary compression (see chapter 10). What if, after implementing study recommendations, you have four reference librarians at the same branch library ranging from six months to sixteen years on the job, now all making the same salary? Will this be acceptable? Do you have money in your project budget to alleviate some of this compression?

9. *How do employees move through these pay ranges (get increases)? Does it make sense to you? How would you change that?*

   This question will help you get a feel for staff members' perspectives on pay increases, job growth and development, and performance management. Should increases be automatic each year or should they be related to performance? Should everyone get the same increase or should it vary depending on performance level (i.e., outstanding performers get a higher percentage than fully competent performers)?

10. *Are there any issues of concern regarding the distribution of job responsibilities in your department?*

    Because compensation is a component of your human resources system, a project often extends beyond the boundaries of a compensation project. The information you learn from this question is often helpful in job design and in activities seeking more alignment of roles with goals or an enhancement of efficiency and effectiveness. This question may not be appropriate for all participants or at all, depending on the scope of your project.

11. *For what positions is an MLS degree necessary? Why? What librarian functions are being performed? What are the essential functions of an MLS librarian in this library system?*

    Motivated in part by the tight labor market for credentialed librarians as well as by financial limitations, some public libraries are looking at the roles of professional librarians—along with those inherent in other employee categories—to ensure that employees are performing the highest-level duties in their classifications and that the lowest-level work is pushed down to the lowest possible level within the organization. So, although we all compose letters on computers, for instance, administrative support personnel, rather than librarians or department heads, should send out the mailings.

    In addition, a library that encourages employees to return to school for a bachelor's degree or an MLS will have some pay policies and practices different from those of a system that recruits only applicants who already hold an MLS degree. Similarly, a system that wants to reward employee longevity may have a different pay plan than one that places a high premium on goal achievement. Finally, systems that are planning to downsize, reorganize to use MLS positions at only the management level, or open branches in many new communities will have different goals and consequently different pay plans. A library system that can't afford to hire any staff with an MLS degree will truly need to design creative pay plans *and* take the time to consider how it services its customers in the most effective way. Finally, if your library is considering requesting that applicants for branch manager positions have an MBA or coursework in business, that too would be important information to have.

Ability to Implement a Compensation Program

12. *What is the financial position of the library system? What resources have been approved or funded to implement adjustments if necessary?*

It is important that funds have been, or can be, set aside to implement at least partial salary adjustments. It simply is not good for morale to conduct a compensation study and then leave it on a shelf. There should be a commitment to at least partial funding, in accordance with resources, and to implementation over time to the extent feasible. As mentioned earlier, consider the costs necessary not only to implement market findings but to address other pay inequities, such as salary compression.

13. *What should the library pay in relation to the market? At the market value? A little below? Above?*

Although most library systems say they would like to pay at the going market rate, some find that their financial position does not allow it or that their benefits are so outstanding they choose to pay a percentage (usually 90 percent) of market rate. One library needed help designing a three-year implementation plan to achieve employee pay at 90 percent of market. Needless to say, it was quite a bit behind the market. Libraries must also take into consideration that in three years, the salary data collected during the study are, for all intents and purposes, out of date. We would not recommend that you base a compensation plan on three-year-old data. Think what has happened to the American economy in the last year alone!

Other library systems are willing to pay above-market rates to attract and retain the best-qualified employees. A recent public sector client wanted a system flexible enough to generally pay at market but to go above the market rate for employees in hot-spot jobs or for high performers.

Finally, be aware of what data you are asking for. A recent study conducted for a county library system in the Washington, D.C., metro area revealed that though the client considered itself a comparator and competitor organization with several other large county libraries, the data obtained showed that implementing market-competitive pay ranges was impossible in the system's current budget situation. The board questioned why these other libraries were included in the first place (a resounding endorsement for early project communications), and the system ended up setting ranges competitive with its local government jurisdictions and two immediately neighboring county libraries only.

Communications

14. *What, if anything, do employees know about this project?*

As an internal consultant to this project, you may not need the answer to this question; however, external consultants would like to know. Often the answer "Employees are fully aware of the study; it's been communicated in a variety of ways" is not consistent with reality when you begin conducting focus groups, interviews, or employee presentations. "What study?" the employees may say. Though this is a digression about employee communications, we can't count the number of times employees have been sent letters or e-mails announcing the study, only to have them later say, "We never got that letter/e-mail." Further digging reveals that the letters were included as paycheck stuffers, but with so many employees using direct deposit, they never open their pay envelopes! Or, an all-staff e-mail was sent, but a known segment of staff never checks e-mail. It is critical to identify the best—and multiple—ways of communicating with staff.

Other

15. *Are there any issues you are aware of that may have an impact on this project?*

    Again, as an employee working within the system, you may not need to ask this question if you are familiar with the library's history and current events. Consultants, on the other hand, ask this question because they know that the compensation study is only one of many events. For example, employees may be jaded because of the results (or lack of results) from prior studies, and other priorities might limit the amount of management and employee time available to work on this project. If a new software system is about to be installed and all employees are to be trained in its use, or if all technical processing functions are going to be outsourced during the project time frame, it's important to know this early on in the process so that the work plan can account for it and answers to employee concerns and considerations can be prepared.

16. *What would be a successful outcome of this project for you? How can its success be ensured?*

    External consultants always want to ensure that they are meeting the goals set by their clients. If you have been appointed project manager or a member of the review committee by senior management in your library system, you should discuss the criteria for success in advance of the project as well.

    Do not limit your inquiry about success criteria to the opinions of senior management. Ask employees this question as well, attempting to gauge their expectations. If they run to extremes (e.g., "I expect a huuuuge salary increase because I don't earn nearly enough" or "Nothin's gonna happen anyway"), you may be able to help them frame realistic goals and talk about management's commitment.

Framework for Posing Context Questions

The preceding were just sample questions. When you prepare for your interviews with management and the board, think through the purpose of each of your questions. Remember that the list of questions may not be the same for each stakeholder group. Think about the following:

> What do you need to know from this stakeholder/constituency?
>
> Why?
>
> What information will the responses to this question give you?
>
> What, if anything, can you do with this information?

At the end of the interview process, will you have all the information you need to understand the compensation and related issues facing the library, to draft a compensation philosophy, and to select and propose the design components of the pay plan?

Thus, for each question, make sure its answer will provide you with information you need and can use. It is generally not a good idea to ask questions that are not relevant to your project. Sometimes it is even detrimental, because those interviewed might think something may change when, indeed, nothing is planned.

After you complete the interviews, you might find it helpful to compile the data in a simple PowerPoint presentation with main categories and subheadings, and review it with management and the review committee. Include a draft of the compensation philosophy with the presentation to encourage discussion and to ensure that it captures the intent of management. The next section of this chapter will give you an overview of what a compensation philosophy is and how to craft one.

COMPENSATION PHILOSOPHY

A compensation philosophy is a clear statement of intent that is developed to guide compensation decisions made during the project and afterward. It should reflect a clear understanding of the library's intentions and desired level of competitiveness with the market. It can also be published and serve as a reference for managers and employees on how the library will handle compensation decisions. In general, a compensation philosophy is a guiding statement. Its components include

> goals and objectives for compensation and the compensation plan at the library
>
> definition of your marketplace
>
> desired degree of competitiveness with your market
>
> value placed on internal equity, performance, longevity, training, career development, and other factors of value to the library

Examples of real-life compensation philosophies adopted by library systems follow.

Example 1: Anytown Public Library

> Anytown Public Library seeks to recruit and retain well-qualified, highly motivated employees. Employees will be compensated for their contribution to the library's mission, for meeting their goals, and for innovation, risk-taking, and continuous improvement.
>
> *Guidelines*
>
> Jobs will be assigned to salary grades and ranges. Each range will be reflective of, and externally competitive with, the appropriate market for that job. The guideline for external competitiveness of salary ranges is the market median of the range minimum. Salary ranges will be revised and updated regularly to reflect the market.

Originally included in this compensation philosophy, then excluded because of potential fiscal constraints, was the following:

> Anytown Public Library provides tuition reimbursement and supports skills improvement and career development for employees.

This philosophy also indicates what Anytown Public Library values in its employees, and hence what it will reward: contribution, goal achievement, innovation, risk-taking, and continuous improvement.

Example 2: ABC Public Library System

> The goal of the ABC Public Library System's compensation plan is to recruit and retain qualified, competent employees to best serve the needs of a growing and diverse community.
>
> ABC Public Library System's salary ranges balance competitiveness with the external market and with internal equity. In general, the comparable market consists of libraries and public jurisdictions in the region. The comparable market for "hot" (in-demand) professional and management jobs may include private industry in the region. "Competitive" is defined as the median salary and/or salary ranges of the market.

This philosophy indicates that both internal and external equity are valued and important to the library. It also differentiates hot jobs by broadening the definition of the labor market to include private sector organizations.

Example 3: Public University

> The goal of Public University's compensation plan is to establish and maintain a market-based salary program with salary ranges that are competitive with a broad mix of industries in the regional marketplace and with public doctoral institutions of similar size.
>
> Jobs will be assigned to salary ranges based on the median value of similar jobs in the marketplace.
>
> Within these salary ranges, employees will be paid for their individual performance and contribution to the campus mission.

This organization's philosophy clearly states the library's commitment to a market-based compensation plan. It defines its market broadly, informing the reader that private companies are part of its marketplace. It also clearly articulates a reward system based on performance.

Example 4: XYZ Public Library

> The goal of XYZ Public Library's compensation plan is to recruit and retain qualified employees. XYZ Public Library's salary ranges will be set at the market to achieve this objective.
>
> ■ The market for professional positions is public libraries in the region.
> ■ The market for nonexempt, nonlibrary positions is local.
> ■ Internal equity is very important.
>
> XYZ Public Library encourages career development and lateral and upward mobility within the library system; it does not provide extra compensation for specialized skills (e.g., computer search skills or second language ability).

A compensation philosophy does not ordinarily respond to a single issue—such as the one for specialized skills in this example. The issue was controversial because some employees were paid for specialized skills while others were not. Implementation of the new pay plan was to have eliminated the need to consider extra compensation for specialized skills. Because the issue was contentious, it was decided to clarify it (and "lay it to rest," according to the human resources director) in the compensation philosophy.

Example 5: A Maryland Public Library

The goal of QRS Public Library's compensation plan is to recruit, retain, and motivate highly qualified employees. Our salary ranges should achieve a balance of being competitive with the external market as well as internally equitable and should reflect the median salary offered by the market. The comparable market for professional library positions is Anne Arundel, Baltimore, Carroll, Frederick, Cecil, and Howard County public libraries. The comparable market for all other positions is a combination of library systems and other local public and private sector employers.

Salaries to new hires should be offered and increases awarded based on a combination of factors including related experience, education, licenses, etc.

This philosophy, a little different from the others, identifies the local county public libraries with which the subject library competes for professional librarian positions and thereby limits the competition to these library systems, exclusive of other public, nonprofit, or private sector employers.

Example 6: A Medium-Sized Metropolitan Area Public Library

The goal of City Library's total compensation plan is to recruit and retain highly qualified employees.

When fiscally prudent, the library's salary ranges will be set at the 60th percentile of the market in order to achieve this objective.

The market for professional positions is public libraries in the region as well as nonprofit [agencies], private [employers], and local governments.

In addition to comparing to librarian positions, comparisons will be made to positions requiring comparable education and experience.

The market for nonexempt, nonlibrary positions is local.

Internal equity is very important.

City Library encourages career development [and] lateral and upward mobility within the library system.

This philosophy defines more specifically at what level of competitiveness the library would like to be in comparison to the market, also clearly defined by categories. This example also speaks to pay equity (see chapter 7) in stating that "comparisons will be made to positions requiring comparable education and experience." These positions may not necessarily be in libraries, but could be in local government, in local higher education, or with other employers.

Example 7: Small, Rural Library

The Library desires to be competitive in its identified market in providing compensation to top-quality, qualified employees. The goals of the Board's compensation plan are to

recruit and retain qualified, high-quality, and high-performing employees in order to provide outstanding customer service to best meet the needs of customers in a fast-growing environment; and establish, ensure, and maintain internal equity among positions as well as individual employee salaries.

To achieve these goals the Board will strive to

Be competitive (pay at market rates) with the defined market in the pay offered to both new and current employees, with a particular focus on hard-to-recruit and -retain management positions;

Maintain internal equity within the assigned salary ranges; and

Provide appropriate training, development, and career opportunities to enhance recruitment and retention efforts.

The Board's management assumes responsibility for the ongoing administration and revision of the compensation plan and philosophy as necessary.

The market for employees comprises local and regional public libraries and non-profit and private sector employers.

At this time, consideration will be taken to ensure that key management positions are competitive with their correlating positions in local government to ensure a strong recruitment and retention effort.

This final example is interesting and relevant for several reasons. First, it calls particular attention not only to the internal equity of positions but to the internal equity of individual salaries as well. Salary compression was a significant and ongoing problem at this organization, as is often the case in public sector organizations where numerous salary studies have been conducted over time but attention has not been paid to the equity of individual salaries. Second, this library felt a particular level of competition with the local county government for the higher-level, management positions. This concern was raised at the project outset by HR, the library's executive director, and the board of directors, and proved a valid concern once findings were analyzed. Though emphasizing upper management in a compensation study is not often well accepted by employees, in this case, because of the true recruitment and retention crisis and because of strong communication and education throughout the project, employees were very accepting of this philosophy and of the findings in general.

COMPENSATION POLICY DESIGN COMPONENTS

In addition to a brief philosophy statement, or as a substitute for it, a more specific policy can be created to delineate details of the compensation plan, including selected criteria and responsibilities of senior management and the board of trustees. An example of such a policy is shown in worksheet 6.

Begin to think about options and personalize a philosophy for your organization. Consider and discuss the following when developing a compensation philosophy:

What are the compensation plan goals and objectives?

How will you define the marketplace?

How will you determine what jobs are worth?

Who is going to manage the system? How will you keep it up to date?

Do you want broad or narrow job classifications? Generic or flexible?

What is the desired degree of competitiveness with the market? Will you define differences in the market for different positions?

ABC PUBLIC LIBRARY'S COMPENSATION POLICY

The goal of [library name] is to [**a.** Insert brief mission.]

> *Example:* We believe that it is in the best interest of both the library system and our employees to fairly compensate our workforce for the value of the work provided. It is our intention to use a compensation system that will determine the current market value of a position based on the skills, knowledge, and behaviors required of a fully competent employee. The system used is objective and nondiscriminatory in theory, application, and practice. We have determined that this can best be accomplished by

[**b.** Select one of the following or draft one appropriate to your situation.]

☐ using a professional compensation consultant and system recommended by library management and approved by the board of trustees.

☐ using internal resources to develop a system approved by library management and submitted to the board of trustees.

Compensation System Goals

[**c.** Select all that apply or develop others appropriate to your system.]

☐ 1. The compensation system will price positions to market by using appropriate local, regional, national, and library-specific custom-made and published survey data.

☐ 2. The market data will primarily include other library systems, local public jurisdictions [if public library], and not-for-profit organizations and will address significant market differences due to geographic location.

☐ 3. The system will evaluate external equity: market pricing of benchmark jobs compared with similar [library name] jobs.

☐ 4. The system will evaluate internal equity: the relative worth of each job when comparing the required level of job competencies, formal training and experience, responsibility, and accountability of one job to another and arranging all jobs in a formal salary grade structure.

[Select one.]

☐ Professional support and consultation will be available to design and implement a new market-pricing compensation system.

☐ The compensation team of [library name] will design and implement the compensation system. Professional resources, including books, local experts, and library or local government colleagues, will be made available to the team as necessary.

☐ 5. The compensation system must be flexible enough to ensure that [library name] is able to recruit and retain a highly qualified workforce while providing the structure necessary to effectively manage the overall compensation program.

☐ 6. The salary structure will be reviewed periodically to ensure market competitiveness. The salaries of one-third of all positions will be reviewed each year on a rolling basis to ensure ongoing market competitiveness.

☐ 7. The assistant director of finance and administration [**d.** or select appropriate title] is responsible for the ongoing administration of the program.

Library Board of Trustees Responsibilities

The board of trustees of [library system name] is responsible for the review of recommendations made by the library director and will give final approval for the new compensation system.

As part of the annual budgeting process the board of trustees will review and approve funds to be allocated for total compensation, which would include base salaries, bonuses or any other variable pay, and all other related expenses including benefit plans as recommended by management.

The board of trustees shall set the salary, salary range, and specific components of the total compensation package for the library director.

Management Responsibilities

The library director is responsible and accountable to the board of trustees. In that capacity the director is charged with ensuring that the library is staffed with highly qualified, fully competent employees and that all programs are administered within appropriate guidelines and within the approved budget.

On an annual basis the library director will review and approve recommended changes to the salary ranges as recommended by

[**e.** Select as appropriate.]

☐ the human resources director

☐ the compensation review team

☐ the assistant director of finance and administration

as determined through periodic market analysis.

The salary budget shall include an allocation for budget adjustments. However, the individual determinations for each employee's salary increase will be the responsibility of the library director. This includes such responsibilities as determining the appropriate staffing levels, titles, position levels, merit and promotional increases, and compensation consisting of salary and other discretionary pay for all positions.

The library director shall ensure that salary ranges are updated and individual jobs are market-priced periodically and that pay equity adjustments are administered in a fair and equitable manner. The

[**f.** Select one.]

☐ deputy director

☐ director of human resources

☐ assistant director

☐ director of finance and administration

☐ other _____

is responsible for ensuring that the total compensation program is managed for consistency and equity.

Signed _____ Date _____

Will adjustments for cost of living be made?

Will you take pay equity into consideration?

What is the importance of internal equity? Individual equity?

From an internal equity perspective, what is most valued?

How is performance recognized and rewarded? How does employee pay progress through the range?

What is the impact of benefits? Longevity? Incentives? Career development?

Who has responsibility for ongoing administration? For revising the plan? For evaluating and assessing fairness?

Do the philosophy and compensation plan align with the library's mission?

This list not only was considered by the director, board, and HR staff during a recent project but also was included in an education presentation to the employee review committee at the beginning of the project. It is very helpful to get employee perspectives on these issues as well as management's thoughts.

To get started with your own compensation philosophy, fill in the blanks in worksheet 6 as follows:

a. Insert a brief goal statement or mission for your compensation philosophy. What do you want the compensation plan to accomplish? Think about recruitment, retention, internal/external equity, and so on.

b. Identify how the compensation system will be developed. Will you use a consultant? Will you work internally to develop the plan?

c. Select/identify goals of the compensation system. Will you focus solely on external equity? If so, who constitutes your market? Will the market be the same for all positions? Will you use published data? Will you include a mix of internal and external equity?

d. Identify who will be responsible for ensuring the ongoing administration and upkeep of the compensation program.

e. Identify who will be responsible for recommending changes and updates to salary ranges. Do you have an internal compensation team? Will the human resources director perform this function?

f. Identify who will have ultimate responsibility and accountability for ensuring the equity and consistency of pay adjustments.

In all cases, if the choices provided do not fit your library, develop your own language. These examples are meant to be illustrative only, as a compensation philosophy should be highly customized to fit the culture, organization, and needs of your library.

As you can see from the worksheet, you will need to gather important information before beginning to design the compensation plan. What you learn from senior management will provide you with the answers to the following:

1. Who is our *market*? That is, who are our competitors for human capital?

2. What is our level of *competitiveness*? Do we want to lead the market, match it, or set our rates behind it? Keep in mind that your choice will not only have an impact on your salary budget, it will also affect your library's culture. For example, an above-market pay policy can contribute to a feeling of selectiveness or elitism—in the very best sense of these words. Employees might feel that they are the best and are delighted to be members

of the library system. A low pay level can contribute to the opposite culture, sometimes leading to below-par contributions and employees seeking to leave. This impact, however, can be minimized given a mission-driven culture and management practices that value employees. Our recent experience shows that if a library includes a reference to a specific point of competitiveness (e.g., 60 percent of the market), the phrase "if fiscally prudent" is included as well.

3. Are we going to base our pay plan on *individuals and their competencies* or *on the job?* This book assumes that *jobs* will be evaluated rather than the individuals performing them. In the event your library selects a method of compensation that is person-based, you will still need to collect market data to establish appropriate pay ranges.

When job-based pay is used, the assumption is that the worth of the job can be determined in the marketplace or via an internally focused job evaluation methodology and that employees (individually and as a group) performing the job are worth (only) as much to your library as the job itself is worth on the market. Chapter 11 presents a broad overview of skills- and knowledge-based pay. In these types of systems, individuals are rewarded for increasing their skills or knowledge.

4. Will pay be based on *performance* or will a *step system* (one that provides for the same annual increase to all but the most unsatisfactory employees) be designed? Or, will you create some combination of the two, where steps are provided to employees but only after a fully competent performance rating is received? Perhaps two steps will be awarded for outstanding performance. Other options are discussed in chapter 10, including an overview of performance-based pay.

5. Is the focus of the compensation plan going to be on *internal* or *external* equity? Both? The intent of an internal-equity-driven system is to ensure that employees performing similar work are paid similarly and that jobs with similar value to the organization share the same pay ranges. Conversely, the goal of an external-equity-focused system is to pay employees in accordance with the market. These concepts will be fully covered in chapters 6 and 7, where the tools are provided to design compensation plans based on these systems.

An advantage of an internally based system is that it can lead to or support a culture of homogeneity and a feeling of fair and equal treatment. On the other hand, because such a system may not attend to the salaries paid in the labor market, the library might have to pay more than necessary to attract and retain good employees just to maintain internal relationships. Conversely, the library might not offer enough salary to attract candidates to fill hot-spot jobs for which recruitment and retention are more difficult.

An important advantage of a compensation plan based on external equity is that it is sensitive to and competitive with the market. That is, pay rates and ranges are aligned with what is paid in the market. A disadvantage, however, is that implementing a compensation plan primarily focused on external equity can lead to the disruption of long-held internal relationships of positions to each other. This change might create feelings of lack of worth and inequity by those holding positions that may not be as highly valued as they were in an internally based system.

A third option—developing a system that reflects both internal and external equity—is our preferred choice of late. There will always be internal relationships of positions that are sacred and cannot be modified because of historical, political, or other internal reasons. By the same token, there will always be positions that no matter how you structure your pay range and build in internal equity will require additional pay to recruit or retain (and these positions change from time to time, making the scenario even trickier to keep up with!). By respecting both the internal relationships and the external market to the extent practical and possible, the resulting compensation system will reflect the reality of your current operating environment and not be just a list of points or a graph of salary data.

6. What role should *base pay* and *benefits* play in relation to total compensation? At the very least, you should have an idea of the overall value of your benefits plan and how it compares with the benefits of your competitors. In addition, you should consider incentives and noncash awards as part of your compensation plan.

7. To what extent is *job security* essentially taken for granted? Unlike employees at private companies, most library employees have not undergone a major downsizing or restructuring effort. Where restructuring has occurred, generally all employees were assured that they would not lose their jobs (although they might have been given different jobs in different locations).

8. Should the pay plan account for *contingent workers*? Although many libraries use substitutes to augment their workforce, should plans be designed that consider a core and a contingent workforce? Is that a possibility in your library system's future?

9. To what extent is your library system going to reward *seniority*? On the one hand, a job is only worth so much, but on the other, what is the message you want to send to employees—especially those with long service and those aspiring to long service?

The following chapters will provide details on establishing internal and external equity and will give you ideas for blending and combining both in order to fit your library's needs.

four | **Job Analysis**

Once you have selected a consultant (or decided to conduct the project yourself), identified your internal project manager, and established your employee committee (or decided not to), you are ready to begin the real project work (believe it or not, all those decisions you've just made are only the beginning!).

Before you make any decisions about your compensation program, you must make sure that you understand the work that is performed by the employees in your library system. Job analysis will provide this information.

Libraries are transformed so frequently that the tasks of yesterday (literally as well as metaphorically) may not be those needed tomorrow. A compensation study often uncovers activities that maintain the status quo instead of those activities that promote the library's goals and plans. A study can also highlight work that is being done but is not recognized at the appropriate level. To enhance the library's flexibility as well as promote employee growth and development, we recommend the following:

1. Look at how work is accomplished—not just individual tasks, but how and by whom (position, not individuals) the work is being done.

2. Review the library's strategic goals to ensure that the work that needs to be done to fulfill them is being done and is placed at the proper level.

3. Ensure that work is being done at the lowest possible level within the organization.

It is generally suggested that you begin your compensation study with a complete and thorough analysis of all library jobs. Conducting this analysis will allow you to

> identify the essential job functions for each position
>
> prepare up-to-date job descriptions that reflect your library system's culture, technology, services and programs, organizational design, demographics, and skills and competencies
>
> gather relevant market data for positions (good job matching requires baseline information about a job's essential functions, level of responsibility, and qualifications)
>
> comply with federal and state legislation

If you select a point factor method of job evaluation (see chapter 6) to determine your internal job hierarchy, it is particularly important to conduct the job analysis early in the process, so you have all the data you need when you begin to evaluate jobs.

This chapter defines job analysis and discusses data to collect and collection procedures. A sample job analysis questionnaire as well as additional questions you may or may not choose to use are also included.

DEFINITION

Job analysis is the systematic process of collecting relevant, work-related information about the nature, scope, and responsibilities of your library's jobs. As a result of job analysis, you will understand and be able to document the knowledge, skills, abilities, and other factors required for each library position as well as the essential functions of each. Job analysis is the foundation on which job descriptions are written and jobs are priced in the market. It is also the tool that will enable you to understand the essential functions of each position. Job analysis can be an eye-opening experience: do not assume that you know exactly what each staff member is doing on a daily basis. It is probably safe to say that you have a good grasp on what you *think* staff members should be doing, but you may not truly realize what they are actually doing from day to day. The job analysis process will give you that detail. It will also provide you with the information you need to ensure compliance with the Americans with Disabilities Act.

USES

Job analysis findings ultimately have several uses, among them being able to ensure the proper classification of positions and having current and accurate information to use in the development of job descriptions. These findings also provide the ability to accurately match your positions to those in other organizations for salary-setting purposes. Job analysis data can and should be used for a variety of purposes supporting human resources and strategic planning, including

> designing jobs
>
> making recruitment, selection, and placement decisions
>
> making reclassification or promotion decisions
>
> setting performance criteria
>
> establishing training, job development, and career counseling programs
>
> designing job families and career paths
>
> ensuring compliance with legal requirements on exempt versus nonexempt status (Fair Labor Standards Act) and overtime eligibility
>
> ensuring compliance with legal requirements on reasonable accommodations (Americans with Disabilities Act)
>
> planning human resources
>
> making outsourcing decisions
>
> determining organization design
>
> analyzing staffing patterns
>
> analyzing workflow
>
> identifying succession planning gaps

Before commencing job analysis, your first step is to consider

> what information should be collected
>
> how the information will be collected
>
> who should be involved
>
> what type of analysis you will use

DATA TO COLLECT

In job analysis, you want to gather information regarding the knowledge, skills, abilities, and other factors pertaining to or required by the job. Always remember (and communicate to employees) that this process is about the jobs at the library, not the performance of the people doing the jobs. Other pertinent factors involved in job analysis include working conditions, especially if they are adverse and involve difficulty (such as excessive or extensive lifting, outdoor work, or work around heavy machinery); supervisory responsibility; or key success factors such as the ability to work as a team member. The amount of data to be collected depends on the purpose of the job analysis process, including whether the findings will be used to determine the internal equity of the library system by applying a point factor system to all jobs. (This application of job analysis to a point factor system is discussed in chapter 6.)

HOW TO COLLECT THE INFORMATION

There are a variety of ways to collect information about jobs: observations, interviews, job analysis questionnaires (JAQs), job descriptions, or work diaries or logs. Figure 4.1 lists the methods used to collect information about the positions in your library system. A description of each method includes the types of jobs for which each method is most appropriate and the advantages and disadvantages of each. A few notes about figure 4.1: observing employees' work firsthand is rightly described as an expensive and time-consuming method of collecting data. The soft benefit of this type of information gathering, however, cannot be understated. The same can be said for conducting employee interviews. Both methods provide employees with an opportunity to be heard and to explain exactly what their job entails. In no other phase of a compensation project do we receive as much feedback from employees as when employee interviews or job audits (observations) are conducted. Employees tell us (either through HR or directly in e-mails or a project hotline) how much they appreciate someone taking the time to speak with them, visit their job sites, and listen to their description of their work. Though you certainly can't expect to interview or observe your entire employee population, you can set a benchmark percentage—perhaps 20 percent of positions—to ensure good representative coverage of a variety of jobs throughout the library.

As you can see from figure 4.1, the questionnaire provides the most consistent advantages. Because one disadvantage is that follow-up by telephone or through face-to-face or small-group interviews may be necessary to ensure clarification or to obtain additional information, we recommend that you select the questionnaire approach augmented with interviews as necessary (in addition to reaping the advantages of employee involvement mentioned earlier). Because the questionnaire method will give you the most information over the widest variety of positions in a short time and because it is cost-effective, the job analysis questionnaire is fully discussed in this chapter. If you decide to add other methods, such as collecting logs or work diaries or observing work, you can easily add them.

JOB ANALYSIS QUESTIONNAIRE

You, the members of the committee, the consultant, or a member of the human resources department can draft a job analysis questionnaire to suit your needs. Suggested topics to include in the questionnaire are found in the following pages. In addition, figure 4.2

Figure 4.1

Comparison of Methods for Conducting a Job Analysis

Method	Description	Best for	Advantages	Disadvantages
Observation	Watching employees perform their jobs, recording tasks and duties observed, and then compiling information into the necessary skills, abilities, and knowledge required for each position	Repetitious, manual jobs	Simple	May not provide sufficient information; time-consuming; costly; requires an observation protocol; requires trained observers; may not represent true picture of employees' duties and responsibilities
Interview	Face-to-face discussion in which an employee is questioned about the skills, abilities, and knowledge needed to perform the job	Management jobs, any job that has changed markedly, and jobs where there is a difference between the employee's and supervisor's perception of the position	Thorough; increases involvement, input, and buy-in of interviewed employees	Time-consuming; expensive; may be redundant if many incumbents in the same job are interviewed
Questionnaire	Incumbents (and often their supervisors or managers) answer questions on a form outlining skills, abilities, and knowledge needed to perform the job; responses are compiled producing a composite statement of job requirements	Analyzing many or all jobs in the library with limited human resources; providing foundation for point factor job evaluation	Increases involvement as all employees complete the questionnaire; least expensive	May require follow-up for clarification; time-consuming for employees to complete and supervisors to review
Work diaries or logs	Employee maintains an anecdotal record of the frequency and timing of tasks over an extended period; the information is reviewed to determine patterns	Most jobs	Thorough	Time-consuming and may not be easy to maintain; may require the diary to be kept over a long time to ensure that periodic (quarterly, annual) tasks are included
Job descriptions	Job descriptions are reviewed (if they are known to be current and accurate) to review the knowledge, skills, and abilities needed to perform the job	Analyzing many or all jobs in the library with limited human resources; providing foundation for whole job evaluation	Inexpensive	Assumes job descriptions are current and accurate; no employee involvement

is a sample questionnaire that you may wish to adopt or use as a starting point for creating your own. The project manager and members of the committee should review the questionnaire after it is drafted. It is important that the questionnaire fit your library. Check the language. Do you use the term "customer" or "patron"? Do you divide your organization into "divisions" or "departments"? Make sure that the language is consistent and that employees will understand exactly what you are referring to. Feedback from the review step will alert you to any language that might be vague or misunderstood. It will also help point out areas of inconsistency and redundancy or highlight questions that do not allow employees to completely describe their jobs. Using this feedback, revise the JAQ as necessary before issuing it to all employees.

Topics

A sample JAQ is shown in figure 4.2. This sample is appropriate if you are also planning to use the information for an internal equity job evaluation method, such as applying a point factor system to each job (see chapter 6). If you choose to use a whole-job evaluation system, you may not need to collect as much detail. The items for which you will seek information should reflect those factors important to, and valued by, your library system. They may include decision making, problem solving, communications, and customer service, to name a few. In our experience, it is helpful to get input on these factors from a variety of stakeholders, including your employee committee, key managers and library leadership, and board members. You can provide these groups with a starter list of factors, and ask them to identify the top ten or top twelve most important. You can also invite them to add their own. We recently encountered several factors we had used before—they were suggested by members of the employee review committee. It turned out that these factors (including building responsibility and certifications required beyond educational degrees) were very important to this particular system. Once you have collected suggestions from all these groups, you can prepare a ranked list of the top fifteen or twenty factors and discuss narrowing it as necessary.

For all purposes, the following topics should be covered in the questionnaire:

1. *Introduction and purpose.* Describe this tool and explain what it will be used for in addition to giving specific instructions for its completion. Even if you are able to distribute the questionnaire to employees at large group meetings (discussed later in this chapter), assume that not every employee will be able or will choose to attend a session and make sure the instructions are adequately detailed to stand alone. Request the employee's name, title, work location (i.e., branch) and department, length of time in current position, length of time in total with the library, and part-time/full-time status. The length of time in the position helps to identify discrepancies that might be found between a relatively new employee and an experienced one in reporting position tasks. For example, it is possible that an incumbent with four months on the job will report a difference in duties and amount of time spent on each when compared with an incumbent with five years in the role. On the other end of the longevity spectrum, it is not necessarily true that the report of the experienced employee is more accurate. It is possible that the veteran may be performing functions that are now obsolete or that have emerged as functions of institutional knowledge or that the veteran simply knows the job very well and handles it in an exemplary fashion. The point is—don't prejudge accuracy of responses based on longevity. Asking for total time employed with the library will give you similar perspective and may help you make decisions that will alleviate potential salary compression during implementation (see chapter 10).

Figure 4.2
Sample Job Analysis Questionnaire

Introduction

The purpose of this questionnaire is to gather information about your job. We are asking you to complete the questionnaire because *you* know the most about *your* job. Because the information you provide will be used in reviewing the internal equity of the library's jobs, it is very important that you give *accurate, thoughtful, and complete answers* to all questions. Your answers, the responses from other employees performing similar work, and your supervisor's comments will serve as the basis for

- summarizing key position information
- ensuring that all jobs are accurately assessed
- determining how jobs within the library compare with each other
- updating the library's job descriptions

**Important: complete the questionnaire with your job in mind,
not your personal characteristics or performance.**

General Instructions

This is not a performance evaluation—we simply want to make sure we understand the duties and responsibilities of the jobs at our library. Think about what knowledge, education, and skills are required for a person to be successful in this job. Before you begin to answer the questions, please take a few minutes to read through the entire questionnaire, reading all instructions carefully. Once you begin to answer the questions, be as objective as possible, responding about your job and *not* your personal situation or performance.

As you respond to the questions, your answers should reflect

what would normally be expected of someone fully trained in the job, rather than a beginner or someone performing over and above what is required

the expected or normal routine of the job rather than special projects, temporary assignments, or out-of-the-ordinary occurrences

the job as it is today, rather than what you expect it to become in the future

In addition:

Complete each section *accurately* and *thoroughly.* Try not to understate or inflate your answers. Please do not use acronyms or abbreviations without defining them at least once.

Choose the *best* response for your job. If no response exactly matches your job, choose the *one* that reflects your job 90 percent or more of the time.

Answer *every* question and provide examples.

Feel free to write comments in any section and to attach additional materials if necessary.

Employees in the same position may complete one Job Analysis Questionnaire together.

After you have completed this questionnaire, please give it to your supervisor by [date]. If you have any questions, please contact your supervisor, our human resources (HR) director, or one of the following members of the review committee: [names]

Completed Job Analysis Questionnaires should be returned to

Your supervisor: _____ by [date] _____

Supervisors to department heads: _____ by [date] _____

Department heads to HR: _____ by [date] _____

As employees of the library, you are an important part of this project. Thank you for your participation.

Name: _____

Job title: _____

Work location: _____

Department: _____

Supervisor's name and title: _____

How long have you been in your current job? _____

How long have you been employed by the library? _____

Are you a(n): ☐ Full-time salaried employee? ☐ Part-time salaried employee? ☐ Hourly employee?

If part-time, how many hours per week do you work? _____

I. JOB SUMMARY

Please provide a brief summary of your position. (Think about how you would describe your job if a friend were to ask you what you do. You may wish to complete this section after you have completed the rest of the questionnaire.)

_____

_____

_____

_____

_____

_____

_____

_____

_____

_____

_____

_____

II. DUTIES AND RESPONSIBILITIES

Please list and describe the essential duties and responsibilities of your job. List these duties in order of importance, listing first those tasks that you consider the most important to your job. Be sure to consider your work assignments over a long enough period to picture your job as a whole. For instance, if your work varies from season to season or at specific times, you may have to view your job over an entire year to accurately estimate percentages. On the other hand, if your duties are basically the same from month to month, you may only have to consider your job over a week or month to accurately reflect percentages.

After listing all duties and responsibilities, indicate the approximate percentage of your time spent performing each job duty on an annual basis. Try to include all duties that require at least 5 percent or more of your time. The total of all duties should be no more than 100 percent; however, do not spend undue time trying to get percentages exact. For any activity that requires less than 5 percent of your time over the course of the year, please use more-general terms and combine all or some of them to estimate a percentage. For example, you may want to list "miscellaneous clerical duties" with a corresponding percentage of 5 percent. Attach additional sheets or materials as necessary.

Job Duty (please describe)	% of Time Annually
1. _____	_____
2. _____	_____
3. _____	_____
4. _____	_____
5. _____	_____
6. _____	_____
7. _____	_____
8. _____	_____
	Total 100%

(Cont.)

Figure 4.2
Sample Job Analysis Questionnaire (Cont.)

III. SPECIAL PROJECTS

Please describe any special projects or assignments you are working on. These should describe work that is not an ongoing part of your position. Include an estimated duration or time frame for each (e.g., three months, summer, etc.) in the column on the right.

Project   **Duration**

_____   _____

_____   _____

_____   _____

_____   _____

_____   _____

_____   _____

_____   _____

IV. EDUCATION/TRAINING

This question asks about the minimum education and training required to adequately perform the duties of your job. Select the minimum level of training and/or education that best describes the job requirements rather than your personal background. Please check only one box.

☐ The job requires some high school education or training.

☐ The job requires a high school diploma or GED.

☐ The job requires additional training or up to one year of job-related course work after high school. An example of additional training at this level is that required to obtain a CDL (commercial driver's license).

☐ The job requires an associate's degree or two years of formal training beyond high school.

☐ The job requires a bachelor's degree or training or education necessary to obtain certificates such as A+, certified electrician, or certified HVAC mechanic.

☐ The job requires additional education in a specialized area, including education or training necessary to obtain CFRE (Certified Fund Raising Executive) or APR (Accredited in Public Relations) certifications.

☐ The job requires a master's degree.

Next, list any licenses or certifications you possess that may be applicable to your current job. Please indicate whether you think the license or certification is required or preferred in the performance of your job. It is not necessary to list education or training requirements covered in the previous section.

License/Certification   **Required or preferred?**

Example: Maryland Driver's License   Required

_____   _____

_____   _____

_____   _____

_____   _____

V. EXPERIENCE

Please indicate the minimum level of relevant experience required to successfully perform your job. Please check only one box.

☐ No previous experience required   ☐ 3–5 years' experience

☐ 6 months–1 year of experience   ☐ 5–7 years' experience

☐ 1–3 years' experience   ☐ 7–10 years' experience

Motor Vehicle Operation

Are you required to operate a library vehicle as part of your job? ☐ Yes ☐ No

If yes, what type of vehicle do you operate? (e.g., passenger car, van, bookmobile, delivery truck, etc.) _____

Bilingual Fluency

Are you required to be fluent in a language other than English as a regular and ongoing part of your job? ☐ Yes ☐ No

VI. COMPUTER SKILLS

Please use the chart below to indicate the types of computer technology and applications you use and describe the types of tasks you perform.

Software	Tasks Performed
Word Processing ☐ Microsoft Word ☐ Other _____	
Spreadsheets ☐ Microsoft Excel ☐ Other _____	
Databases ☐ Microsoft Access ☐ Electronic databases ☐ Other _____	
E-mail	
Internet	
Circulation System [insert name of the appropriate systems relevant to your library]	
Other Automated Library Systems/Modules (acquisitions, cataloging, etc.)	
Other	

(Cont.)

Figure 4.2
Sample Job Analysis Questionnaire (Cont.)

VII. CUSTOMER RELATIONS

A   Please provide information about the nature and extent of your regular contact and interaction with customers. Customers include internal customers, defined as other library employees, vendors, or contractors, or external customers, defined as those who use the library's services.

This question focuses on the type of interaction the position has with customers as well as on the level of responsibility for customer satisfaction. Please check the *one box* that identifies the level of customer relations generally required in your job. You should report all contacts that are required on a regular basis.

- ☐ The job requires understanding and communicating routine, work-related information and requires normal courtesy and tact in dealing with others.
- ☐ The job requires understanding and communicating moderately complex information and identifying and resolving routine problems to ensure that customer satisfaction and service are maintained through daily interactions with internal and external contacts.
- ☐ The job requires understanding and communicating complex information or resolving complex problems; the job includes some accountability for ensuring customer satisfaction within the assigned area.
- ☐ The job requires persuading or gaining cooperation and acceptance of ideas and/or the resolution and/or negotiation of conflicts; the job has significant accountability for ensuring customer satisfaction within the branch or department.
- ☐ The job requires supporting controversial positions or negotiating sensitive issues; the job includes responsibility for monitoring and establishing business procedures to ensure customer service and satisfaction.

Please provide examples of the customer relations activities involved in your job.

_____

_____

_____

B   Please check the one box that best describes the level of responsibility the position has for ensuring customer satisfaction. Remember that customers can be both internal and external users of the services provided by the position.

- ☐ Understands and communicates routine customer requests and provides work-related information in a timely, efficient, and friendly manner; shows courtesy, respect, and tact when dealing with others. Position interacts effectively with others in everyday contacts and has limited effect on external relations and library image.
- ☐ Ensures that customer satisfaction and service are maintained through daily interactions with internal and external contacts. Performance impacts the overall image of the library to some degree, though positive or negative consequences are relatively short-term and contained. Understands and communicates knowledge of customers' priorities and needs.
- ☐ Has significant accountability for ensuring customer service and satisfaction within the branch or department by establishing and monitoring business procedures. Positive or negative impact on public relations or the library's public image is significant. Proactively monitors internal and external customer service and satisfaction and ensures implementation of actions to remedy customer service problems.
- ☐ Performs all aspects of the preceding three items, plus assists in making decisions that may impact donor support, information presented at public meetings or other sensitive areas, including assisting in resolving or de-escalating conflict.
- ☐ Directs public relations policy. Positive or negative impact on public relations or the library's public image is significant and diplomacy is required. Proactively ensures the implementation of outstanding internal and external customer service and satisfaction. Makes decisions that impact donor support, information presented at public meetings or other sensitive areas, including resolving or de-escalating conflict and developing win/win solutions for the library and customers. Builds long-term relationships with external customers and high-level stakeholders, including elected officials and donors.

Please provide examples of the customer service activities involved in the job.

_____

_____

_____

VIII. SUPERVISION

A. Supervisory Responsibility

Does this position supervise employees? If not, please skip to the next section.

Please check the *one box* that best describes the supervisory responsibility of your position.

☐ The position has no responsibility for the direction of others. (If this answer is checked, please skip to the next question.)

☐ The position functions as a lead worker performing essentially the same work as those supervised, but providing some guidance or training to others.

☐ The position supervises people within a branch or department. Responsible for training, instructing, and scheduling work. May have input into performance evaluations.

☐ The position has direct responsibility for supervising and managing a branch or department's strategic work objectives and assists in resolving the most complex problems.

☐ The position directs supervisors in overseeing multiple work functions within a division. Makes recommendations on hiring and disciplinary actions. Evaluates work objectives and effectiveness and recommends modifications to staffing patterns as needed. Resolves the most complex problems.

Please indicate the *number of employees* who report directly and indirectly to you. (Indirect reports are those who report through another supervisor or manager.)

	Full-time salaried	Part-time salaried	Hourly	Volunteers
Direct				
Indirect				

List the *titles* of employees you directly supervise and check the type of supervision given.
(Use a separate sheet or add rows if more space is needed.)

Job title	Complete performance evaluations	Approve leave	Plan work	Assign work	Instruct and train	Review work

(Cont.)

Figure 4.2
Sample Job Analysis Questionnaire (Cont.)

B. Supervision Received

This question measures how your immediate supervisor influences the work activities of the position. The freedom to act and the ability to make policy, procedural, and daily operational decisions should be considered in responding to this question.

☐ Work is assigned and performed under direct supervision; position functions independently on routine work, but questionable cases and situations are referred to immediate supervisor.

☐ Work is assigned and performed under general supervision with little functional guidance, following established procedures; situations are rarely referred to a supervisor unless a change to policy or procedure is involved.

☐ Position functions under general direction of a supervisor or manager and uses a wide range of procedures to meet job responsibilities. The position plans and arranges own work and refers only unusual cases to supervisor.

☐ Position functions under broad administrative direction; sets standards for a department or division; is directly accountable for results.

IX. DECISION MAKING

This question is in two parts. The first relates to decision-making authority and the second to the impact of the decisions made.

A. Decision-Making Authority   (Check only one box.)

What decision-making authority exists in this position?

☐ Has the authority to make routine or recurring decisions or suggestions based on rules or procedures.

☐ Consults with supervisor or others before making nonroutine decisions and share responsibility for the decisions.

☐ Consults with others on very difficult decisions and shares responsibility for decisions.

☐ Provides final approval on decisions that affect department or area of responsibility. Provides input on library policy decisions.

☐ Participates in decisions about organization policy and strategy or about significant transactions.

Please give a specific example.

_____

_____

_____

B. Decision-Making Impact

What *impact* does this position's decisions have on library operations, including impact on other library employees and on customers? Think about decisions you make on a regular basis. Assume in answering this question that all normal care and judgment are exercised and that normal work guidelines and rules are followed. Check only one box.

☐ Poor or incorrect decisions affect primarily the position's own work or an individual customer, are easily detected, and have little impact.

☐ A poor or incorrect decision may cause short delays in getting work done in the immediate area and affect the work of others in the immediate work group or one or a few library customers.

☐ Errors or incorrect decisions may cause major disruptions of a library service or project, impacting a large department, numerous customers, a branch, or an entire function.

☐ Errors or incorrect decisions may result in injury, damage to property or the library's reputation, or financial loss.

☐ Incorrect decisions impact systemwide plans and policies and may have significant impact on the library over the long term. This includes high-stakes projects such as large grants, working with large donors, etc.

Describe the *positive or favorable effects* this position has on the performance of the area or department or on the library as a whole when performed well.

_____

_____

_____

Describe the *negative or unfavorable effects* on the area, department, or the library as a whole that might result from an error made by someone in this position who possesses good job knowledge or uses sound judgment. If someone in this position made a major error, who would ultimately be accountable?

_____

_____

_____

Please give a specific example of the types of decisions the position has the authority to make. For example, what documents does the position have final authority to sign (requisitions, payroll, purchase orders, etc.)?

_____

_____

_____

X. COMMUNICATIONS

This question asks about the communications involved in this position. The first section asks about what kind of interaction is required by the position. The next sections ask you to think about who this position communicates with as well as the frequency of those communications.

A. Type of Interaction

☐ Interaction involves routine information exchange and/or simple service activities requiring common courtesy (e.g., answering questions, directing calls, giving direction in response to simple requests).

☐ Interaction requires moderate tact and cooperation (e.g., scheduling and/or coordinating multiple personal calendars, responding to questions that require some research to provide the correct answer).

☐ Interaction requires substantial sensitivity and cooperation (e.g., basic project interaction, providing information to members of the public who from time to time may be upset or angry).

☐ Interaction involves considerable explanation and persuasion leading to decision, agreement, or rejection on complex issues; diplomacy is required (e.g., problem-solving discussions regarding responsibilities, finance, work flow, or facilitation of service; important contacts involving difficult matters of agreements or controversies such as contract negotiation or arrangement).

☐ Interaction requires expert skills in persuasion, influence, and motivation of personnel at the highest level; issues are complex and require diplomacy and negotiation (e.g., controversial operating relationships, final decision-making and problem-solving discussion regarding library objectives and goals, presenting highly controversial issues, and negotiating major contracts).

B. Level of Contact

Check the box that most closely describes the level of contact that is required on a normal basis to complete this job.

☐ Level of contact is extremely infrequent with virtually no outside contact or contact beyond the immediate work unit/area.

☐ Level of contact is primarily with clerical and technical staff members and first-level service representatives.

☐ Level of contact is primarily with library customers, guests, professionals, vendors, and/or supervisors.

☐ Level of contact is primarily with managers and/or department heads, and/or community representatives, media representatives, and community leaders.

☐ Level of contact is primarily with library leadership, CEO, donors, community leaders, business and industry leaders, or elected officials.

C. Frequency of Contact

How often does this position have recurring contact with any of the following groups or organizational levels, and what is the primary reason for these contacts? Some examples have been provided for you in the first column; please expand on or clarify *who is contacted* in this column. Use the third column of the chart to state the purpose and nature of each contact.

(Cont.)

Figure 4.2

Sample Job Analysis Questionnaire (Cont.)

Who (department, group, or other entity)	Frequency (frequently, occasionally, rarely, never)	Purpose (e.g., deliver messages, negotiate, staff meetings, exchange information via telephone, advise, etc.)
Library board		
CEO		
Division directors		
Customers		
Other institutions, schools, nursing homes, day-care centers, businesses, etc.		
Government officials (city, county, state, etc.)		
Other departments, employees, administrative offices		
Vendors/contractors		
Other (please describe)		

XI. COMPLEXITY

This question identifies the *typical* nature and diversity of work performed as well as the level of judgment and analysis necessary to resolve *typical* problems encountered. Please check the *one box* that best describes the most typical level of complexity of this job. Work is:

- ☐ Routine and well defined with clearly stated and detailed rules or procedures. Judgment is exercised on routine matters and guidance is readily available.
- ☐ Generally well defined with clearly stated directions, but involves some nonroutine or unusual assignments that may require the use of new approaches or occasional independent judgment.
- ☐ Diversified and moderately complicated, requiring judgment to select options and apply established practices and procedures. Involves regularly making choices about how to address problems.
- ☐ Complex and varied; employee in position must develop new solutions in a variety of situations. Work is governed by broad instructions, objectives, and policies. Requires considerable judgment in developing approaches and techniques.
- ☐ Varied and requires analysis of major library issues and problems as well as a complete knowledge of a wide variety of disciplines, operations, and practices. Position consistently uses independent judgment to develop and implement ideas.

XII. WORKING CONDITIONS

Working conditions are described as the physical effort required to perform the duties of the job and the environmental conditions under which the job duties are typically performed.

A. Physical Effort

Check the one box that best describes the physical effort demanded by the job.

- ☐ The work requires no unusual demand for physical effort.
- ☐ The work requires light physical effort in the handling of light materials or boxes and tools or equipment of up to thirty pounds in nonstrenuous work positions and/or continual standing or walking at least 60 percent of the time.
- ☐ The work demands occasional strenuous effort. For example, employee has to handle moderately heavy boxes, moderately heavy tools, equipment, or materials of thirty to sixty pounds.
- ☐ The work requires constant physical effort including some lifting or handling of moderately heavy to heavy tools or materials of sixty pounds or more.

B. Environmental Factors

Check the one box that best describes the environmental factors of the job.

- ☐ The work environment involves everyday risks or discomforts that require normal safety precautions typical of such places as offices, meeting and training rooms, libraries, and residences or commercial vehicles (e.g., use of safe workplace practices with office equipment, avoidance of trips and falls, observance of fire regulations and traffic signals, and/or working in moderate outdoor weather conditions).
- ☐ The work involves risks or discomforts that require special safety precautions (e.g., working around moving parts, carts, or machines and/or working in adverse weather conditions).

XIII. EMPLOYEES PERFORMING SIMILAR JOBS

Employees performing the same job and electing to complete a group questionnaire should sign below. By signing this questionnaire you are indicating agreement with the descriptions provided. Employees performing the same jobs are *not required* to complete a group questionnaire and may complete the document individually if desired.

Name:	Signature:	Date:
Years in current position:	Years at library:	☐ Full-time salaried ☐ Part-time salaried ☐ Hourly

(Cont.)

Figure 4.2
Sample Job Analysis Questionnaire (Cont.)

Name:	Signature:	Date:
Years in current position:	Years at library:	☐ Full-time salaried ☐ Part-time salaried ☐ Hourly
Name:	Signature:	Date:
Years in current position:	Years at library:	☐ Full-time salaried ☐ Part-time salaried ☐ Hourly
Name:	Signature:	Date:
Years in current position:	Years at library:	☐ Full-time salaried ☐ Part-time salaried ☐ Hourly

Attach additional sheets if necessary.

XIV. SUPERVISOR'S COMMENTS

This portion of the questionnaire is to be completed by your supervisor.

As a supervisor, it is important that you review this questionnaire and identify any discrepancies between the employee's responses and your own knowledge of the job. Remember, this questionnaire is intended solely for the purpose of accurately describing the position, *not the individual or his or her performance.*

If you would like to add a note or suggest a correction to any answer, please do so next to the employee's answer and identify your entry with your printed initials, without changing the employee's answer.

In addition, please complete the following:

1. Do you agree with the answers provided by the employee? If not, please explain.

_____

_____

_____

2. List any important job duties this person performs that may have been omitted. Please add them under the appropriate section as well.

_____

_____

_____

3. Additional comments:

_____

_____

_____

Supervisor's name: _____   Supervisor's title: _____

Supervisor's signature: _____   Date: _____

Department head's name: _____   Department head's title: _____

Department head's signature: _____   Date: _____

2. *Job summary or overview.* Provide space for employees to include a brief narrative summary (three to four sentences) of their position (see part I of figure 4.2). It might help for employees to think of how they would describe their job to a friend.

3. *Essential functions.* Here, employees list those primary functions—performed on a regular basis—that make up the job, including duties and responsibilities that define the job or without which the job could not be properly performed (see part II of figure 4.2). Duties equaling less than 5 percent of the job on a regular basis should not be included in this section. Essential functions are also critical to meet Americans with Disabilities Act (ADA) requirements, because these are the functions that an incumbent must be able to perform to fill this position. (There is more on ADA requirements in chapter 5.) Like all sections of this questionnaire, this section can be approached in a number of ways and levels of detail. We have found that employees spend the most time on this section and struggle with it the most. If you are skeptical, try listing all your job duties and responsibilities and then assigning a percentage of time for each. It's not easy! However, this is also the most crucial part of the document as it provides the foundation of the position and allows evaluators later in the process to determine the knowledge, skills, and abilities necessary to perform these functions. Don't be surprised when employees' responsibilities add up to more than 100 percent. The focus should be less on the math and more on the relative importance of each of the functions. If one task requires 40 percent of the person's time and another requires 10 percent, it is easy to spot the priority level of these responsibilities, regardless of whether the true percentages should be 38 percent and 7 percent. Also stress to employees that they need not be *exact* in calculating their percentages. We have seen lists with percentages calculated to three decimal points. *Not* necessary! The employee does not need to perseverate to this level nor do the evaluators need this fine a cut.

4. *Special projects.* Employees should list additional functions, special projects, or tasks that may be performed but are not essential to the job (see part III of figure 4.2). Include functions performed very rarely in terms of the entire scope of the position or those assigned as a one-time occurrence.

5. *Education and training.* Employees check a box corresponding to the level of education and/or training required for the position (see part IV of figure 4.2). This and the next section are often difficult for employees in that they must remove their own individual qualifications from the picture and think about what is required to effectively perform the job. For example, a library clerk may have a bachelor's degree, but this degree is not required for the job. Ask employees to check the one box that is the closest match. Note that it's not always possible to write a questionnaire that has an exact match in every category for every employee. In addition to educational degrees, libraries are now seeking candidates or employees with specific certifications that add value to certain positions. This is the appropriate place to collect this information, as it often coincides with education or training an employee may be obtaining. Examples of certificates that libraries may value and recognize in their pay systems are state library associate training certification; HVAC, engineering, or electrician certifications; and information technology (IT) certifications, including A+, MCSE (Microsoft Certified Systems Engineer), and security certifications. Make sure the language and examples in this section match your organization's culture and values, and include any relevant state requirements.

6. *Experience.* Employees check the box corresponding to the appropriate amount of experience required for the job (see part V of figure 4.2). Again, employees must think about the number of years of experience required to perform the work successfully,

which may or may not match the years of experience they themselves possess. We have also included sections on whether the position requires operating a library vehicle and whether the position requires bilingual skills. There may be other types of education or training important to your library that you may want to include as well.

7. *Computer skills.* Technology plays a huge part in any job in today's libraries. This section collects data about the specific software and programs used in the position, as well as the tasks performed with each (see part VI of figure 4.2). This section is not designed to address the intricacies of IT positions; these data are collected in other sections of the questionnaire, including job complexity and education and experience required.

8. *Customer relations.* Customer relations are increasingly important in the library world. Employees check the box that most closely describes their customer service responsibilities (see part VII, versions A and B, of figure 4.2). We have included two different versions of this part, depending on the focus of customer service in your library.

9. *Supervision.* This section may cover several subtopics: the level of supervision that is required for the position, the level of supervision the position provides, and the number of employees supervised. Employees may check boxes but are also given space to provide relevant examples (see part VIII of figure 4.2). Again, check language carefully. Are your employees familiar with terms like "work unit" or "division"? Or do you use "department" and "group"? Do you refer to a "supervisor" or a "manager"? Or both?

10. *Decision making.* This portion of the questionnaire addresses the types of decisions made in the position, including the authority the position has to make decisions, and the impact of those decisions on the library (see part IX of figure 4.2).

11. *Communications.* The type and level of interaction the library's positions have with others are critical to providing excellent service. This section asks employees to think about what type of information they communicate, to whom, and how often (see part X of figure 4.2). You could choose to include one or two of the three sections in this category, depending on your needs.

12. *Complexity.* This section discusses the nature and diversity of the work performed as well as the level of problem-solving involved in dealing with problems typical to the job (see part XI of figure 4.2).

13. *Working and environmental conditions.* Employees check boxes relating to the amount and type of physical effort required to do the job as well as the type of working environment in which the job is performed—that is, normal office conditions versus working outdoors in adverse weather (see part XII of figure 4.2).

If you read the first edition of this book, you know that new sections have been added to this version of the Job Analysis Questionnaire. No single library system needs to use every factor presented here; tailor the questionnaire to cover the areas of focus in your library.

Additional topics may be included, depending on your needs. If you have not conducted a study for some time (or ever), we recommend erring on the side of collecting *more* data rather than less, even though it represents a larger time commitment on the part of employees completing the questionnaires and supervisors reviewing them. Factors added to recent client job analysis questionnaires include

> *Budget*—Does the position have responsibility for any budgets? To monitor only? To develop? What amounts?

Facilities—Does the position have responsibility for any buildings? At what level? Opening and closing only? Being on call if an alarm goes off in the middle of the night?

Systems responsibilities—Does the position have responsibility for a function that affects operations systemwide? At what level? This could include IT positions as well as program development, training, or human resources, for example.

Tools and equipment—Does the position require using hand tools? Power tools? Other trade tools? Office equipment?

Finally, it is very helpful to include an "Other Comments" section. What more could employees possibly have to add, you might wonder? We rarely review a questionnaire that does not have something written in this section. Suggested wording for this section could be as follows: "If you believe that the questions above do not provide you with adequate opportunity to fully explain the duties and responsibilities of your job, please provide additional information below." Sometimes just having the opportunity to use this space prompts employees to remember some crucial aspect of their work they may have previously omitted.

Respondents

It is important to give the questionnaire to all rather than a sample of employees. Although this adds time and cost to the project (including paper and copying costs as well as the extra time for employees to complete and management to review each questionnaire), it does, in fact, increase involvement. It allows all members of your workforce to have input into the process and to be heard about their jobs. Many employees are delighted to be given the opportunity to share information about their jobs with others—even in a written format. In fact, this may be the first time many employees have been asked to think about, reflect on, and document their job duties. Sometimes job descriptions for the library's positions are woefully out of date—even to the point of being completely obsolete. The information gathered from the questionnaires will provide details about current job duties and responsibilities—and will furnish an impetus for you to update your system's job descriptions at the end of the compensation study.

Offer the option for employees in the same position to complete the questionnaire as a group. This supports the concept of teamwork, and employees find it interesting to learn more about their organization as a whole and their department or position in particular. This collaborative approach also cuts down on the volume of paperwork and supervisory review. See part XIII of figure 4.2 for an example of a chart that can be included in the JAQ to ensure you know which employees are included in the group. However, do not make it mandatory. There may occasionally be one employee in a group of circulation assistants, for instance, who is actually performing another job. There may also be the employee who *thinks* she is performing another job but is truly functioning as a circulation assistant. In either case, it will benefit you, and employee morale, if the employees are not required to complete a joint questionnaire. Group completion does help minimize embarrassment if an employee has problems with reading and writing; however, other arrangements can be made to help with literacy issues. A group should only complete the questionnaire if all members are performing essentially the same tasks. Differences, if any, should be noted. There may be situations, as mentioned earlier, in which several employees share the same title but are, for one reason or another, performing different jobs. The employees in these groups may not be aware of these differences.

In such cases you may need to offer guidance to groups of employees who wish to complete questionnaires together.

Throughout the questionnaire, employees should be encouraged to supply examples or attach any additional information that they believe will help explain their jobs. Although attachments are more rare than commonplace, employees have taken the liberty to provide everything from a chart of accounts to a five-page recitation of daily activities—in five-minute increments. Employees may attach examples of reports, spreadsheets, or other documents they've developed or produced. Some employees have even attached T-shirts, bookmarks, and other marketing materials they developed. This information occasionally adds to an understanding of the employee's tasks and activities. Although it will not substantially affect your understanding of the job, allowing the employees to attach this information creates more buy-in, and they appreciate the opportunity to share something about their jobs. This indeed is an important reason by itself to encourage the attachments.

Kickoff Meeting and Instructions

When possible, invite all employees involved in the study to a communications meeting before they complete the questionnaire. This meeting can be offered in several sessions if large numbers of employees are involved or if employees are at different locations. The meeting allows you the opportunity to describe project steps, discuss the employees' roles in the project, and give employees the opportunity to ask questions. Having a meeting of this type during the initial steps of the project sends quite a few important messages to employees. First, it lets them know that this is an open process—that the project steps aren't secrets. Employees often (and rightly so) feel nervous or apprehensive during compensation studies. They may worry about pay being cut or about losing their jobs. These communication sessions give you the chance to address those questions and concerns and to manage expectations. Our practice is to include these two lines: "No one will lose his or her job as a result of this study," and "No one will lose pay as a result of this study." Of course these promises require the commitment of library management before they are made public, but they can be repeated in communications throughout the project and go a long way toward putting people at ease, at least in terms of job security. The second sentence, about no one losing money as a result of the study, bears a little more discussion, which is included in chapter 10, "Implementation."

The flip side of the anxiety that may be created by the project is the expectation that everyone will receive large pay raises. One way to allay fears and manage expectations is to identify a set of related guidelines as mentioned earlier and supported by the philosophy presented in this book. However, though employees will not lose pay or their jobs, they should also not plan to book a Caribbean cruise or go on a shopping spree. Explain that until the market review has been performed and the data analyzed, it is impossible to tell what the results of the study will indicate and how or if those findings can be implemented.

An additional benefit of having a kickoff meeting with employees (and the purpose of mentioning it in this section) is the opportunity to centrally distribute and review the questionnaire along with guidelines for its completion. Employees usually have many questions about the completion of the JAQ. Again, there is often some fear associated with "doing it wrong." It's important to explain that these questionnaires are an avenue for learning about the duties and responsibilities of the job and that employees' individual performance, skills, abilities, education, or experience are not at issue. It's hard to remove the individual employee from the job he or she performs, but that is exactly what must be done to get objective job content information. In addition to providing hard copies of the document, you can provide a link on your intranet for employees to obtain the file electronically. Though they will eventually need to print it out to submit it to their supervisor, many employees prefer doing the actual writing on a computer. This makes the completed questionnaires much easier to review as well, as handwriting does not have to be deciphered.

Emphasize that employees filling out the questionnaire should evaluate what is really needed to do the job *by a fully competent performer*—not a superstar, an underachiever or overachiever, or a new employee. Remind employees that you are looking for the minimum qualifications required for their specific jobs, not what they individually might possess in terms of education, years of experience, and so forth. Nonetheless, and probably not surprisingly, employees may exaggerate the requirements of the position or share *their* years of experience and education versus those required by the job. Conversely, employees may underestimate the requirements of their jobs and check lower-level descriptions. For example, several library assistants indicated on their questionnaires that five years of experience and an MLS would be required to perform their job in a competent manner. In contrast, a branch manager stated that an associate's degree and two years' experience in business would enable a person to run the branch efficiently and effectively. Because the potential exists for both extremes, it is advisable and helpful to have a review by knowledgeable people—experienced consultants if you are using them or members of a review team. Also especially helpful (although not always the definitive resource) is supervisory review.

If your project schedule allows, give employees up to two weeks to complete the questionnaire, and ask them to turn it in to their supervisor. In addition, we have found that offering one hour of work time in which to complete the questionnaire is helpful. This may eliminate some of the "I had to complete this on my own time at home because the desk is so busy" complaints. Depending on how many and which questions you include, the questionnaire can be lengthy, and the questions require some thought. Though the questionnaire itself may not take an entire two weeks to complete, employees sometimes find that if they take a first pass at their responses, then revisit those responses in another three to four days, they are more likely to find gaps and omissions.

Confidentiality and the Questionnaire

Unlike an organizational or cultural assessment, the JAQ is not a confidential source document. It is designed to collect information about a job and what is required of an employee to perform it. The questionnaires will be reviewed by others, so be up front with employees about that. In addition, if the job description writers or those evaluating the position need more information, they will need to return to respondents. Remember to emphasize that employees are writing about their jobs, not their own performance or opinions. What employees do on a daily basis should not be controversial or in any way secret.

There is one exception to this statement about confidentiality—and it applies to an optional part of the questionnaire. For example, in addition to a library system wanting its compensation and pay plan updated to reflect the market or internal equity, it may also want to design a performance management system, provide recommendations on library staffing and structure, or facilitate an organizational design process. To save time and costs, as well as to provide a quick preliminary overview of the issues at hand, an extra sheet could be added to the JAQ asking a variety of pertinent questions. Figure 4.3

Figure 4.3

Confidential Questions on Staffing Levels

Name (optional): _____

Department: _____

Position: _____

1. Are there any aspects of your job that you think you should be doing that you are not doing? If so, what and why?

    _____

    _____

    _____

2. Are there any aspects of your job that you really should not be doing because they do not provide a return to the library equal to your investment of time and effort, are not necessary, are repetitive, are outdated, are inefficient, etc.? If so, what and why?

    _____

    _____

    _____

3. Are there any ways you think the library could operate in a more efficient and effective manner? If so, what and how?

    _____

    _____

    _____

shows confidential JAQ questions for a large urban library system that wanted to design optimal staffing levels for small branches, large branches, and the central (main) library departments. For an organizational redesign study designed for a small system neighboring a major metropolitan area, a confidential section was added to the JAQ, as shown in figure 4.4.

In both of these instances a variety of options were provided to employees for returning the information in a confidential manner. Options included faxing, e-mailing, or mailing (anonymously) directly to the consultant. Employees were also told they could return this page with their questionnaire if they were comfortable with this option and chose to do so. Finally, the instructions reminded employees about the phase of the project to which these questions related and stated in bold letters, "It is not necessary for supervisors to review or comment on these responses." Note, however, that questions such as these may not be appropriate if the study is conducted by internal library personnel only because it may be difficult to ensure confidentiality and therefore the candidness of responses. These types of projects request only the employee's perceptions and comments. Employees' names must be optional, and all information must be kept confidential, with only summary findings reported. Expect to receive a very high rate of response on such addendums—over 50 percent and often as high as 90 percent.

Supervisory Review

Although parts I–XIII of the sample questionnaire in figure 4.2 are to be completed by the employee, part XIV allows for a review by the employee's supervisor. The supervisor is asked not to make any changes to the JAQ but to provide comments. Here the super-

Figure 4.4
Confidential Questions for an Organizational Redesign Study

Name (optional): _____

Department: _____

Position: _____

1. What are your department's goals? Are they being met? Please describe.

    _____

    _____

    _____

2. Does your department provide good customer service? Please describe.

    _____

    _____

    _____

3. Are there any aspects of your job that you think you should be doing that you are not now doing? If so, what and why?

    _____

    _____

    _____

4. Are there any aspects of your job that you really should not be doing because they do not provide a return equal to your investment of time and effort, are not necessary, are repetitive, are outdated, are inefficient, etc.? If so, what and why?

    _____

    _____

    _____

5. Do you feel you possess the appropriate skills for a changing work environment (e.g., knowledge of PC applications such as databases, the Internet, etc.), or could you use some training in a specific area? If so, what type of training would be helpful?

    _____

    _____

    _____

6. Are there any ways you think the system could operate in a more efficient and effective manner? If so, what and how?

    _____

    _____

    _____

visor can comment, for example, on whether the respondent may have overestimated or underestimated when responding to different sections or if the employee forgot to include something critical to the job.

Supervisors typically have one week to review the JAQs of the employees reporting directly to them. The amount of work involved for the supervisor, of course, depends on the size of the library system. In some library systems, a second level of review also takes place, usually by the department head, division director, or assistant director responsible for that area (e.g., public services or administration). In smaller library systems, the assistant director or library director may review all JAQs.

Having reviewed each questionnaire, if the supervisor disagrees with an employee's response to a certain question, he or she should initiate a conversation with that employee about the job in addition to providing comments on the JAQ itself. Often, jobs evolve in many small ways over time. It is not unusual that the supervisor neither notices nor keeps track of all the changes. In many cases, employees, and the responsibilities of their jobs, just grow over time. This is not unusual for library systems, which in recent years have seen vast changes in technology, outsourcing, fund-raising, restructuring, customer demands, demographics, numbers of available workers, and so on playing prominent roles in day-to-day library life. It happens so often and so quickly that by the time one formal change might be made to a job or job description, it might be time to make another. Therefore, the job description should be reviewed by both the employee and supervisor on an annual basis, usually at the time of the annual performance review. On agreement, if warranted, it should be updated and submitted to the human resources department or other individual responsible for maintaining job descriptions. In this case, the supervisor will have not only the job description but the most current assessment of the work performed in the job from the incumbent herself or himself. The conversation should be about communicating job expectations and should not be confrontational. Supervisors and employees should view this as an opportunity to ensure that everyone is on the same page—a critical point when performance reviews are taken into consideration.

Sorting Completed Questionnaires

Once you have received all the questionnaires from your employees and you have reviewed them—what's next? First, you should be aware that you probably will receive a very high return rate of questionnaires from employees—typically more than 95 percent. After the JAQs have been submitted to a central location (usually the human resources office or your designated project manager), the next step is to sort them by current position title and by current salary grade. It is also advisable to separate branch positions from main library positions (if applicable). These may be combined later, but at this point it is important to note any major differences in the scope or nature of the positions attributable to location or size. For example, you should put all JAQs for circulation clerks in grade 2 assigned to the main library in a separate stack from the circulation clerks in the same grade who work in branch libraries. You should also separate positions that have more than one level; for instance, you may have two or three levels of branch managers or library assistants assigned to different grades.

Next, sort the questionnaires in order of current grade, lowest to highest. Having all the JAQs sorted this way will allow you to go through them quickly and obtain an overview of the system, the positions in it, and the interdependencies among them. It also enables you to see any potential problem areas and highlights areas where more information is needed. Obviously, a person with sufficient knowledge of your system should do this sorting.

If you are a member of an internal project committee, you might want to form a subcommittee to perform this process and make it easier for the reviewers or your consultant. It will make your project go faster, and, if you have a consultant, the cost will ultimately be lower because he or she will not have to struggle to figure out who's who.

It is strongly recommended that you make copies of your completed questionnaires before sending them on for review. You don't want to have to ask employees to complete the questionnaires again if they should somehow get lost in the process.

The next step is to use the information gathered from the JAQs and employee interviews to prepare job summaries. (Job summaries are discussed in detail in chapter 5.)

Interviews with Employees

Although the topic of conversation is their job, confidentiality must be ensured when employees are interviewed. As mentioned earlier, when designing a new compensation system, even when working with a steering or review team, it is often necessary to interview employees to learn more about their jobs.

After all JAQs are received, they should be reviewed with an eye for the following:

> disagreements between supervisor and employee perceptions of the job, particularly those highlighted by the supervisor's comments on the questionnaires
>
> positions in which the employees have widely different tasks
>
> positions for which more information is necessary to fully understand them

You must also identify jobs that have undergone major changes, that have a significant rate of turnover, or that have not been reclassified for a long time even though there were requests to do so. Ultimately you should interview a representative percentage of employees (approximately 20 percent, depending on the size of the library system and the feasibility and affordability of this task). If there are multiple incumbents in a job title, they can be interviewed as a small group rather than individually. This process not only provides an even greater understanding of the job but also involves more employees directly in the process, thereby enhancing their knowledge of how others do the job and fostering additional ownership and commitment to the project.

Keep in mind that all data that you collect in this phase of work will be crucial in classifying positions, identifying appropriate salaries, and updating job descriptions. Though these tasks are labor intensive, they are well worth the effort in terms of return on investment. The next chapter discusses job descriptions in detail and is an excellent example of a direct outcome of collecting current and accurate job content information.

five | Job Descriptions

While you have current and accurate job information for all library positions, it is the perfect time to write new or update your current job descriptions. Rarely will you have this information in one place at one time—take advantage of it!

A job description is a summary of the most important features of a job. It identifies the job and describes the general nature of the work as well as the specific tasks, responsibilities, outcomes, and competencies required to perform the job. Your objective is to provide information in a consistent format that summarizes job tasks in an accurate, clear, and useful way without being so specific as to limit the flexibility of the employee in the position or the flexibility of the position in your system. All parties—the employee, his or her supervisor, and your human resources professional—should have input into the process and reach consensus that the final job description is an accurate representation of the work being performed. Because job descriptions are often used during an external market analysis (see chapter 7), they should also provide enough information to ensure that the persons or firm conducting the study will be able to make high-quality job matches.

Before writing job descriptions, you should understand the components and decide whether you want to use generic or specific descriptions (discussed later in this chapter).

HOW TO DRAFT THE JOB DESCRIPTION

The easiest way to draft job descriptions is to use the information obtained in job analysis and apply it to an appropriate template. The job analysis questionnaire completed by employees and reviewed by supervisors offers a wealth of information about each job. Drafting job descriptions is the first place to capitalize on this information. Worksheet 7 includes three templates for job descriptions that you can choose from to adapt and customize for your use. All you need to do now is to group the questionnaires according to title and complete each template by filling in the components (explained in the following sections). The job description should be drafted and submitted to the supervisor and to human resources for review. It is prudent to obtain employee sign-off as well, to ensure accuracy from their perspective as well as to promote commitment and buy-in. This employee sign-off and review can be built into your annual performance review process, so that each year the employee and supervisor confirm the accuracy of the job description and suggest changes as necessary based on changes in the job over the last performance rating period. This step also ensures that employees are very clear on the expectations of the job and alleviates some of the "well, you never told me I was supposed to do that" comments during the performance review!

TEMPLATE A

Job title: _____ Salary range: _____

Department: _____ Reports to: _____

Position summary: _____

_____

Essential Functions	**Percentage of time spent on each**

1. _____   _____%

2. _____   _____%

3. _____   _____%

4. _____   _____%

Other Functions

1. _____   _____%

2. _____   _____%

3. _____   _____%

Minimum Job Requirements

Education: _____

Experience: _____

Specific skills: _____

Specialized knowledge, licenses, etc.: _____

Supervisory responsibility, if any: _____

Working conditions: _____

TEMPLATE B

Title: _____ Grade: _____

Work location: _____ FLSA status: _____

Date created: _____ Job summary: _____

Essential Functions

1. _____

2. _____

3. _____

Required Knowledge, Skills, and Abilities

1. _____

2. _____

3. _____

Education and Experience

1. _____

2. _____

3. _____

Physical and Environmental Conditions

_____

_____

_____

_____

_____

_____

_____

_____

_____

The above job description is not intended as, nor should it be construed as, exhaustive of all responsibilities, skills, efforts, or working conditions associated with this job.

Reasonable accommodations may be made to enable individuals with disabilities to perform the essential functions of this job.

(Cont.)

WORKSHEET 7 ■ **Basic Job Description Forms** (Cont.)   `WEB`

TEMPLATE C

1. **Who?** (the position or incumbent) _____

2. Does **what** work? (including review of others' work) _____

_____

_____

   a. essential _____

_____

_____

   b. nonessential _____

_____

_____

3. **Where?** _____

4. **When?** (or how often) _____

5. **Why?** (purpose or impact of work) _____

6. **How** is work accomplished? _____

Often consultants perform the task of writing descriptions. Alternatively, an individual from the human resources department may undertake this assignment, or it could be a function of the compensation committee.

The preceding advice assumes that you are starting from scratch in developing job descriptions. If you have kept your job descriptions up to date, you certainly don't need to reinvent the wheel here, unless you want to ensure that all are in a consistent format. Even if your job descriptions are in good shape, this is still a prime opportunity to compare the job analysis questionnaires to the job descriptions to ensure they include all tasks and knowledge, skills, and abilities.

Job Description Components

Regardless of the format you select, job descriptions typically include the following components:

Job summary—a brief description that summarizes the overall purpose and objectives of the position and the results the employee is expected to accomplish; some summaries include the amount and the degree of freedom or independence the employee has to act or the name of the position to which a person holding this job reports

Essential functions—the tasks, duties, and responsibilities of the position that are most important to get the job done; required to comply with the Americans with Disabilities Act (ADA)

Additional or nonessential functions—the desirable but not absolutely necessary aspects of the job and the job duties for which accommodation can reasonably be made

Knowledge, skills, and abilities—the specific minimum competencies required for job performance: *knowledge* is the body of information, such as library science, one has acquired; *skills* include problem solving, communicating orally, and the like; *abilities* are those personal characteristics an employee has that may be necessary to excel on the job, such as the ability to make decisions or effectively supervise others

Supervisory responsibilities (sometimes included in essential functions rather than a separate section)—the scope of the position's authority, including a list of jobs that report to the incumbent (It may be better to make references to "assigned staff" in lieu of specific position titles, as these would have to be changed every time a structural, staffing, or organizational change takes place. The same goes for including a reference to which position this position reports to.)

Working conditions—the environment in which the job is performed, especially any unique conditions beyond those found in a normal office or library environment, and the physical effort required of the position (from minimal in an office setting to the more intense physical effort required of HVAC engineers or delivery drivers); in conjunction with the essential functions, required by the ADA

Minimum qualifications—minimum (as well as desired, but you must include the minimum) educational levels, experience, and licenses required to perform the job

Worksheet 7 contains the preceding components in templates A and B. Another format for job descriptions is shown in template C.

The Language of Job Descriptions

When writing job descriptions, the language should be consistent among all jobs in your system. Use action verbs with an implied subject (that is, the *who* implied is the holder of the position) and explicit outputs (the *what* of the job). For example:

evaluates children's literature

labels and processes materials

supervises assigned staff

assists patrons with locating materials and information using electronic and online databases and resources

performs circulation tasks including registering patrons, checking materials in and out, and answering questions regarding library policies

develops departmental goals and objectives

Furthermore, consider this tip from the director of an academic library: "Be smart," she said, "in how you write job descriptions and the language you use." In her world, job descriptions go through the university's human resources department for approval and grade assignments. She suggested using the right terminology when writing them, especially when they involve information technology skills. What is the right terminology? The right terminology is what the rest of the university (or, if yours is a public library, the county) is using when evaluating its information technology jobs. For example, if the librarian is managing an integrated library system (having, of course, many complex records, etc.), write that the job is database manager. Use the terms *systems*, *web master*, *technical trainer*, and so forth when describing the duties of the members of your workforce. They are likely to be more highly compensated that way. A branch manager in a large urban library system recently recounted a very similar example. This library's classification is conducted by the municipality's office of human resources. The branch manager stated during a focus group that he finds himself trying to "crack the code" of the human resources office's desired terminology so that he can get positions reclassified.

Broad versus Specific Job Descriptions

Should job descriptions be broad or specific? In other words, how much detail should be included? An example of the type of flexibility we are referring to is a manager asking a "clerical assistant grade 2," who spends most of her time checking books in and out, to help out in the materials processing department, where there is a vacancy for someone at the grade 2 level. A library system that has broad job descriptions would call this position "clerical assistant" or "library assistant" with possible duties including checking books in and out, processing books, aiding customers by troubleshooting computer problems, counting money, record keeping, filing, receiving and checking in shipments of materials, having familiarity with the library's automated circulation system, and so forth. A library system with specific job descriptions and titles would refer to that same position as two separate positions: circulation clerk and materials processor; a person holding either of these positions would rarely fill in or help out the other's department.

Although little that's been said so far about job descriptions is controversial, this is one area where some human resources professionals disagree. However, we favor broad job descriptions for several reasons.

First, library systems are constantly undergoing change. New technologies, flattened job hierarchies, networked communications, and increased responsibility for decision making to promote high levels of customer service are a way of life in today's libraries. These trends probably will not stabilize or slow down soon. Therefore, broad job descriptions provide some flexibility in the roles employees play and the tasks they need to accomplish.

Second, the state of the current economy has created larger candidate pools when hiring for library jobs. When bringing on new employees, as with current employees, managers and supervisors need flexibility to assign employees appropriately to accomplish necessary tasks. Of course, care should be taken to ensure that new work assignments are reviewed carefully and that a similar type, level, or complexity of work is assigned to an employee in a given salary grade. If an employee is consistently assigned lower- or higher-level duties, that employee's position should be reevaluated.

Third, although this might have been implied already, job descriptions that are too narrow can serve as a roadblock or bottleneck to making changes or meeting customer needs (i.e., "It's not my job"). Even though many job descriptions have disclaimers, including the "other duties as assigned" statements, an employee may view the description as all-encompassing. Obviously, this can cause employee relations issues if not resolved early on.

Fourth, job descriptions that are very specific can become obsolete before the ink is dry. Keeping them current can be a full-time job. With myriad technological changes presenting themselves to library staff each day, it is impractical to list—and therefore limit yourself to—every electronic database or Internet search tool a librarian may need to use at a certain point. Keep these statements broad and you'll save time by not having to constantly revise job descriptions. For example, some library systems assign positions to a specific branch. In some locations, that really ties the library director's hands when it comes to optimizing staffing patterns, providing coverage, or indeed providing for development opportunities and cross training for incumbents. One option is to include a disclaimer (discussed later in this chapter) stating that all positions are eligible for systemwide transfer.

Fifth, library systems should think about the degree to which they need employees who are technical specialists versus generalists when making hiring decisions. This does not refer to the dreaded "g" word (generalism) that several years ago made a public library client quake (although that client is now leaning more in that direction, with some branches having full-service desks at which all customers, adults and children alike, are served by the same librarians). Rather, generalists are flexible employees who can float into various departments, handle a variety of tasks, and tackle special assignments. One library client in a medium-sized metropolitan area with eighteen branches has a position (with three permanently assigned staff members) specifically called Public Service Floater. These staff members cover any public service duties in any department in any branch in the system. When interviewed during the compensation study conducted for this library system, these staff members clearly advocated for the benefit of having such a broad knowledge of the library system and being able to provide coverage in any public service area. They also spoke about how much they enjoy having a real feel for the big picture of the library system versus one specific function or department. Of course not everyone wants to or can work in a different branch every day, but having this capability built into the system for certain positions is a clear advantage in terms of staff coverage, cross training, and institutional knowledge.

Finally, as education stimulates the growth of new skills and abilities, many employees enjoy being flexible and having an opportunity to try out their new knowledge. Some enjoy and thrive on it for its own sake; others value it because they know it makes them more marketable.

Given the economic pressures of rapid organizational and technological change, fiscal conservatism of local governments, the downturn in the overall economy, increased competition from retail and online booksellers, and customers' demands for fine-tuned customer service, job descriptions need to allow for broader—not more limiting—application. Some may resist this idea because people don't like to change. Employees like knowing exactly what to do, and some may have difficulty handling ambiguity. Clear communication and training are the answers to ensure that employees are comfortable handling new assignments. Once-skeptical employees turn into advocates after reaching a comfort level with a new task, process, or technology.

Many supervisors find it more difficult to manage in this environment. It is far easier to manage (though not as easy to obtain highly productive and innovative results) in accordance with a clearly delineated document that specifies what employees should do and how they should do it. It is actually harder to give employees the freedom and flexibility needed to do their work to meet today's challenges. This type of flexibility has for some time been demanded by the Gen Xers and continues to be important to the Gen Yers/Millennials who are increasingly filling the ranks of our employees. In addition, having flexible job descriptions can help make the most of the increase in part-time staff that libraries are encountering as baby boomers, military personnel, and other post-career candidates search for meaningful and rewarding part-time employment.

Customizing Job Descriptions

Customize job descriptions in accordance with your needs. Peter Vaill, an expert in organizational development and change management, popularized the concept of "permanent white water" in his book *Managing as a Performing Art*.[1] This phrase characterizes a work environment that doesn't fit into the old model of change with its inherent uncertainty followed by a longer period of adjustment and stability. Instead, in a state of "permanent white water," one major change is followed by another, and so on. The periods of calm between the turmoil don't seem to exist for many in the work world today. If you're working in such an environment, fluid, flexible job descriptions are essential. If your library or system is smaller and more stable, perhaps more content-specific job descriptions would be appropriate.

Recently, a suburban public library system with eight branches sought to promote certain values and behaviors that were important to the system. Figure 5.1 shows what planners incorporated into *each* job description under the essential functions section.

Another forward-thinking system developed sets of behaviors for each library position that were used as part of the performance management process. References to these sets of behaviors were included in the job descriptions, thus creating consistency and accountability in the overall compensation and classification systems. These job descriptions included statements such as the following:

> trains, coaches, and evaluates staff in information service behaviors, collection development and maintenance procedures, programming techniques, and other areas as necessary
>
> greets customers and responds to reference and readers' advisory requests using model reference and readers' advisory behaviors

Job descriptions can—and should—be tailored to fit the needs, expectations, and culture of your library system.

Figure 5.1
Essential Job Functions for All Jobs at XYZ Library

Serves on branch or system committees and participates in workshops, seminars, and training as requested

Notifies the supervisor with suggested ways to improve the efficiency and effectiveness of personnel and procedures and systemwide goals and objectives

Maintains good public relations with the community through contacts with public officials, community leaders, Friends of the Library, appropriate school personnel, and the public

Learns new skills and technologies to retain proficiency in areas of expertise

Is dependable and punctual

Maintains a positive, friendly, and cooperative attitude and provides consistent customer service

Upholds all library policies and procedures as defined in the library's *Policies and Procedures Manual*

Completes time sheet and other necessary forms and reports accurately and in a timely manner

In addition to the specific duties and responsibilities of this job, it is the responsibility of every employee to comply with the library's values statement, customer service guidelines, and all other policies detailed in the *Employee Handbook* and the *Policies and Procedures Manual.*

Disclaimers

Although using generic job descriptions is highly recommended, there is no way around dealing with the infamous "other duties as assigned" section. Regardless of how broad your library's job descriptions will be, they still must contain enough information to add value. No longer can we look at a five-year-old job description and assume it is still accurate. As you read this, you may feel this way about some of your job descriptions that are just two or three years old.

To remind employees and supervisors alike that job descriptions are subject to change and that they are not meant to be all-inclusive, consider adding—or customizing—one of the following disclaimers.

> The above job description is not intended as, nor should it be construed as, exhaustive of all responsibilities, skills, efforts, or working conditions associated with this job. Reasonable accommodations may be made to enable qualified individuals with disabilities to perform the essential functions of this job.

> This and all library positions are eligible for systemwide transfer.

> Management reserves the right to assign or reassign duties and responsibilities at any time.

> This job description reflects the current essential functions of this position; it is understood that other tasks or duties may be assigned as the work environment dictates.

> Features of this job are described below. Job duties and tasks may be subject to change at any time because of reasonable accommodation or other reasons.

Figures 5.2, 5.3, and 5.4 show sample completed job descriptions with a variety of disclaimers. Make sure the disclaimers you choose fit your culture and work environment.

EMPLOYEE AND SUPERVISORY REVIEW AND BUY-IN

After collecting information on each of your jobs and writing the job descriptions, you will have plenty of information to begin a compensation study; however, there is one step remaining: employee and supervisory review. When job descriptions are still in draft format, make certain that employees and their supervisors have an opportunity to review them. Allowing all constituencies input into the process is beneficial for several reasons, including helping to ensure that you have captured the essence of the position without missing any relevant duties or tasks, providing supervisors and all employees with a document they can live with, and promoting employee and supervisory buy-in of the job descriptions themselves and of the overall compensation project. If employees feel confident that the job descriptions are accurate and current and that they have had the opportunity to provide input, they will likely feel more confident that positions are placed fairly and equitably in a new compensation plan. Even experienced consultants obtain agreement from the client on the job description format up front, draft the descriptions from the data collected from employees, and submit the draft descriptions back to the client. If you are writing or updating your job descriptions with in-house staff, allow time for one round of revisions and showing employees and supervisors a final draft, if necessary.

Figure 5.2
Sample Job Description: Circulation Clerk

Date: 7/08

Job Summary

Charges, discharges, and renews library materials; provides information to customers concerning library services and circulation policies; sorts and routes returned library materials to proper locations; processes daily operations report; checks materials for wear or damage; performs other duties as assigned.

Essential Functions

1. Charges, renews, and discharges library materials to/from customers, assisting them with self-checkout machines as needed
2. Provides general information about library hours, services, policies, and materials, referring reference questions to appropriate staff
3. Registers customers by issuing and updating library cards
4. Sorts and routes returned materials to proper location
5. Receives and records fines and lost materials information
6. Checks library materials for damage and makes minor repairs
7. Maintains orderly circulation and service areas
8. Maintains periodical collections, sorts gift items, and prepares new books for circulation as directed
9. Performs other duties as assigned

Required Knowledge, Skills, and Abilities

1. Knowledge of general library procedures, policies, and operations
2. Knowledge of circulation policies, processes, and procedures
3. Good interpersonal and communication skills

4. Ability to perform numeric and alphabetic sorting and filing
5. Basic computer skills, including Microsoft Word, Excel, Outlook, and Internet
6. Familiarity with library's automated circulation system
7. Ability to work evenings, weekends, or other irregular hours

Education and Experience

1. High school diploma or GED
2. No previous experience required

Physical and Environmental Conditions

Work occasionally requires stooping and bending. Occasional light lifting such as three or four reams of paper, four or five books, or other materials (up to twenty pounds) may be required.

There are usually no major sources of discomfort; work is essentially conducted in a normal office environment with acceptable lighting, temperature, and air conditions.

Some positions require considerable physical exertion—such as regularly lifting heavy items (up to eighty pounds) such as carts or crates full of books—on a highly frequent basis and/or assuming awkward positions.

Parking booth duties may include routine discomforts from exposure to moderate heat, cold, moisture/wetness, and unpleasant air conditions.

The above job description is not intended as, nor should it be construed as, exhaustive of all responsibilities, skills, efforts, or working conditions associated with this job.

Reasonable accommodations may be made to enable individuals with disabilities to perform the essential functions of this job.

FINAL APPROVAL

As the final authority for review and approval of all job descriptions, some library systems appoint a committee such as a board and human resources staff committee, a committee that includes a cross section of staff members, or a labor (if unionized) or staff association committee. Select the method that best fits your culture and politics for review, but ultimately designate one person for final approval (e.g., a senior human resources professional if the library system has one or the library director or assistant director in a smaller system). In addition, this person could be held accountable for updating the job descriptions periodically—however, all employees and supervisors should play a role in this process. As previously mentioned, employees and supervisors should review job descriptions at least annually as a part of the performance management process.

Figure 5.3
Sample Job Description: Technical Services Assistant

Date: 5/08

Job Summary

Performs a variety of clerical and administrative duties related to the acquisition, receiving, and processing of library materials; performs other duties as assigned

Essential Functions

1. Places online orders for all types of library materials, including books, videos, CDs, audiocassettes, etc., using the library's automated program
2. Creates/edits item records for all formats of material
3. Processes/packages all formats of material
4. Obtains price and availability information via various electronic resources
5. Creates, maintains, and updates supplier lists in automated system
6. Prepares materials for return
7. Distributes material for delivery to branches, including repairing, repackaging, or transferring materials
8. Provides assistance to acquisitions and cataloging staff as directed
9. Serves on branch or system committees and participates in workshops, seminars, and training as requested
10. Notifies the branch manager with suggested ways to improve the efficiency and effectiveness of personnel and procedures and systemwide goals and objectives
11. Maintains good public relations with the community through contacts with public officials, community leaders, Friends of the Library, appropriate school personnel, and the public
12. Learns new skills and technologies to retain proficiency in areas of expertise
13. Maintains a positive, friendly, and cooperative attitude and provides consistent customer service
14. Performs other duties as assigned

In addition to the specific duties and responsibilities of this job, it is the responsibility of every employee to comply with the library's values statement, customer service guidelines, and all other policies detailed in the *Employee Handbook* and the *Policies and Procedures Manual.*

Required Knowledge, Skills, and Abilities

1. Ability to gain working knowledge of library policies and procedures
2. Ability to act as a representative of the library to the public
3. Knowledge of technical services policies and procedures
4. Ability to learn to maintain and organize library materials and records
5. Ability to learn to operate relevant computer systems, including hardware and software, and office machines
6. Strong communication skills, both verbal and written
7. Basic math and language skills

Education and Experience

1. High school diploma or GED
2. Six months or more of related experience

Physical and Environmental Conditions

1. Work requires light physical effort in the handling of light materials up to thirty pounds in nonstrenuous work positions or continual standing or walking 60 percent or more of the time
2. Work environment involves everyday risks or discomforts that require normal safety precautions typical of such places as offices or meeting rooms (e.g., use of safe workplace practices with office equipment and avoidance of trips and falls)

This job description is not intended as, nor should it be construed as, exhaustive of all responsibilities, skills, efforts, or working conditions associated with this job.

Reasonable accommodations may be made to enable qualified individuals with disabilities to perform the essential functions of this job.

This and all library positions are eligible for systemwide transfer.

LEGAL COMPLIANCE

Your library's job descriptions must be in compliance with state and local legislation and with federal laws such as the Equal Employment Opportunity (EEO) Act, the Pay Equity Analysis Act in Canada, and the Americans with Disabilities Act (ADA).

Figure 5.4
Sample Job Description: Librarian

Position number: _____

Date: 8/08

Job Summary

Assists customers in locating and using the available resources of the library and provides timely and accurate information and answers to research questions; performs other duties as assigned

Essential Functions

1. Provides reference assistance to customers and library staff in person, by phone, and via e-mail including explaining the arrangement of the library, identifying the types of materials available, guiding users to sources of information, and providing instruction in the use of various library reference sources
2. Assists with collection development, maintenance, and management in assigned area
3. Participates in library projects, committees, and activities as assigned
4. Participates in community outreach programs including library tours and participation in community organizations
5. May specialize in a particular area such as children's materials, periodicals, reference, media, business and technology, or other specialty and may serve as in-house subject matter expert in assigned area
6. Supervises, trains, and evaluates the work of assigned staff, including library associates and clerical staff
7. May be located in the central library or a branch
8. Performs other duties as instructed and assigned

Required Knowledge, Skills, and Abilities

1. Knowledge of reference practices and procedures, including readers' advisory and reference interviews
2. May require knowledge of specialty subject area
3. Good interpersonal, communication, and organizational skills
4. Research skills including online database searching
5. Ability to use relevant library hardware, software, and other equipment

Education and Experience

1. Master's degree in library science from an ALA-accredited college or university *or* equivalent technical training, education, and/or experience
2. No previous experience required

Physical and Environmental Conditions

1. Work requires light physical effort in the handling of light materials or boxes and tools or equipment up to thirty pounds in nonstrenuous work positions and/or continual standing or walking 60 percent or more of the time
2. Work environment involves everyday risks or discomforts that require normal safety precautions typical of such places as offices or meeting rooms (e.g., use of safe workplace practices with office equipment and avoidance of trips and falls)

This job description is not intended as, nor should it be construed as, exhaustive of all responsibilities, skills, efforts, or working conditions associated with this job.

Reasonable accommodations may be made to enable individuals with disabilities to perform the essential functions of this job.

Americans with Disabilities Act

Effective July 1992, the Americans with Disabilities Act (ADA) requires employers to identify "essential job functions." Essential job functions are those parts of a job that cannot be easily reassigned or delegated to another employee. That is, employees who do not have an impairment that would prevent them from doing so must perform these essential job functions. Once the essential functions are defined (via job analysis), you are required to make reasonable accommodations that will allow an otherwise qualified person with a disability to perform the essential job functions. "Essential job functions" and "reasonable accommodations" have to be determined on a case-by-case basis. (The sample JAQ in figure 4.2 accounts for a delineation of "essential job functions" as well as working conditions.) There are many books and publications, as well as advice from your attorney, that can help you learn more about the ADA. This section is designed to give you an overview of your responsibilities in this area so that you can write job descriptions that are useful and in compliance.

You may be wondering if your library system is required to comply with the provisions of the ADA. The answer is probably yes. Title II extends the prohibition of discrimination on the basis of disability to all activities of state and local governments, including those that do not receive federal financial assistance. By law, Title II of the ADA covers programs, activities, and services of public entities. Public entities are defined as

> any state or local government
>
> any department, agency, special-purpose district, or other instrumentality of a state or local government
>
> certain commuter authorities as well as Amtrak

Title II does not include the federal government, which is covered by sections 501 and 504 of the Rehabilitation Act of 1973. Title II is intended to apply to all programs, activities, and services provided or operated by state and local governments. If it is difficult to ascertain whether a library is a public entity, as some appear to have both public and private features, review the following criteria with your attorney:

1. Is the library operated with public funds?
2. Are employees considered government employees?
3. Do you receive significant assistance from the government by provision of property or equipment?
4. Is the library governed by an independent board chosen by members of a private organization? By an elected board? By a board appointed by elected officials?

Experience indicates that all public libraries are public entities and are covered by the provisions of the ADA. Academic libraries that are a part of a public institution of higher education and K–12 school libraries most likely need to comply with the ADA as well. Private and special libraries should check their legal requirements under the ADA with their attorneys.

Definition of Essential Functions

According to the Equal Employment Opportunity Commission (EEOC) regulations implementing the ADA, a job function may be considered essential if any of the following conditions exist:

> The position exists to perform that function.
>
> There are a limited number of available employees among whom the performance of that function can be distributed.
>
> The function is so highly specialized that the incumbent in the position was hired for his or her ability to perform that function.

The EEOC considers various forms of evidence when determining whether a particular function is essential. This evidence includes

> the judgment of the library director, assistant director, or senior human resources professional
>
> written job descriptions prepared *prior to* advertising or interviewing for the job
>
> the amount of time spent on the job performing that function

the consequences to the functioning of the library system or to public service of not requiring the incumbent to perform the function

if unionized, the provisions of a collective bargaining agreement

work experience of prior employees in the job

work experience of current employees in similar jobs within the library system

Consult with your attorney concerning other questions you might have about compliance with the ADA.

The next two chapters will focus on establishing the internal equity of your library's positions as well as the external competitiveness of positions in your market.

NOTE

1. Peter Vaill, *Managing as a Performing Art: New Ideas for a World of Chaotic Change* (San Francisco: Jossey-Bass, 1989).

six | Point Factor Job Evaluation System for Internal Equity

One of your goals is to create a compensation plan that is externally competitive, internally fair, and supportive of your library's compensation strategy. This chapter discusses internally focused job evaluation systems that support the library's values. The next chapter will provide the information you need to assess equity with the external labor market. Chapter 9 provides tools to help you design your compensation plan using the data you have gathered. Ultimately, jobs will be assigned to grades and pay ranges in your compensation plan based on job content and market value and/or internal equity, not on employee value or individual performance. Although individual-based compensation systems are mentioned in chapter 11, this chapter and the next focus on *job-based* pay. An exception is librarians in academic libraries eligible for faculty status. Job evaluation relating to these librarians will be discussed later in this chapter.

JOB EVALUATION

The underlying purpose of job evaluation is to create a job hierarchy, be it internally or externally focused, in which the relative importance of each job (not job holder) within an organization can be easily identified. Job evaluation does not determine rates of pay—that comes later. Job evaluation produces a ranking of jobs used by the library system in descending (or ascending) order, from the job that has the most accountability for setting and achieving strategic goals and objectives to one that is responsible for routine and clearly established tasks. Regardless of what process you use for job evaluation, this list will reflect the value of *your library's positions*. This list will (and should) look at least slightly different in each library system, as it reflects the internal equity of positions within a particular system. Though professional librarians are placed higher in the hierarchy than library pages in every system, your system may place your training coordinator higher than professional librarians while another system may have that position on par with library associates.

As just described, even within a relatively consistent industry such as library services, the relative order of jobs will change from institution to institution. For example, research skills and the knowledge of esoteric subject matter will likely be more valued in an academic or research library than in a branch of a local public library. In addition, the scope and responsibility of similar outreach efforts can range, for example, from involvement with local groups like the Kiwanis, community center, and Rotary Club to creating community partnerships, establishing literacy programs, developing senior and young adult programs, tracking homework assignments, and designing programs—all while directing the bookmobile to senior centers, day-care centers, and nursing homes. Thus, the same position in two different library systems will be used and valued differently and, subsequently, will be assigned to very different salary ranges based on the scope of the job, level of responsibility, and contribution of the position to the library's mission.

Formal job evaluation systems were created in the 1920s and first used in the 1930s. They are used in both the public and private sectors, and fall into two large categories—quantitative or nonquantitative approaches. The most commonly used job evaluation systems are whole-job ranking and point factor. Market pricing/slotting is another method of job evaluation, but because of its external focus (in contrast to the internal focus of these plans) it will be discussed in greater detail in chapter 7. Whichever type of system is used, the evaluator(s) must have a comprehensive understanding of the work involved in each position being evaluated. The questionnaires discussed in chapter 4 provide a consistent method for collecting this information.

Whole-job ranking is generally more subjective than a point factor system. It seeks to make comparisons between whole jobs as opposed to comparing components of jobs. Point factor plans, on the other hand, break down jobs and compare different parts or components with each other by applying a systematic method of job factors and degrees.

Following are brief descriptions of these types of internally focused job evaluation systems. Included are some of the pros and cons of each as well as of the externally focused method of job evaluation (market pricing). Figure 6.1 summarizes these advantages and disadvantages.

Figure 6.1

Comparison of Job Evaluation Methods

Method	Advantages	Disadvantages
Whole-Job Ranking (nonquantitative)	More flexible than point factor and other classification methods Less time-consuming than factor-based methods Supports trend toward broader class definitions Simplest method overall	Can become subjective and not as defensible Depending on the size of the library, can be as time-consuming as other methods Most effective for smaller units; judgment calls in larger units are open to inconsistencies Although can show that one job is more important than another, there is no indication of how much more important (relative worth or value) Requires that job ranker be highly knowledgeable about all jobs
Point Factor Method (quantitative)	Defensible and objective measure of job worth Fairly easy to communicate and understand Supports internal equity when factors are applied consistently to all jobs Ensures accuracy, quality, and reliability	Does not easily adapt to market conditions, dual career ladders, or professional trends Time-consuming because of complexity and detail Can be too focused on "policing" (point counting) Factor and level definitions are often difficult to distinguish and may not apply to every classification or occupational group Maintenance and updates can be expensive
Market Pricing/ Slotting Method (externally focused)	Maintains market competitiveness More flexible than other methods Market data are available for most jobs	Can be time-consuming Slotting non-market-priced jobs can be subjective May reflect biases in the market (e.g., gender pay inequity)

Whatever job evaluation system you select, it should be flexible enough to adjust and adapt to changes within the library's world of work as well as the marketplace in general. The systems that appear to be the most useful are those that are

> efficient (i.e., do not require a large staff to maintain and allow for quick decision making)
>
> based on a limited number of objective, predefined job characteristics
>
> developed in conjunction with all key stakeholders (including managers, union representatives, and employees)
>
> easily communicated to all employees

Whole-Job Ranking

Whole-job ranking is the simplest method of job evaluation. It involves looking at each job as a whole and positioning it in a hierarchy by ranking it against other jobs using job descriptions, job titles, and the evaluators' knowledge of position duties and responsibilities as well as the "perceived complexity and difficulty of the job relative to other jobs in the organization."[1] The outcomes of all job evaluation, to some extent, are open to the interpretation of the evaluators, though this has more impact in whole-job evaluation as there are no predefined levels or degrees of job components to which evaluators may match a given job. The result of this method is a listing or ranking of jobs in order of relative importance. This method is limited in that it does not attend to the relative difference between positions—just that one is higher than the other. In addition, jobs are ranked without reference to any specific criteria. Sometimes ranking systems are as simple as gauging whether the job under study should be assigned a grade equal to, above, or below the position being rated.

As mentioned earlier, whole-job ranking can be seen as a subjective process. Raters shouldn't, but might be, influenced by current pay, the personality of the incumbent, or the perceived prestige of the job (though this is not exclusive to whole-job evaluation—point factor systems can also be made to come out as the evaluators think they should). It is also difficult to conduct whole-job ranking in complex, large library systems that have many varied positions. Nonetheless, ranking can be a reliable job evaluation system, as those doing the ranking generally know, with some degree of accuracy and reliability, which jobs are worth more than others in the library, while considering the placement of new or changed positions as well. Whole-job ranking, although not frequently used as the sole method of job evaluation, is often used instinctively as a check-in for reviewing the findings of point factor job evaluation. Be aware that the federal Equal Employment Opportunity Commission (EEOC) cautions that use of the whole-job evaluation approach is not "a valid defense should the employer ever be challenged about either the disparate impact [on] or the disparate treatment of employees in a job classification."[2]

Point Factor Plans

M. R. Lott created the point factor method of job evaluation in 1924. This method is based on the analysis of jobs in terms of separately defined factors that are of value to the library or for which the library is willing to pay. A point factor system comprises compensable factors (most often defined by the organization), numerically scaled factor degrees within each of the compensable factors, and weights assigned to each factor reflecting the relative importance of each to the library. Once the scaled degrees and weights are established for each factor, each job is measured against each compensable factor, using the same factors for each job, and a total score is calculated for each job. The total points assigned to a job help to determine the job's relative value and location in the hierarchy of a pay structure. These points for each job can be arranged in an overall hierarchy from high to low or low to high, thus depicting the relative value of all library positions.

Point factor systems based on compensable factors are the most widely used internally focused job evaluation systems. Although they can be complex because of the time and effort necessary for development and application, existing point factor systems can be purchased and adapted to your specific needs and values. Point factor plans offer a rationale for the differences in the ranking of jobs, provide quantitative documentation, and are objective. It is the recommended system for clients who want a more defensible internal equity system for evaluating each job than that provided by whole-job ranking. Keep in mind that because a point factor job evaluation system alone will not provide you with enough information to set salary ranges, it is advisable to obtain market data for at least 30 to 40 percent of your total jobs (most likely representing far more staff). In this manner you will have market rates to use in updating or designing your salary ranges, and then the ability to slot jobs into the market-based ranges following the application of the point factor plan.

DESIGNING AND APPLYING A POINT FACTOR SYSTEM

Because it is the most widely used method of job evaluation for internal equity, the remainder of this chapter takes you through the process of designing your own customized point factor plan. It outlines the steps you will need to follow to evaluate your jobs for internal equity. The following steps would be used whether you custom design or adapt an existing point factor plan:

1. charter and train a job evaluation committee
2. select compensable factors
3. select factor weights
4. identify degrees in each factor
5. evaluate jobs (apply the point factor system)
6. order and review final rankings
7. present findings

Step 1: Charter and Train a Job Evaluation Committee

Whether you choose to design your own point factor system or purchase and modify an existing one, you may elect to go through the process with a committee. Evaluating jobs with a committee has pros and cons. On the positive side, you will create a real understanding of both the process as well as the jobs in the library for those serving on the group. Many employees are very familiar with the work being done in their own immediate work area but may only be somewhat familiar with the work in their larger department or division and the library as a whole other than at a very superficial level. We have had very positive experiences in conducting job evaluations with a committee because they are learning, at a very detailed level, what positions do what work throughout the entire organization. It often provides a new perspective and newfound appreciation for the work other employees do. Employees serving on the job evaluation committee will also gain a ground-level view and understanding of the job evaluation process the library uses to classify positions. Finally, employees tend to trust the process—and results—much more readily when they know that their peers and colleagues were involved throughout the study instead of management conducting the entire project behind closed doors or "in secret." The disadvantages of using a committee include an increased amount of time necessary to evaluate jobs, as consensus needs to be reached on each factor. Confidentiality can also be a concern—these staff members will be discussing the job evaluation points and outcomes at a level that other staff will not be privy to. Just as with the larger review committee, a job evaluation committee needs to be educated about the importance of confidentiality in this process. If you choose to work with a committee on job evaluation, invite no more than three to five people, a subgroup of the review committee, to serve on a job evaluation team.

The art of job evaluation is to reconcile varied and legitimate views of the same position. Of course, you can't expect the committee to know how to evaluate jobs at the outset of the project. You must train the committee first and allow for practice before beginning this process. You can easily design training and practice from the information provided in this chapter. We recommend a brief PowerPoint or other format for training, supplemented by job evaluation guidelines that employees can have on hand as they evaluate—almost serving as a cheat sheet for the process. Figure 6.2 provides an example of guidelines for evaluators using a point factor job evaluation system. In addition, these guidelines serve as a charter for this portion of the project work. They lay out not only the process of job evaluation but also how committee members will work together (i.e., reaching consensus, maintaining confidentiality, respecting all opinions, etc.).

Step 2: Select Compensable Factors

Start with the articulation and definition of compensable factors. A *compensable factor* is any job attribute that provides the basis for determining the worth of a job. Most generic compensable factors include required skill and effort, responsibility, and working conditions. Within each factor are other aspects of job content; for example, experience, knowledge, and required licenses or certifications might be found within the skill factor.

It is helpful to get buy-in from management and the review committee as a whole when identifying, defining, and weighing compensable factors. The factors need to reflect your library system's values and direction and enable you to differentiate levels of responsibility within the library. Many libraries have chosen point factor plans as their job evaluation method. No two have ever identified the same set of factors, nor have any two ever assigned the same weights to the factors once the factors have been selected. Most use some or all of the following factors and subfactors:

- education/training
- experience
- certifications/licenses
- customer relations/service/satisfaction
- communications/key interactions/level of contact

Figure 6.2
Sample Job Evaluation Guidelines

ANYTOWN LIBRARY
Job Evaluation

Purpose

To establish and maintain internal equity.

How

Ascertaining the relative values of jobs through a systemized method of job grading. The process includes consistently assigning a degree to the factors listed below for all library positions.

- Education/training/certification
- Experience
- Customer satisfaction and service
- Supervisory responsibility
- Number of employees
- Complexity
- Decision-making impact
- Physical effort
- Environmental factors
- Building responsibilities

Job evaluation focuses on the nature and requirements of the *job itself, not* on the skills, performance, background, or characteristics of the job holder.

The product of job evaluation is a ranking of Anytown Library's jobs, from the job that makes the greatest contribution to the library to the job that demands the least of an incumbent. The product is expressed in points to facilitate the comparison of value.

Guidelines

- Evaluate the job requirements, not the incumbent, his or her performance, or personality.
- Evaluate the demands of the job at an acceptable, full-performance level, following an orientation period, not what would be nice to have or what outstanding performers can do.
- Evaluate what is required regularly, not what might occur only periodically or for special projects.

- Think about what you would require if hiring someone new into the position (i.e., minimum levels of education, experience, etc.).
- Select a degree within each factor that appropriately describes the job; the degree selected includes the values of all lower-level degrees.
- Consider the value of the job to the library *now*, not the future value of the position or what its value might be to any other organization.
- Measure the value of the job according to each separate factor rather than trying to make the position come out where you might think it ought to.

Job Evaluation Procedures

1. The selected jobs will be evaluated by the library's Job Evaluation Committee.
2. All committee members will have copies of the completed Job Analysis Questionnaires to be evaluated.
3. If requested or necessary, a committee member will provide a brief overview of the responsibilities and duties of the position.
4. We will discuss each position. If we believe that additional information is needed to evaluate a particular position, that position will be tabled until the information can be obtained.

   Given sufficient information, degrees will be assigned to each factor. They will be assigned factor by factor, one job at a time.

   It is important that consensus be achieved on each degree.

5. All committee members will fill in the agreed-upon factors on the blank worksheets provided; one person will be designated to keep the master list to transfer to a database.
6. An additional sheet to note questions or disagreements on factors for individual jobs may be used to provide documentation as appropriate.

- supervision
    - level of supervisory responsibility
    - number of employees supervised
    - level of supervision received
- job complexity
- problem solving
- decision making
    - authority
    - impact
- working conditions
    - physical effort
    - environmental factors

A streamlined job evaluation system includes the following factors:

- education and experience
- complexity
- impact
- customer relations
- working conditions

What factors are selected or excluded depends entirely on your library's culture and environment. If every position in an academic library requires a minimum of a bachelor's degree, education may be included but weighted less than in other systems. If your public library system has just begun work on a major customer service initiative as described by your strategic plan, customer service might be a very important factor in your job evaluation plan.

Once factors are identified, a clear definition of each must be written. Measure results and observable outcomes rather than tasks or subjective opinions. State ideas clearly and as concisely as possible; be specific. Write the factors to encourage evaluators (and employees, as they will see these factors in the job analysis questionnaire) to think about the *position*, not the person. Even including such simple statements as "the *job* requires X" can help keep the focus on position requirements in contrast to individual attributes and performance. Think about what you're attempting to learn with each factor. For customer service, are you attempting to measure the level of interaction positions may have with internal and external customers (i.e., communicating basic information about library hours versus negotiating contracts with county engineers for new facilities), or does your customer service factor focus on creating partnerships with local nonprofits to offer programs to special needs teens or on explaining to customers how to use databases? This exercise will help ensure you are getting the information you need from employees and will help you design the factor degrees (discussed in step 4). As an example, if *communications* is a factor, the factor description might read as follows:

> This factor measures the type and level of communication the position has with both internal and external customers. Internal customers are defined as other staff members, vendors and contractors, or library board members. External customers are defined as those who use the library's services or partner with it (and might include vendors, city/county officials, board members, etc.).

Determining which factors are important to your library system is a good exercise for the review committee. It fosters good dialogue about what factors are really important to the library and should be used as measures of relative job worth. Aim to include only one issue or consideration per factor. That is, limit your definition of each factor to as few measurement dimensions as possible. For example, do not include problem solving and decision making or scope and effect in the same factor definition. Doing so makes it more difficult to find the appropriate fit for each position. Describe issues only once—that is, in only one factor. Do not evaluate the same issue in more than one factor. For example, if customer service is a factor, don't measure it again in the problem-solving factor. It bogs down your system with built-in redundancies and adds time to actual job evaluation. You may want to start the committee discussion with a core list of factors and then have others up for discussion by the group. Committee members may also suggest factors not previously thought of. For instance, in one suburban Maryland library system, budget responsibility was becoming an important job duty for many positions as management was pushing this responsibility farther down into the organization. Committee members in this system suggested the factor and helped develop the language for each degree (i.e., monitoring budgets versus developing budgets, etc.).

Step 3: Select Factor Weights

Once factors have been selected, assigning factor weights is neither as difficult nor as daunting a task as it might sound. Follow these steps:

a. Involve the review committee. It encourages some real thinking about not only what factors are important but *how* important they are. If customer service is a high priority in your mission and values statements, it should be weighted more heavily than, for example, supervisory responsibility. If you have included too many factors in your system, that will become apparent in this step. If no factor is worth more than 5 to 7 percent, you may have diluted your system too far. It is important to note that you can collect information in the questionnaire without creating a factor around that topic in the job evaluation system. For instance, as mentioned earlier, perhaps budget responsibility is a piece of information you would like to collect about each position. You can include a question about the level of budget responsibility in the questionnaire but not include a factor for budget responsibility in your job evaluation plan. You will still have this information for use in informing the level of complexity and decision making inherent in the position and will have the specifics of budget responsibility for use in developing or updating position descriptions.

b. Take into account the nature of the work performed by all the positions that will be covered under the job evaluation plan. The positions generally range from entry-level, such as page or shelver, to the experienced and professional, such as department manager.

c. Rank in order of importance the factors selected.

d. Determine the initial weights of each factor as a percentage of 100.

It may help to create a worksheet similar to worksheet 8. This worksheet lists the factors and leaves space for the ranking and percentage of weight that should be assigned to each. Ask each member of the review committee and management to complete the worksheet individually. Gather the individual responses, and use a flip chart to share them if you are working with a group. Factor by factor, list everyone's answers. Mean, median, and mode of responses are easy to spot.

WORKSHEET 8 ■ Factor Weights   WEB

Please rate the importance of each factor to meeting the mission, goals, and objectives of the library. Then, assign a weight of importance for each factor by allocating from 1 to 100 percent to each so that the total of the weights assigned to each factor is 100%.

Factor	% Weight Example	% Weight Your Library
1. Education/training	10	_____
2. Experience	10	_____
3. Customer relations	20	_____
4. Supervisory responsibility	10	_____
5. Number of employees supervised	5	_____
6. Level of supervision received	15	_____
7. Complexity	20	_____
8. Decision-making authority	0	_____
9. Decision-making impact	0	_____
10. Physical effort	5	_____
11. Environmental factors	5	_____
TOTAL		**100%**

With the assistance of a facilitator, the group can then discuss each factor and work to reach consensus. You can move toward consensus by reviewing each factor one at a time and asking the person who gave the factor the lowest and the person who gave it the highest percentage of weight to talk about their rationale. Generally, most people respond within 5 to 10 percent of each other on each factor, and reaching consensus is not difficult because the people in the room are very familiar with the library and its values.

Step 4: Identify Degrees in Each Factor

Once you have established and weighted each factor, break down each into levels or degrees. Following is an example pertaining to experience:

Factor name	Experience
Factor description	This factor measures the amount of previous experience normally required to achieve fully competent performance in the position.
Degrees	1. less than 6 months
	2. 6 months to 1 year
	3. 1 to 3 years
	4. 3 to 5 years
	5. 5 or more years

This suggests that when evaluating positions you should look at how much experience is required of the incumbent prior to taking the job with the library. For example, you might hire a circulation or library assistant with little or no relevant experience, and therefore the position would be assigned degree 1. On the other hand, the experience requirement for the director of outreach position might be four to five or more years. Thus, the position would be assigned degree 4 or 5. Make sure these degrees fit your culture. If you do not have any positions that require less than a high school diploma or GED, do not include a degree level in the education factor of "less than a high school education." As another example, perhaps all positions require a basic level of customer service responsibility in that all are required to be able to answer certain directional or informational questions for customers. If this is the case, do not include a "no customer service responsibility" option in your system.

Your next step is to create a draft of the highest and lowest degrees in each factor. Again, look for fit with your organization. If it is determined that a PhD would not be a minimum qualification for even the highest-level job in the library, then PhD would not be included as a degree within the education factor. Similarly, if incumbents in all positions are required to hold at least an associate of arts or sciences degree, this would be the lowest level (degree) indicated for the education factor, rather than "some high school education."

Once the highest and lowest degrees in each factor are defined, it is then necessary to determine the number of intermediate degrees needed. For example, if the system has "some high school education or training" as the lowest degree in the education factor and "master's degree in library science" as the highest degree, the final scheme for degrees of the education factor might be

1. The job requires some high school education or training.

2. The job requires a high school diploma or GED.

3. The job requires additional training or up to one year of job-related course work after high school (e.g., commercial driver's license).

4. The job requires an associate's degree or two years of formal training beyond high school.

5. The job requires a bachelor's degree, training, or certification (e.g., A+, electrician, HVAC).

6. The job requires additional education in a specialized area, such as CFRE (Certified Fund-Raising Executive) or APR (Accredited in Public Relations).

7. The job requires a master's degree in library science and MCSE (Microsoft Certified Systems Engineer) certification.

Note: If you are determining degree levels for an academic or a special library, you may need to add another degree level (number 5) if additional training is a requirement—for example, a biology degree in a medical library or a law degree in a law library.

The appropriate degree level in each factor would then be assigned to each position based on *what is needed* to successfully perform the job. The individual employee's level of experience, education, or performance is *not* taken into consideration when assigning degrees to each position. In addition, it is important to remember that you must consider the job in its present state, not what would be nice to have or what you may reorganize into in five to seven years.

When defining degrees of compensable factors, be aware that having *too many* degrees can result in having to

> force artificial distinctions between degrees
>
> require very detailed job analysis questionnaires or other forms of job documentation
>
> increase the amount of time necessary to evaluate jobs

Conversely, having *too few* degrees can present a problem as well. You may experience difficulty assigning a degree if there's too large a progression from one level to the next, and the number of degrees you have may not fully cover all the work performed.

Although you should try to have only one issue per factor, you may not always achieve that aim. For instance, you may find that, in the interest of streamlining your point factor system, it may be practical to combine factors—for example, *complexity* and *problem solving* as one factor. This one factor identifies the extent to which the job must use analytical and problem-solving skills in performing varied activities as well as the amount of independent judgment used by the incumbent. The benefit of such a factor is that you are gathering more in-depth information about each job. However, one drawback to combining factors is that it may become increasingly difficult to identify *one* specific factor that best fits each job. Therefore, you may find that it is helpful to break factors down into component parts. For instance, if you are attempting to identify decision-making skills, you could refer to *decision-making authority* (the independence an incumbent may use in making decisions without referring to a supervisor) as well as *decision-making impact* (the potential outcome and effect of the types of decisions made by the incumbent). That is, will the decisions generally affect individuals or their immediate work areas, or is the impact of decisions organization-wide? There are examples of this in the sample Job Analysis Questionnaire in chapter 4.

If a factor includes more than one issue, describe them in *each* degree. That is, if a given issue is in one degree, it needs to be described in each degree within the factor. Again, consider the example of a combined factor that includes the issues of *complexity* and *problem solving*. In the following example, each of the four factors addresses both job complexity and the problem-solving skills required.

1. Work duties are well defined with clear instructions or standard routines. Work is highly structured, and independent judgment may be used in routine matters such as changing the order in which tasks are completed. Guidance is readily available.

2. Work regularly involves making choices about how to address problems in the work situation. Work involves moderately complicated procedures and tasks requiring independent judgment to select options or interpret data.

3. Work is complex and varied. It requires selection and application of technical or detailed skills to develop new solutions in a variety of work situations. A considerable degree of independent judgment is required to vary from established procedures and to develop methods for accomplishing work objectives.

4. Work is extremely complex and varied and requires a complete knowledge of a wide variety of operations, practices, and disciplines. Work consistently involves dealing with situations, facts, and problems that have not been previously addressed. Work consistently involves a considerable degree of independent judgment to develop and implement ideas.

Step 5: Evaluate Jobs

Depending on the number of positions in your system and the available time of committee members, you may or may not be able to evaluate all positions with a committee or subcommittee. Our recent experience has shown that although it is still best to evaluate your positions with some library staff involvement, evaluating with the entire committee can be substantially more time-consuming than is practical, for both you and the other committee members. A recent job evaluation project with a subcommittee of a project's employee committee took two and one-half days, even though the library has had a job evaluation system in place for years and was only doing an update. If possible, select a group of no more than four or five people, not including an HR representative and your consultant (if you are working with one). As with the larger employee committee, try to include representation from a variety of levels and departments in the library, not just upper-level management or only reference librarians.

You may choose to evaluate only certain positions with a group (strive for at least half of your total positions). When developing a list of positions to evaluate with the group, try to select positions that cover a large percentage of library staff. For instance, evaluating the library associate, department head, librarian, and circulation assistant positions will most likely cover many staff members. In addition, try to select positions that encompass all levels of responsibility within the library. In other words, don't evaluate only the management or professional positions and skip over lower-level or entry-level positions. Following both of these tips will ensure that your job evaluation process is fair and equitable and covers the largest percentage of library staff possible. For example, a large urban library system with a central location as well as twelve city and suburban branches evaluated the following positions:

Main Library	*Branch*	*Other*
page	page	terminal operator
page/clerk	clerical technician	data editor
clerk I	clerk I	stock handler
clerk II	clerk II	
clerk III	clerk III	
clerical supervisor	clerical supervisor	
clerical technician	library assistant	
library assistant	staff librarian	
staff librarian	senior staff librarian	
senior staff librarian	department head	
unit head	division head	
assistant department head		
department head		

A small library with two branches in a rural/resort area evaluated the following:

manager, adult services	building maintenance/services manager
manager, automated systems	manager, technical services
manager, youth services	bookmobile manager
electronic outreach librarian	cataloger
circulation manager	library associate
jail librarian	technical assistant—automation

accountant/bookkeeper	senior administrative specialist
library aide—bookmobile	library aide—circulation (part-time)
janitor/security	library aide—technical services
library aide/bookkeeper	library aide—mending (part-time)
library aide—circulation (full-time)	page
ILL assistant (part-time)	

Though the amount of paper can become a bit overwhelming, we recommend having copies of the questionnaires available for the group. Each person does not need a complete set, but a copy for every two people for single-incumbent jobs will be helpful. For jobs with more than one person, divide the questionnaires among the committee members to ensure that all information is reviewed. To help the committee focus on the evaluation process and on each of the jobs to be evaluated, it may be helpful to ask committee members to summarize the information in the questionnaires they have reviewed to make sure the group is aware of the various perceptions of the work revealed by employees completing the questionnaires. Having someone from HR serve on the evaluation committee will also ensure that group members get a good feel for how the position being evaluated fits into the larger organization. For example, is the position in a job family with positions doing similar work slotted above and below it in the current classification structure?

Select Degrees

The method of job evaluation discussed in this chapter involves, broadly, applying the same point factor system to all the library's jobs. That is, first individually and then collectively, the members of the committee will, job by job, select the degree in each factor that most closely describes but does not exceed the job being evaluated.

Often the trickiest part of job evaluation is knowing whose opinion to listen to. You will have at your disposal, of course, the employee's understanding of the duties and responsibilities of the job as well as the supervisor's comments and feedback. You may also have notes from employee interviews. It is also a good idea to refer to the current job descriptions for the positions (unless you know these to be woefully out of date). Finally, group members will have perceptions and opinions. Perhaps a group member works in the same department as the job being evaluated; perhaps HR has input on their understanding of how the department is structured and which positions do what work. In any case, those are a lot of voices to listen to at once, and rarely will they all agree. How do you know which to listen to and take as the real story?

There is no right answer to this dilemma. Sometimes the employee will have overstated or understated the duties and responsibilities of the job. Sometimes the supervisor will have provided no comments or feedback. Sometimes the job description doesn't agree with either the employee *or* the supervisor! This is where the art and science of compensation and classification come to the forefront, and where consensus becomes truly imperative. We have worked with many committees where the process involved calling supervisors or employees on the phone and/or asking them to stop by the job evaluation meeting room for a few minutes to provide further clarification.

When members of the committee disagree, the group should work toward consensus. Consensus does not necessarily mean that everyone is in full agreement. Rather, it means that each member of the committee believes that he or she has had the opportunity to be heard, can live with the decision, and does not choose to block consensus.

WORKSHEET 9 ■ Job Evaluation Rating by Position, Factor, and Degree   `WEB`

Job Title	Education/training	Experience	Customer relations	Supervisory responsibility	Number of employees supervised	Level of supervision received	Complexity	Decision-making authority	Decision-making impact	Physical effort	Environmental factors	Total

Anyone can block consensus. When this happens, suggest that the committee move on to the next position and revisit the unresolved position(s) at another time. The converse is also true, because job evaluation is sometimes a subjective and human process. That is, instead of blocking consensus, some group members may go along with the majority when they shouldn't.

Finally, keep in mind that the first draft of a job evaluation should be just that—a draft. Only after reviewing the resulting hierarchy will committee members and library leadership be able to spot outliers and "sore thumbs." Chances are, however, that by using a group process, you will create a job hierarchy that is fairly close to the reality of internal equity at your library.

Back to the process! After discussion, apply the point factor plan to the jobs to be evaluated. Use and modify worksheet 9 to structure this process to fit your job evaluation system. Write the name of the job to be evaluated in the left-hand column. For example, you might start with library assistant I, II, and III. Some libraries choose to evaluate jobs by job family, some by grade level, some by department. Choose whichever method will fit your process best.

Next select the appropriate degree for each factor in each job. The degree for education/training for the library assistant I might be "1" (high school education or equivalent), and 1 may be selected as well for the education/training factor for library assistant II because no additional education may be required for incumbents in or applicants for this level of library assistant. The educational requirement for library assistant III might increase to a degree of 2 if post–high school education or an associate's degree is the minimum requirement for entry into this position. The application of the point factor plan for the library assistant positions would continue as degrees were reviewed and selected for the remaining factors—experience, customer relations, and so on. After degrees for each factor are assigned to the positions in the library assistant job family, continue in a

WORKSHEET 10 ■ Job Documentation Justification   `WEB`

Position: _____ Department/Location: _____

Date: _____

Factor	Degree	Justification/Discussion Points
1. Education/training		
2. Experience		
3. Customer relations		
4. Supervisory responsibility		
5. Number of employees supervised		
6. Level of supervision received		
7. Complexity		
8. Decision-making authority		
9. Decision-making impact		
10. Physical effort		
11. Environmental factors		

similar manner with another job family, if this is the approach you've chosen to take with the list of jobs to be evaluated. Remember, now you are only selecting the *degree* for each factor. In other words, points have not been assigned or even defined yet. You have determined the factor weights, but at this point you are focusing on the degree (numbered 1 through 5 or 1 through 4 and the like, depending on the factor).

During the job evaluation process, you may find that one or more factors for certain positions generate a great deal of discussion. If you can reach consensus only reluctantly, it is a good idea to make note of the discussion and its outcome. A "justification" worksheet (worksheet 10) is a good way to document the process in case the position needs to be revisited later. It also provides a way of ensuring that all parties have their opinions heard and noted. It can be used as backup documentation to explain or justify why you selected the degree you did for that particular factor. There is no need to use this sheet for factors on which consensus was easily achieved; you can limit its use to those degrees that were controversial selections or to those instances when the decision to select one of two degrees was a difficult one.

Assign Points to Factors and Their Degrees

Having identified compensable factors and defined the degrees associated with each, you now have sufficient information to assign points to each degree. In determining points, the number of points of the first degree (degree 1) is the same as the factor weight or value (that is, the percentage of the total 100 percent allocated to it in worksheet 8). For example, if education is weighted at 20 percent, degree 1, "ability to read and write," would be 20. You can determine the top degree by multiplying degree 1 (20 points) by 10. Thus, the last degree, "completion of an MLS degree," would be 200. With a factor of 20 percent, the first and last degrees for education would be

EDUCATION FACTOR	Degree	Point Value
	1	20
	2	
	3	
	4	
	5	200

Next, to find the value of the degrees between degrees 1 and 5, subtract the value of the first degree from the last degree:

$$200 - 20 = 180$$

Then, divide the difference (180) by one less than the number of degrees:

$$5 \text{ (degrees)} - 1 = 4$$

$$180 / 4 = 45$$

Add the result (45 in this case) to each degree, beginning with the second:

EDUCATION FACTOR	Degree	Point Value
	1	20
	2 (20 + 45)	65
	3 (65 + 45)	110
	4 (110 + 45)	155
	5 (155 + 45)	200

For another example, assume that the experience factor is assigned a factor weight of 10 percent. There are four degrees from which the committee can select to evaluate the experience required:

EXPERIENCE FACTOR	Degree
	1 (less than 6 months)
	2 (2 months to 1 year)
	3 (1 to 3 years)
	4 (3 to 5 years)

Following the same principles established for the education factor, degree 1 would be allocated 10 points (the same as the factor weight) and the final degree, 4, would be assigned 100 points (10 times 10). Subtracting 10 from 100, 90 points remain. Dividing 90 by 3 (one less than the number of degrees) tells us that 30 points would differentiate one degree from another, assuming equal value between degrees. The degrees allocated to experience would then be as follows:

EXPERIENCE FACTOR	Degree	Point Value
	1	10
	2	40
	3	70
	4	100

Repeat the process for all other factors, ultimately creating a chart that might look something like this:

FACTOR	DEGREE				
	1	*2*	*3*	*4*	*5*
Education	20	65	110	155	200
Experience	10	40	70	100	
Complexity	. . .	. . .	. . .	. . .	. . .

These examples assume that the difference between degrees in each factor is identical. You may, however, elect to have even more customized factors; that is, you determine a different increment between degrees in certain factors. For instance, perhaps the increment from a high school diploma to an associate's degree is worth relatively less to the library than the difference from a BA/BS degree to the completion of an MLS degree. The only rule in developing these increments is that as the degrees ascend within the factor, the value of the degrees should either remain constant or increase (not decrease). For example, in an education factor, the increment between degree 1 (some high school education) and degree 2 (high school diploma or GED) is 30 points. The increment between the next degree (AA degree or additional training beyond high school) should be 30 points or more, and so on throughout the factor.

Figure 6.3 shows a completed job evaluation plan with factor weights and points assigned to each degree. This example shows varying rather than even increments between degrees.

For the final summary of the job evaluation process, design a spreadsheet that looks very similar to worksheet 9 used by the committee. An example of a completed hierarchical ranking is shown in figure 6.4. The points associated with factor and degree weights have been entered into the spreadsheet, replacing the degree numbers originally entered during job evaluation. By position, enter the points for each degree in each factor. If you keep a copy of the original job evaluation results on an electronic spreadsheet while you are evaluating, you can do a simple search and replace for each column so that all 1s under education become 20s, and so on. The result is a ranking of the library's positions by total points from the one with the most to the one with the least number of points, or vice versa, depending on how you sort the data.

Step 6: Order and Review Final Rankings

Once you have a completed draft hierarchy of all evaluated positions, build in time for review and validation of findings before final approval. Often jobs look very different when rank ordered than they do while evaluating them one at a time. This review should be conducted with HR and/or library leadership rather than with the employee committee. No matter the level of confidentiality or professionalism of committee members, it is very difficult to see draft findings that may place their own position higher in the hierarchy only to see a final version that has changed to their detriment. The same may be said for draft salary survey findings (see chapter 7). In any case, make sure to review

Figure 6.3

Job Evaluation System

Introduction

The following job evaluation system has been custom-designed for Anytown Library to reflect the factors of value within the library. To ease use and understanding of the job evaluation process, this system has been designed to follow and reflect the factors as outlined and defined in the Job Analysis Questionnaire. Individual factors will be given weights (see chart below) to reflect their importance to the library. Evaluators will then assign each position a degree within each factor for each library position.

Variables: Weight   3,000 points   Number of degrees

Compensable Factors	Weight	Maximum Points	Number of Degrees
1. Education/Training	10%	300	7
2. Experience	7%	210	6
3. Communications/Key Contacts			
A. Nature of Contact	7%	210	5
B. Level of Contact	7%	210	5
4. Customer Satisfaction and Service	15%	450	4
5. Supervision			
A. Supervisory Responsibility	6%	180	5
B. Number of Employees Supervised	4%	120	5
C. Supervision Received	5%	150	5
D. Number of Volunteers	1%	30	4
6. Complexity and Problem Solving	15%	450	6
7. Decision Making			
A. Authority	7%	210	4
B. Impact	8%	240	5
8. Working Conditions			
A. Physical Effort	4%	120	4
B. Environmental Factors	4%	120	4

Degree Values

Compensable Factors	Degrees						
	1	2	3	4	5	6	7
1. Education/Training	30	60	90	130	180	235	300
2. Experience	20	40	70	110	160	210	
3. Communications/Key Contacts							
A. Nature of Contact	40	70	110	150	210		
B. Level of Contact	40	70	110	150	210		
4. Customer Satisfaction and Service	80	200	325	450			
5. Supervision							
A. Supervisory Responsibility	0	30	70	120	180		
B. Number of Employees Supervised	0	20	45	80	120		
C. Supervision Received	20	50	80	110	150		
D. Number of Volunteers	0	10	20	30			
6. Complexity and Problem Solving	25	80	160	250	350	450	
7. Decision Making							
A. Authority	25	75	140	210			
B. Impact	25	50	90	150	240		
8. Working Conditions							
A. Physical Effort	5	25	65	120			
B. Environmental Factors	5	25	70	120			

Number of Employees Supervised (Direct and Indirect)

1. 0
2. 1–5
3. 6–10
4. 10–20
5. 21+

Factor/Degree Descriptions

Education/Training

1. The job requires less than a high school diploma but does require *some* training.
2. The job requires a GED or a high school diploma.
3. The job requires up to one year of job-related course work after high school.
4. The job requires an associate's degree or two years of formal training beyond high school.
5. The job requires a bachelor's degree.
6. The job requires additional education beyond a bachelor's degree in a specialized area.
7. The job requires a master's degree.

Experience

1. No previous experience required
2. Six months to one year of experience
3. One to three years' experience
4. Three to five years' experience
5. Five to seven years' experience
6. Seven to ten years' experience

Communications/Key Contacts

Nature of Contact

1. Interaction involves routine information exchange and/or simple service activities requiring common courtesy (e.g., answering questions, directing calls, giving direction in response to simple requests).
2. Interaction requires moderate tact and cooperation (e.g., scheduling and/or coordinating multiple personal calendars, responding to questions that require some research to provide the correct answer).
3. Interaction requires substantial sensitivity and cooperation (e.g., basic project interaction, providing information to library patrons who from time to time may be upset or angry).
4. Interaction involves considerable explanation and persuasion leading to decision, agreement, or rejection on complex issues; diplomacy is required (e.g., problem-solving discussions regarding responsibilities, finance, work flow, or to facilitate service; important contacts involving difficult matters of agreements or controversies).
5. Interaction requires expert skills in persuasion, influence, and motivation of personnel at the highest level; issues are complex and require diplomacy and negotiation (e.g., controversial operating relationships, final decision-making and problem-solving discussion regarding library system objectives and goals, presenting highly controversial issues and negotiating major contracts).

Level of Contact

1. Level of contact is extremely infrequent with virtually no outside contact or contact beyond the immediate work unit/area.
2. Level of contact is primarily with clerical and technical staffs, and first-level service representatives.
3. Level of contact is primarily with library patrons, guests, professionals, vendors, and/or supervisors.
4. Level of contact is primarily with managers and/or department heads, community representatives, Friends groups, or media representatives.
5. Level of contact is primarily with assistant directors or the executive director, community leaders, business and industry leaders, elected officials, and/or financial agencies.

Customer Satisfaction and Service

1. Work requires understanding and communicating routine, work-related information, and requires normal courtesy, respect, and tact in dealing with others. Position interacts effectively with others in everyday contacts. Has limited or no effect on external relations and library image.
2. Ensures that customer satisfaction and service are maintained through daily interactions with internal and external contacts. Performance impacts the overall image of the library to some degree, though positive or negative consequences are relatively short-term.
3. Job has significant accountability for ensuring customer service and satisfaction within the branch or department by establishing and monitoring business procedures. Positive or negative impact on public relations or the library's public image is significant.
4. Job has substantial accountability for ensuring customer service and satisfaction systemwide by establishing and monitoring business procedures. Positive or negative impact on public relations or the library's public image is major.

Supervision

Supervisory Responsibility

1. Job has no responsibility for the direction of others.
2. Job functions as a lead worker performing essentially the same work as those supervised. May assist in training. May supervise or train volunteers.
3. Job supervises work within a unit or agency as a first-line supervisor. Makes recommendations on hiring and disciplinary actions. Evaluates program/work objectives and effectiveness and realigns work as needed. Responsible for training, instructing, and scheduling work within a unit or an agency. Conducts performance evaluations.
4. Job oversees multiple work functions within a branch, a unit, or an agency. Makes recommendations on hiring and disciplinary actions. Evaluates work objectives and effectiveness and recommends modifications to staffing patterns as needed. Conducts performance evaluations.
5. Job has direct responsibility for supervising and managing the operations of multiple departments and resolves the most complex problems.

(Cont.)

Figure 6.3
Job Evaluation System (Cont.)

Supervision Received

1. Work is performed under general supervision where the position functions independently on routine work; questionable cases and situations are referred to the immediate supervisor.

2. Works under general supervision with little functional guidance; rarely refers cases to supervisor unless a change to policy or procedure is involved.

3. Position functions under general direction and uses a wide range of procedures in meeting job responsibilities. The position plans and manages own work with minimal direction.

4. Position is under broad administrative direction; sets standards for a department or branch; is directly accountable for results.

5. Position is directly responsible to the board of library trustees and/or the library director; sets systemwide standards; is directly accountable for results.

Complexity and Problem Solving

1. Work of a relatively routine nature; requires only the ability to understand and follow instructions.

2. Work involves a choice of action within limits of standard policy and procedures.

3. Work requires judgment in the adaptation and interpretation of established practices, procedures, theories, and/or concepts to solve problems and situations for which the solution is not clearly defined.

4. Work is governed generally by broad instructions and objectives usually involving frequently changing conditions and problems requiring some judgment, initiative, creativity, and/or ingenuity.

5. Work requires the ability to plan and perform involved or technical work presenting new or regularly changing problems, to work from broad instruction, and to deal with complex factors not easily evaluated. Work requires considerable judgment, initiative, creativity, and/or ingenuity in areas where there is little precedent.

6. Work requires the ability to act independently in the formulation and administration of policies and programs for major divisions or functions.

Decision Making

Authority

1. The position has the authority to make routine or recurring decisions or suggestions based on rules or procedures.

2. The position consults with supervisor and/or others before making difficult and/or nonroutine decisions and shares responsibility for the decisions.

3. The position provides provide final approval on decisions that affect department or area of responsibility. The position provides input on library policy decisions.

4. The position makes decisions about organization policy and strategy or about significant transactions.

Impact

1. Incorrect decisions affect primarily this position's own work, are easily detected, and have little impact.

2. A poor or incorrect decision may cause short delays in getting the work done in the position's area and affect other employees or library customers.

3. Errors or poor decisions may cause major delays or disruptions to a library service or project.

4. Errors or incorrect decisions may result in injury, damage to property or the library's reputation, or financial loss.

5. Incorrect decisions impact systemwide plans and policies and may have significant impact on the organization over the long term.

Working Conditions

Physical Effort

1. The position is physically comfortable. The individual has discretion about walking, standing, and the like.

2. The position occasionally requires stooping or bending. Occasional very light lifting, such as three or four reams of paper, four or five books, or other materials (up to twenty pounds) may be required.

3. The position routinely requires lifting of moderately heavy items, such as equipment or boxes (up to forty pounds), and/or very long periods of walking on a routine basis, and/or standing for long periods and/or frequently requires stooping and bending.

4. The position involves considerable physical exertion, such as regular lifting of heavy items (up to eighty pounds) such as carts or crates full of books, on a highly frequent basis and/or assuming awkward positions.

Environmental Factors

1. There are no major sources of discomfort (i.e., essentially normal office environment with acceptable lighting, temperature, and air conditions).

2. There are occasional minor discomforts from exposure to less than optimal temperature and air conditions. The position may involve dealing with modestly unpleasant situations, such as occasional exposure to office chemicals and/or extensive use of video display terminals.

3. There are routine discomforts from exposure to moderate heat, cold, moisture/wetness, and unpleasant air conditions. The position may involve routine exposure to soiled materials and light chemical substances such as cleaning solutions.

4. There are routine exposures to significant levels of heat, cold, moisture, and air pollution. The position may involve exposure to chemical substances and physical trauma of a minor nature such as cuts, bruises, and minor burns.

Figure 6.4
Sample Hierarchical Ranking with Points

ANYTOWN PUBLIC LIBRARY
Job Evaluation Results

Job Title	Education/training	Experience	Customer relations	Supervisory responsibility	Number of employees supervised	Level of supervision received	Complexity	Decision-making authority	Decision-making impact	Physical effort	Environmental factors	Total
Central library manager	350	230	250	240	192	192	288	264	212	0	0	2,218
Adult coordinator	350	173	312	192	155	192	230	212	212	0	0	2,028
Facilities manager	200	230	250	192	115	192	288	212	212	0	0	1,891
Children's coordinator	350	173	312	144	38	192	230	212	212	0	0	1,863
Personnel manager	300	230	312	96	38	192	288	159	212	0	0	1,827
Assistant facilities manager	200	230	188	144	38	144	230	159	212	120	120	1,785
Trust and public relations manager	300	230	312	144	38	144	230	159	212	0	0	1,769
Senior branch librarian	350	173	250	144	155	144	173	159	159	0	0	1,707
Juvenile coordinator	350	173	312	0	0	192	230	212	212	0	0	1,681
Department heads	350	173	250	144	115	144	173	159	159	0	0	1,667
Branch librarian	350	173	250	144	76	144	173	159	159	0	0	1,628
Supervisor of circulation	250	173	250	144	115	144	173	159	159	0	0	1,567
First-class engineer	200	230	125	0	0	144	230	159	212	120	120	1,540
Assistant branch librarian	350	116	250	144	38	144	173	159	159	0	0	1,533
Outreach department manager	350	116	188	144	76	144	173	159	159	0	0	1,509
Children's department manager	350	116	188	144	38	144	173	159	159	0	0	1,471
Network and microcomputer administrator	300	173	188	96	38	96	230	159	159	0	0	1,439

the draft hierarchy after a few days' sabbatical, bringing a fresh perspective that is usually helpful. You can list all jobs by

total points

factor and degree (that is, all jobs that received a degree of 1 in the factor of education; all jobs that received a degree of 2 in education, etc.)

department total points—for example, in a public library environment, this will usually translate into

■ branch jobs
■ main library jobs

- finance and administration jobs
- maintenance and delivery; bookmobile drivers
- job family (e.g., circulation staff, librarian)
- management

Review the hierarchy to see if it makes sense and *fits* your library. Consider the following:

> Having gone through this process, and given your knowledge of the library and its jobs, are you comfortable that each job contributing at the same or similar level is ranked with a similar point total?

> Do any jobs stick out like a sore thumb (and therefore not belong where they were slotted)? This is OK. Sometimes a position just doesn't fit in a given place, regardless of what the points say. As consultants we always tell clients that we can provide reliable data and informed recommendations until the cows come home, but the clients have to *live* with this system after we leave. Any system has to work for your library's culture and environment and staff.

After a final draft is developed, review the hierarchy with the full committee. We often include only the job titles in hierarchical order, not the actual points, as people can get hung up on points and lose the big-picture perspective. Also, from our experience, many information system or IT jobs stick out as sore thumbs because the market often requires slotting them into a higher grade in the library's structure than they would be if decisions were made based on point totals alone.

Once each committee member has had an opportunity to reflect on the results and make notes on inconsistencies found, discuss and review the feedback with the group. These two steps—individual review and group review—are important to validate the final results and should not be overlooked.

Experience has shown that some jobs will clearly be ranked inappropriately. It happens in all committees. Talk it through together and review the degrees again. Some degrees may have been erroneously assigned, and that's OK. Now is the time to make any necessary changes.

After committee review, the project manager should review the final list with department heads. Depending on the culture of your library, share all or partial (their own organizational unit) findings with department heads, either individually or as a group. If a department manager uncovers a problem, review it for validity and determine whether to present it again to the review committee. Often, the problem involves a misperception of the job or an issue that can be easily resolved during the meeting. Other times, it's a legitimate problem that will need to be addressed by the committee. Regardless of the outcome, don't forget to follow up with the department head. Other than just making good common sense, this helps to build commitment to the process and buy-in from leadership.

Step 7: Present Findings

After all the changes are made to the hierarchy and the differences are reconciled, it's time to present the plan to senior management, the library director, and others for their review and feedback. Although some project teams might seek final approval at this point, it is best to wait until you have the results of your market pricing (see chapter 7). Market findings might influence some assignments and rankings, and senior managers are often hesitant to approve anything before having all the data—especially market information on difficult-to-recruit or other hot skills positions. However, at this point, do not change rankings again. Although the market rates may put a position in a higher or lower ranking, wait until you have all the data, and highlight jobs that have inconsistent job evaluation and market findings for conversation and pay-policy considerations.

LIBRARIANS WITH FACULTY STATUS

For professional librarians in academic libraries who hold faculty status, the job evaluation exercise will not be relevant. Where librarian salaries are tied to faculty salaries, you will not need to market price their salaries either. An academic department or the college's human resources department will do that for you.

Generally, although not always, when librarians in academic settings hold faculty status, it is a nontenure appointment. Sometimes, although they are not eligible for tenure, librarians are eligible for "permanent" status after a defined number of years of service. In a system where all other exempt professional and administrative employees are termed "at-will" or "regular" at best, this is a benefit and a compromise position for not being on a tenure track.

In these institutions, as with faculty positions, there are defined qualifications for librarian rank, typically librarian I to librarian IV. Level I is reserved for an entry-level, master's-prepared librarian. Movement to level II is typically based on performance, continuing education, and experience and is more or less automatic for quality, high-performing librarians. Many librarians remain at this level because the requirements for advancement to the rank of librarian III are substantial. For example, one university library requires the following:

> Evidence of leadership, resourcefulness, innovation, and dedication. . . . Professional participation . . . should include refereed publications, papers presented at professional meetings, committee appointments, and holding office in professional organizations or similar activities that contribute to the advancement of the library profession or to an academic discipline related to the individual's position. Service at this rank should be characterized by leadership or significant participation of high quality.

The same library adds the following requirements for advancement to librarian IV:

> The Librarian IV must also demonstrate significant achievements in at least two areas of professional activity. Significant achievement in professional organizations at this rank can be demonstrated by activities such as holding a major office, serving as a committee chair, engaging in extensive committee work, or similar activities that contribute to the vitality of the library profession or to an academic discipline related to the individual's position. The involvement, effort, and contribution must be at a level that is recognized by others in the field.
>
> At this rank academic research and publication activities will be judged by both quality and extensiveness of activities. These activities should go beyond the occasional and reflect expertise recognizable by others in the field.

Promotions, as you can see, are based on professional activity as well as job performance—very different from the typical criteria or compensable factors in a public library. However, these requirements clearly convey the values of this academic library. This type of policy not only communicates the library's values but also is clear about what it will evaluate and reward.

NOTES

1. "Alternative Approaches to Job Evaluation: Determining Internal Equity," *FLA Solutions* [e-newsletter] 13, no. 3, www.foxlawson.com/newsletter/pdfs/volume13_3.pdf.
2. Ibid.

seven | **Market Pricing**

While chapter 6 details an internally focused job evaluation system and its application, this chapter looks outward. It presents an overview of how to collect external salary data and market price positions and reviews which jobs should be the focus of a custom survey, which libraries and other organizations should be surveyed, and why. A sample spreadsheet you can use to analyze data is included.

Market pricing is what it sounds like: determining a "price" or pay rate for library positions in the marketplace to facilitate the development of competitive pay rates. Libraries and other organizations use market pricing to establish pay structures and rates that are market sensitive. That is, they see what employees in comparable positions are paid. They also track movement of market rates to adjust or revise their pay structures. This provides a rational, objective basis for setting pay rates. Market pricing uses the labor market, adjusted by your compensation philosophy, to set rates at, above, or below the going market rate.

Whether or not you have created an internal ranking of library positions based on their value to your system, as outlined in chapter 6, you still need to collect salary data for the library's jobs. During the market-pricing phase of this project, you will gather information regarding the rates paid to employees holding similar positions in your market.

This chapter reviews how you can design, conduct, and analyze custom surveys to learn of your competitors' pay rates. You should consider developing two or more surveys. One will be sent to the libraries in your labor market as you have defined it. These libraries, be they public, academic, or special, will have positions that are similar to those of your library and that are library-specific. The libraries you survey will be familiar with your terms for library positions and can easily determine the extent to which their jobs match yours. However, that is not the case with other surveys, which will be sent to organizations, local government jurisdictions, colleges, school boards, and nonprofit or for-profit organizations in your local labor market. Therefore, a more generic survey or surveys should be sent to those identified participants that better reflects the types of positions in these organizations. In addition, a pay equity survey can be conducted. All these surveys and the types of jobs included will be discussed in this chapter.

The basic steps of market pricing are to

> establish your time line for this part of the project
>
> select benchmark positions to survey
>
> identify survey participants
>
> decide if you will ask any questions about pay practices and benefits
>
> design the questionnaire
>
> use other, published market data sources if available
>
> follow up with participants and verify or quality control responses
>
> analyze and, if necessary, adjust data
>
> prepare and send reports to participants

Although these steps don't always happen in exactly this order, and they may be iterative, what follows is a "walk through" of each step of the process.

STEP 1: ESTABLISH A TIME LINE

First determine when you absolutely must have the cost of your new compensation plan finalized for inclusion in the budget planning and approval processes. Once you are ready to assess the fiscal impact of your new compensation plan, you will essentially be finished with the project. From the date of your presentation for approval by the board of trustees, local governing body, or academic administrators, work backward to determine your starting date. Depending on the timing of your survey, and in consideration of other activities that may be occupying staff time (end of fiscal year activities, technology installation, technical processing study, or salary planning), as well as the length of your survey and whom you are surveying, you should plan at least eight to twelve weeks to develop and send out the survey, compile and tabulate findings, and analyze results. When planning your time line, don't forget that you will need to develop the salary structure and implementation plan (see chapters 9 and 10) and obtain approvals as well.

Generally you can schedule survey activities parallel with other tasks (e.g., employee interviews, creating and applying a point factor job evaluation plan) and begin this step very early in the project. (See the appendix for a complete project time line.) For example, if you plan to cost out your new pay plan and implement it on July 1, depending on your approval process, the survey should be ready for mailing no later than January 1 so that you have figures for the budget process beginning in April or May. Larger, more-complex systems and academic libraries generally require more time for completion of market pricing than do smaller ones. Scheduling also depends on your budget planning process and time line. Working with two Maryland Eastern Shore libraries recently, we had two drastically different deadlines for budget figures, even though both systems' fiscal year begins July 1. One needed information in early January; the other did not need the figures until mid-March.

The survey process is very time-consuming and, without fail, will always take longer than you plan, so build in plenty of time. Determine how much time you will need to draft the survey and have it reviewed by the committee and any other individuals involved in the approval process. Keep in mind that there will be suggestions for revisions, especially regarding the benchmark jobs selected and summary position descriptions. Make sure you plan time to follow up with participants after receiving their responses. Of two things you can be certain: there *will* be questions, and you *will* need to verify the data once they are received. Develop a detailed work plan and stick to it. Finally, allow time for one, two, or maybe three weeks of extensions. There will be participants who simply don't have time to complete the survey by your targeted deadline but do want to participate. It is crucial, and to your benefit, to have some time built in to allow for these extensions.

STEP 2: SELECT BENCHMARK POSITIONS TO SURVEY

Select the positions in the library's structure that will serve as benchmark jobs to be included in the survey sent to other organizations. Benchmark positions are easily understood, are used by other libraries or area employers, and should represent all levels and types of work performed throughout the library structure. It is important to include jobs that have many incumbents, although you will also include several single-incumbent positions such as department heads, assistant directors, and the library director. In selecting benchmark jobs, consider the following guidelines. Surveyed jobs should be

easy to describe

varied in terms of required education and experience

commonly used by other employers

representative of all levels of work in the library

stable and not in the process of changing (so that matches are comparable)

representative of a large percentage of the employee population

jobs for which you are having trouble recruiting and retaining (i.e., hot skills jobs, department heads, MLS librarians)

representative of library and nonlibrary (finance, human resources, maintenance, security) jobs

Because you will be sending out a survey to nonlibrary participants, make sure to include jobs those participants will have data for—for example, an entry-level clerk, accountant, office manager, systems administrator, network manager, or facilities manager.

Although you might like to survey every single one of your library's positions, please don't (unless your system is very small and including all jobs does not result in a survey of overwhelming length). As you draft the survey instrument, consider the reader of or responder to your survey—the one who will ultimately decide whether to complete it. Respondents may be overwhelmed if you ask for information regarding too many positions or ask too many questions in general. Remember, the average HR manager or compensation analyst completes many salary surveys each year—don't make yours the most difficult to get through!

Include the most important benchmark jobs—those most important to your library and those that encompass the majority of your employable population, such as librarian (BLS and MLS), library associate, circulation clerk, and so forth—and cover the system both vertically and horizontally. An example of the jobs surveyed for a large urban library follows.

division directors

accountant

acquisition clerk

branch manager (various levels)

circulation manager

communications director

fund development officer

IT manager

IT specialist

librarian I

librarian II

manager, facilities

manager, outreach services

physical processing assistant

technical services manager

graphic artist

circulation assistant

circulation lead worker (team leader)

electrician

help desk technician

library associate I

library associate II

literacy specialist

mailroom technician

maintenance supervisor

manager, human resources

network manager

purchasing specialist

security guard

shelver

stationary engineer

In this same large system, a series of three other local surveys went out to local universities and community colleges, public school systems, hospitals, county governments, and other nonprofit agencies. The following is the combined list of benchmarked jobs for that local survey:

accountant	IT manager
graphic artist	IT specialist
cashier	literacy specialist
chief financial officer	mailroom technician
civil engineer	maintenance supervisor
clerical or customer service lead worker (team leader)	manager, facilities
communications director	manager, human resources
counselor	network manager
county engineer	office clerk (entry-level)
dean	planner
delivery driver	public works director
electrician	purchasing specialist
fund development officer	security guard
help desk technician	stationary engineer

A WORD ON PAY EQUITY

Pay equity is defined by the National Committee on Pay Equity as evaluating and compensating jobs (even dissimilar jobs) based on their skill, effort, responsibility, and working conditions, not on the people who hold the jobs (men or women). Pay equity is also known as comparable worth and equal pay for work of equal value and is a solution to eliminating wage discrimination and closing the wage gap. In 2006, we were privileged to be involved in an important study with the North Carolina Library Association. The impetus behind the project was to assess pay equity of library positions in the state. Briefly, the project involved surveying every public and academic library in the state as well as every local government and institute of higher education in North Carolina. As you will notice in the accompanying list, several of the positions listed in the survey that went to local governments, nonprofit agencies, or other nonlibrary employers were not "library" positions. What does a planner or a public works director or an engineer have to do with market rates for your library positions? More than you might think. Many libraries are beginning to focus on the importance of pay equity, just as the ALA-APA (American Library Association–Allied Professional Association) has developed its "Advocating for Better Salaries and Pay Equity Toolkit."

We assisted a suburban Maryland library system with a pay study designed to assess the equity of the library's positions with those of the local county government. In this case, no other employers were included in the market study—the focus was solely on ensuring pay equity with the local county government, a source of much comparison of salaries and competition for library employees. In this case, we actually sat with library HR staff and county HR staff and matched library job descriptions with county job descriptions.

In looking at pay equity you generally do not focus on similar work; rather, you need to look for a similar *level* of work and responsibility as well as a similar level of education, experience, and training requirements. For instance, a planner in a local government typically requires a master's degree, as does a professional librarian. The planner and librarian both may be hired directly after achieving these degrees. In addition, a planner and a librarian have a similar level of responsibility, independence, supervisory responsibility, job complexity, or all of these. Of course individual cases may differ, but in many public library systems this is an accurate match in responsibility for a professional librarian. This, in a nutshell, is pay equity. This particular library system went on to match all its positions with similar-level positions in the county government, then advocated (and obtained!) funding to ensure that the salary ranges were also equitable.

The databases resulting from the North Carolina study can be accessed by every public and academic library (in addition to the university and government participants) to assess pay equity in their own jurisdictions. Many of our current and recent clients are opting to include a sampling of positions in their salary surveys (as in the accompanying list) to check, if not fully assess, pay equity.

A small regional library benchmarked the following jobs to survey:

library director	librarian
deputy director	library associate I (BA/BS entry-level)
branch manager I	circulation clerk
branch manager II	page/shelver
senior librarian	custodian
information services manager	bookkeeper
technical processing assistant	administrative assistant
computer/network technician	delivery driver

We have developed surveys including as few as seven positions for a small library. How many jobs should you survey? If market pricing is your only method to evaluate jobs and create a salary structure, you should collect data for *at least* 50 percent of your jobs. If the market data are augmenting a point factor or other job evaluation plan, obtaining market data for 25 to 30 percent of the jobs will suffice, though in all honesty, the more the better, within the framework of keeping the survey manageable by other libraries and employers.

In theory, using information gathered during job analysis is critical for ensuring that jobs are matched properly to jobs in other organizations. In practice, however, it is not always practical to wait for the results of the job analysis process in order to develop a salary survey. In many cases, library systems simply do not have the time in their project schedules (or budgets) to conduct these processes end to end. In many (or most) cases, you will need to develop and distribute the survey *while* you are conducting your job analysis. We have found that the best solution to this dilemma of timing is to ensure that the survey draft receives thorough review and approvals—by your committee members, library leadership, and human resources staff. However you decide to proceed, you will need to draft an up-to-date summary for each job included in the survey to facilitate the respondents' ability to accurately determine if they have an appropriate match. Examples of two such summaries follow.

> *Cataloging manager*—Responsible for cataloging materials and for bibliographic database management; creates original cataloging as necessary; develops and maintains authority files; supervises two full-time cataloging assistants; requires master's in library science and two years' library or cataloging experience

> *Acquisitions supervisor*—Supervises acquisitions operations and staff; orders materials in a timely fashion from the most cost-efficient source; responsible for understanding, setup, and maintenance of the Data Research Associates acquisitions program used for ordering, receiving, and serials check-ins; establishes or revises acquisitions procedures; requires associate of arts degree *or* two years of job-related experience beyond high school

If you have up-to-date position descriptions, use these to create a first draft and then do several levels of thorough review of the draft survey. If position descriptions are outdated and not helpful in this effort, work with the committee or HR staff to develop the draft descriptions for the survey, and make sure to include the same type of review. If you are lucky enough to have a project time line that allows you to have completed questionnaires before issuing a salary survey, by all means use these questionnaires to help draft the survey descriptions. In all cases, we recommend thorough and multiple reviews to ensure that you are asking for the right positions and data before sending the survey out to other libraries and employers.

STEP 3: TARGET SURVEY PARTICIPANTS

When selecting survey participants (those from whom you would like to obtain data), review the list of organizations identified during your library manager interviews (chapter 3) and refer to your compensation philosophy. Consider other libraries and other local organizations that hire your former employees and those you use as a pool from which to draw job candidates. Think locally, regionally, and nationally, as appropriate, for the type of position. Think library, educational institutions, nonprofits, public sector, and private sector, again depending on the position and your competition for qualified applicants. Think comparators and competitors. If appropriate, think pay equity. For a slightly structured approach to selecting participants, brainstorm with the committee to complete worksheet 11.

Your selection of survey recipients will depend on the labor market in your community and your direct competitors for human resources. For example, one library system included several local hospitals and health-care systems as participants, as they were the employer of choice for nonexempt staff and certain professional positions because of their flextime and other benefits. Therefore, it became important to obtain information about the pay practices, benefits, and salaries of those institutions. Another client included many of the large local distribution centers and banking call centers/customer service centers as these were a big draw for administrative, clerical, and physical labor positions. Information about obtaining data from private sector companies is given later in this chapter.

Seek an appropriate balance between libraries and other competitors for employees. About 75 percent of the recipients of public library surveys are other public libraries. In academic libraries, 75 percent of those surveyed are other academic libraries, the local school board, and one or two public libraries. This has yielded an excellent response rate from the libraries surveyed (at least 75 to 80 percent or more return), approximately 65 to 75 percent from school boards and other public institutions, and about 20 to 50 percent from private companies. Because the response rate is typically lower from private organizations, it is best to design a separate, shorter survey that contains only general-industry benchmark jobs (e.g., secretary, clerk, accountant, information technology specialist, department manager) and does not use library jargon. Also be prepared to research and use published sources of private sector data.

How many organizations should you survey? A good rule of thumb is to survey twelve to fifteen libraries, public sector agencies, or nonprofit organizations and five to eight private companies. Keep the following in mind:

> Not every organization will respond.
>
> Not all respondents will be able to match (that is, provide data for) every surveyed job.
>
> You can augment the data, especially data for the generic nonexempt and exempt positions, from published sources (see step 6, later in this chapter).

Like you, potential participants are very busy and often receive many requests to participate in salary surveys. They will want to evaluate the cost and benefit of investing their time to complete the survey. To help increase participation, determine an appropriate

WORKSHEET 11 ■ Survey of Positions and Types of Employers   [WEB]

Library Positions	Type of Employer to Survey	Organization to Survey	Contact Name

Nonexempt
  Circulation
  Administrative support
  Accounting
	Local
	  City government
	  County government
	  School boards
	  Hospitals/health care
	  Local college/university/
	  community college
	  Local for-profit companies
	  (competitors and
	  comparators)		

Professional
  Accounting/finance
  Human resources
  Marketing
	Local, some regional
	  City government
	  County government
	  School boards
	  Hospitals
	  Local college/university/
	  community college
	  Nonprofits
	  Local for-profit companies
	  Libraries		

Librarian
  Entry-level MLS
  Experienced MLS
  Branch manager I, II
  Specialist
  Children's
  Technology
  Trainer
  Catalog
  Department manager
	Local, regional, some national
	  Public libraries
	  College libraries
	  School boards
	  Special libraries		

See chapter 8 for suggestions on survey sources for library executives.

contact in advance. For libraries, you can use your professional network. For general-industry participants, contact your local chapter of the Society for Human Resource Management or WorldatWork (formerly the American Compensation Association) or the local chamber of commerce. For public sector connections, call the local chapter of the International Public Management Association for Human Resources (formerly the International Personnel Management Association), the National Association of Counties, or the International City/County Management Association, or just call the organization and ask for the human resources director. Capitalize on your contacts and network. If you know someone from a library association committee or even a nonprofit board you serve on, give that person a call.

Before mailing the survey, call the person yourself or ask someone in your library who has had prior contact or dealings with the organization to call and solicit participation. Let the person know that the survey is coming and explain why participation is important and appreciated. An e-mail is also appropriate—just make sure to follow up if you do not receive a response. If you are planning to send your survey electronically, make sure you have an accurate e-mail address so your survey does not end up in a spam or junk-mail folder.

You can send the survey electronically, by mail, or both. We have had much success using web-based surveys—participants seem more apt to complete an online form than a paper survey. However, if a participant asks for a hard copy survey, by all means provide one. Survey tools like Zoomerang or SurveyMonkey are easy to use and administer; alternatively, your web developer or other IT staff may be able to launch your survey design online for you. In any case, offer to receive responses in the easiest way for the participant—mail, fax, or e-mail. If necessary, offer to work through the survey with the participant face-to-face or by phone. In addition to encouraging participation, this will help ensure the reliability of job matching.

Offer participants a report (summary of findings) at the conclusion of the survey. You might also offer respondents something more tangible such as a T-shirt from your summer reading program, tickets to a fund-raiser, membership in your Friends program or book group, and the like. There is no ethical reason not to do so, and you know how guilty some people feel when the American Whatever Association sends those mailing labels. We have also provided small-denomination gift cards from Amazon.com, Target, or Starbucks. Check with your HR director to see if offering such rewards constitutes a conflict of interest.

STEP 4: DECIDE IF YOU WILL ASK ABOUT PAY PRACTICES AND BENEFITS

As previously mentioned, base salary is only one aspect of total compensation. You may also want to ask questions about incentives and benefits. You might wonder, "Why even ask about incentives if we don't really have the ability to offer them?" Because general industry and even some government jurisdictions offer other cash awards (e.g., the city of Baltimore now offers incentives for certain positions, as do departments of the University of Maryland), you will want to be aware of this trend and have an idea of how it affects the total compensation package offered. You can obtain this information by asking the following:

> Are employees in a certain position or positions eligible for an incentive?
>
> If so, what percentage of base salary are they eligible to earn?
>
> What is the average earned?

You might have a similar feeling about whether to ask about benefits, especially if you are tied to a university, college, or county government and are not able to make independent decisions about the benefits offered. Nonetheless, some library systems want a true picture of total compensation that includes both salaries and benefits; competitive information about salaries is sufficient for others.

In addition, while you might not have any control over the design of your benefit plans, you may use the knowledge you gain to

> lobby for changes to your benefit plans in the future
>
> inform employees about the value of benefits to them (public library benefits are often very generous)

determine if the value of benefits offered by your competitors (whether they be much richer or less generous than yours) should be a factor in the level of pay you offer to employees

In some instances benefits are worth a substantial amount—sometimes as much as $2,000 to $4,000 per year over those offered by competitors. Because the cost of benefits continues to escalate dramatically, two things are happening:

Libraries are not always able to absorb large health-care premium increases and have begun increasing the percentage of the employee contribution.

Even with price-shifting modifications to existing employer/employee contribution rates, benefits will continue to serve libraries as an invaluable tool for recruitment and retention—especially if employees can spend benefit dollars in a flexible manner.

Survey for benefits data only if you will use the information. It is a major undertaking for both the library commissioning the survey and for respondents. That is, reporting benefits information is time-consuming for respondents, and inputting and analyzing benefits information will take almost as much time as the salary segment of the study.

We find one question in particular to be very helpful in getting a big-picture view of benefits in comparator organizations without having to analyze the minutiae of each benefit component. The question is this: What is the cost of benefits as a percentage of salary *of benefited employees* in your library system? Along with asking the total payroll budget, this question will give you a feel for how your system ranks in terms of benefits as a whole. If all responses are within 5 percent or so of your response, you can at least see that your benefits are comparable and competitive, even if one system provides two additional paid holidays versus your two additional personal days. Be sure to ask participants to indicate the cost of the entire benefits package as a percentage of *total salaries/wages of those who receive benefits*, including employer contributions to health insurance (family coverage), retirement, workers' compensation, life insurance, short-term disability, and FICA. The total probably corresponds to the overhead rate you normally add to each employee's compensation, on average, for budgeting purposes.

If you do ask specific questions regarding health insurance plans, make sure to ask what percentage of the premium is paid by the employee for individual or family plans as well as the actual dollar amount of the premiums. It does no good to know that employees in Library X pay 20 percent of their individual health insurance premium if you do not know the total premium amount. Health insurance plans differ widely, of course, and 20 percent of HMO Plan A may be $50 more per pay period than 20 percent of PPO Plan B.

You may also decide to ask some questions about general pay practices. These should be issues of particular interest to your system. For instance, if many of your current employees are hitting their range maximum, you may want to ask other systems how they handle longevity. Other questions may focus on the following:

job evaluation systems

salary structure design (i.e., steps or no steps? how are increases awarded?)

basis for merit or performance adjustments (performance appraisal or automatic step), frequency, and size of increase

COLA increases and their frequency and amounts

bonus or other incentive/award plans

salary differentials or other pay practices for compensating staff assigned to work evenings, weekends, or holidays

We have designed surveys that include very broad or very general questions in this section. It really depends on your information needs. If you want general information on how comparators have structured their compensation systems, keep the questions broad. If recruitment of bilingual library associates is an issue in your system, you may want to ask, as one recent client did, what if any premium is paid for bilingual skills. Other libraries will probably be interested in this information too and will want to receive the summary of your findings. Just remember to limit your questions to a feasible number.

STEP 5: DESIGN THE SURVEY

Keep the following basic design principles in mind when preparing the survey questionnaire. Although they might sound like little things, they do make a difference.

- The final questionnaire should be easy to read, be easy to respond to, and look appealing. You want respondents to want to flip through it for an overview, and then take the time to read it in more detail.
- Include clear, concise instructions as well as a contact number or e-mail address where participants can ask for clarification or help.
- Make it look professional, including a cover letter or e-mail explaining why you are seeking respondents' participation and what they will receive in return.
- Number the pages.
- Keep the size of the survey, including the number of positions and other questions, reasonable and not overwhelming.
- Ask for participants' names and telephone numbers and include yours.
- Underline or *otherwise highlight* keywords.
- Note in your cover letter if you have additional or open-ended questions at the end of the survey.
- Design your data collection format (Excel spreadsheet or other) to parallel your questionnaire. (This will facilitate data entry and analysis.)
- Pilot test your survey with your own data *before* you issue it.

The questionnaire should ask the following for each benchmark job:

- *Base salary*—Ask for the average/actual salary for a position as of a certain date (i.e., January 1 or July 1). This number represents the current salary being paid to incumbents in a given position. If there is only one person in the position, the number is the individual's actual salary. If there are multiple staff in a position, this number will represent the average of their combined salaries. Many public and academic libraries, school boards, public jurisdictions, and nonprofits have a fiscal year that begins July 1. If this is the case in your situation, it makes sense to ask for data effective on that date.
- *Salary range*—Request the minimum, midpoint, and maximum of the salary range to which the position is assigned. Although the average or median of all base salaries reported for each position is referred to as the "market rate," the range helps verify the lowest and highest actual base salary paid and will provide a good measure of how respondents are paying in relationship to

their range. Keep in mind, though, that pay ranges reflect the policies and compensation philosophy of other organizations, which might or might not reflect your own. A word on range midpoint—some library systems have a defined range midpoint, while others do not. If this information is not provided by the participant, you can calculate a mathematical midpoint simply by adding the minimum and maximum and dividing by two.

Hiring rate—We have begun including this question in recent surveys. Though it doesn't apply to every job or even every library system, some employers use hiring rates that are different from range minimum to recruit for positions that are particularly hard to fill or retain in their systems. For instance, if a library is seeking MCSE-certified IT technicians, it may be willing to pay a higher entry-level rate for candidates with this certification. Though libraries and other employers, particularly academic libraries and school systems, often pay higher than range minimum for candidates with previous years of directly related experience, this question is designed to address a different issue. Finally, a higher hiring rate may be used by libraries that haven't conducted a study in some time. These organizations will likely have outdated, unrealistic minimum salaries and therefore need to have a higher rate to attract new hires.

Type of job match—Ask participants to report if their job is bigger than, equal to, or smaller than your job summary (expressed in percentages: between 20 percent smaller and 20 percent larger than yours) and to describe the difference on a separate sheet so you can determine if the percentage difference is appropriate. Your summary job descriptions and cover letter will indicate the scope measures, so the differences should not be difficult for respondents to provide. Perhaps your library's position requires a BA/BS and the participant's does not. Perhaps your position does not supervise any employees but the participant's matching position does have supervisory responsibility. These are just two examples of how positions may differ in their degree of match but still be essentially the same position because of the job duties and responsibilities involved.

Other position information—You should request the following additional information for each position: the job title used in the respondent's organization, the number of hours normally worked each week, the number of incumbents in the position, and exempt or nonexempt status in the responding organization.

Decide up front whether you would rather have the salary data in hourly or annual format and specify to participants what you are requesting. Our practice is to request hourly data: libraries, governments, and other employers define a full-time workweek differently (35, 37.5, or 40 hours, for instance). If you have hourly figures, you can easily convert these to full-time figures based on *your* full-time workweek.

Other general demographic questions are very helpful in comparing your library to other libraries or employers. Whether the library has unions, the total number of employees (full- and part-time), the number of branches, whether the system has a main library, and the total operating budget—all are good statistics to have in making comparisons between library systems.

Think about what you really need to know and how these data will be helpful to you. Don't ask questions that fall into the "nice to know" category but whose answers won't necessarily be used for your project. Remember, the participation rate will be adversely affected if the questionnaire is too lengthy or cumbersome to complete.

In your instructions make it clear that participants should read the job summaries provided and understand what is involved in the job in your organization before matching it to the surveyed jobs. Explain that respondents should not rely solely on title, because organizations use titles differently. One organization's administrative assistant is a $28,000-per-year support person, while another's is a $42,000 executive assistant. One public library in Maryland refers to employees holding a bachelor's degree and who have completed the state's training program as "librarian," while other libraries will only use that title for employees who hold a master's degree. To help participants make accurate job matches, define how the job fits into your organization's structure; to whom a person in that job reports; whether the job holder supervises others and, if so, how many; and what education and experience are required to do the job competently. In summary, job matches are based on *job content*, including

- education and experience requirements of the job
- licenses or certifications required by the position
- scope (budget size, number of employees, or other scope data appropriate to the position)
- breadth of job
- supervisory responsibilities

They are *not* based on

- title
- current grade
- incumbent salary
- incumbent performance
- length of tenure of incumbent
- market considerations

If the respondent's job matches at least 85 percent of your job summary, then it's probably a good match to include in the survey and in your subsequent analysis.

Approval

Once you have designed a complete draft of the survey, you will need to have the appropriate people (the library director, an employee committee, or both) review it. Your focus during the approval process should be to

- ensure that position summaries are accurate and that they represent the actual work being performed and the minimum qualifications for the job rather than what skills the incumbent(s) might possess
- minimize the number of jobs surveyed (It's easy to keep adding just one or two jobs to the total list. Over time, this can make your survey too lengthy to produce a good participation rate.)

You can reduce the time spent on final approval processes if you seek review from the committee electronically. Because this is a critical point at which much time can be lost, *set a return date* and adhere to it. A few days to a week should be sufficient to review the changes.

While the committee is reviewing the survey, you can concentrate on the following administrative tasks:

Verify your contact list to ensure that the appropriate people are contacted and informed about the survey. Ensure that you have accurate e-mail addresses if surveys are to be sent electronically.

Set up your data collection file (whether it be a spreadsheet or database application), and input your library's data for comparative purposes later.

Pilot Test

Once the survey has been designed, reviewed by the appropriate parties, and approved, pilot test it. Have human resources, the assistant director, or your finance director complete the survey as a respondent. Although one person should be specified to enter the actual data for your library, multiple users can proofread, quality control, and otherwise vet the survey before issuing it to participants. This step serves as the final check before the survey is distributed to other organizations. On completing the survey, your internal respondents will be able to tell you about any glitches or problems they encountered. Final changes and revisions to ensure ease of completion can then be made before your external market attempts to complete the survey. Though time is often of the essence in a compensation project, please do not minimize the importance of pilot testing the survey *before* sending it out to participants. This is the time to make sure that the survey is easy to understand and complete, flows easily, and gives you what you need without too much work by participants.

Cover Letter

Draft a cover letter or e-mail to go along with the survey itself. Let participants know why you are contacting them, provide some background information about your library, and inform them of the due date for their data. Don't forget to provide phone, fax, and e-mail contact information if participants have questions and to allow them to provide their responses by their method of choice. Most will opt for a web-based option if it is provided.

Ask survey participants to respond within two weeks. Experience proves that the majority will take longer, so allow time for this in your project work plan. Plan to follow up with phone calls during the beginning of the third week after the survey is distributed.

STEP 6: USE OTHER MARKET DATA SOURCES

So far you have read about the information you will need to collect for a special custom survey—a survey designed to meet *your* specifications and time line. There are, however, other ways to obtain information on what employers pay for jobs.

Published Surveys

Participating in or purchasing published surveys may be less expensive than conducting one of your own, either independently or through consultants. Published surveys will, however, be more generic and less focused on your specific jobs or market for employees. You may need to find several surveys to adequately cover all the library's benchmark positions. Given today's competitive marketplace, you should not consider using a survey that is older than two years. For information technology and other difficult-to-recruit jobs, the data can become outdated even more quickly. Depending on what is available in your local area and the extent to which you are able to conduct market pricing research, a few sources for published data follow. Note that some can be expensive.

The U.S. Department of Labor's Bureau of Labor Statistics (BLS) provides good salary data on library and nonlibrary jobs alike. The data are available and can be sorted by region or metropolitan area, so you should be able to find data in geographic proximity. Be sure to note the date of the data provided, as BLS is typically one to three years behind. The data are still usable, but they will need to be aged (typically about 2.5 to 3 percent per year) to account for cost of living adjustments and other salary range increases applied industry-wide. In addition, published surveys are available for purchase from such commercial entities as the Economic Research Institute, Mercer, Hay Group, Abbott Langer, and PricewaterhouseCoopers.

Telephone/Fax/E-mail Surveys

The library world is a nicely networked market. You could design a brief survey for obtaining limited information on a few jobs, such as one conducted on behalf of a public library client in the Northeast. A year following the implementation of a major new pay program, management wanted to follow up to make sure they were still on track with their entry-level salary for newly minted MLS librarians. A brief survey was faxed to library systems included in the original survey, asking for returns within one week and offering the options of returning completed surveys electronically, via fax, or over the telephone. This garnered 100 percent participation. Participants' reports were prepared and sent to all respondents, even though it was just a small, quick survey.

Recruiting Ads or Calls/Job Applications

You can go to local employers, ask for an application for a friend, and ask a few questions about starting salary or benefits while you are there. This is a quick way of getting information that would be difficult to obtain by survey. This method should be used to verify or corroborate information you have, rather than as a primary source.

Industry- and Professional-Group Surveys

These surveys are designed and conducted by professional, marketing, or recruiting groups or others. The American Library Association, state library associations, and other industry professional associations often survey constituents and make that information available. These are generally good sources of salary data for specific jobs of interest to a certain industry. Check with your local universities or colleges because they may produce salary surveys as well. The College and University Professional Association for Human Resources (CUPA-HR) publishes a survey that academic libraries might find useful. Also check with your human resources staff or the human resources staff at the college, university, city, or county level. These individuals often belong to professional organizations, such as the Society for Human Resource Management or its local or regional chapters, that often produce annual salary surveys. Finally, local or statewide organizations, such as your state library association, association of counties, or a municipal league, may produce salary surveys. State governments are also good sources of data—the division of library services in Maryland, for instance, compiles and distributes an annual survey of public library positions. You may ask, "If my state does the same, why do I need to do all this other work?" Although the data included in the Maryland survey are quite helpful, they are typically not deep or specific enough to help libraries develop comprehensive compensation systems. Not every position is included, for instance, and job descriptions defining what is required for each position are not included, so you would be making position matches based on title alone. Also, of course, your review of data would need to include employers other than libraries and perhaps libraries outside your own state.

Keep in mind that salaries and benefits from respondents will often vary based on the size of the organization and sector of the economy. For example, it is likely that the pay rates for a small public library will be lower than those for a university academic library. Likewise, the academic library rates will be lower than those of a local utility company. If you decide to include a professional association survey in your data, contact the survey sponsor and learn as much about it as possible. If you can't get answers to your questions, be careful how you use the data.

Be leery of a variety of surveys published by information technology, marketing, human resources, and finance groups as well. Although many of them may look terrific, they may not be valid sources of salary information. If a survey doesn't include background on how the survey was conducted, publish a participant list or effective date of the data collected, or outline quality control standards and procedures for cleaning data, you can't consider the data valid.

Websites of Potential Participants

Often, when there is a lack of participation in a key area, say, community colleges or local hospitals, you can find useful salary information on their websites. Some organizations publish their entire salary and grade structures and provide job descriptions online, ensuring that you will be able to make quality matches. Take this information with a grain of salt, however, because without speaking directly with someone in the human resources department, you can't be sure if the data are truly up to date, if the organization is hiring (as is common practice) well above range minimum, and the like.

Be very wary of collecting salary data from the Internet unless the source is reputable and reliable. You will be able to find a salary for any position you can dream of on the Web, but ask yourself these questions:

> Are these data from your geographic area?
>
> What organizations are included? (Libraries? *Fortune* 500 companies?)
>
> What are the budgets of these organizations?
>
> How many employees do they have?
>
> Are they comparable to your library?
>
> Can you match a job description or position summary to one in your library? Does it include differentiation for years of experience or education required?

Not all information found on the Internet is questionable; however, make sure the information is really a match before incorporating it into your findings.

STEP 7: FOLLOW UP AND VERIFY RESPONSES

Not only will you need to follow up by calling the organizations to remind them to participate, you will also need to contact them to help you "clean" the data after they complete and return your survey. Cleaning the data is almost literally just that. You need to review the data sent by survey participants and clean them up. For example, if the respondent reported annual rates and you want hourly, you will need to convert the data to your hourly format (if you know the respondent's hours worked per week). If the respondent writes that a particular job is about equal to yours, yet it pays 50 percent more, you should call and verify the match or the numbers provided. Similarly, call to find out the true numbers if the respondent put the same number (salary data) in the columns headed minimum, midpoint, and average. It is important to thoroughly review all data to make sure that they fit and make sense and that, to the fullest extent possible, all information requested is provided. This step will ensure that the data you move forward with in the analysis step will be of the highest quality.

Mistakes in data entry can happen. You need to check responses for reasonableness. That is, do the data make sense? If the response indicates that circulation assistants are earning more than the branch manager, you will need to follow up to ascertain the accuracy of the response. An error may be as simple as a participant's typo; however, the only way to be sure is to speak directly to someone from the organization.

Essentially, you should review the data at least twice, though you will most likely end up reviewing it many more times. First, each participant's response should be thoroughly reviewed position by position, looking for inconsistencies. Second, after the data are entered into a spreadsheet (see step 8 later in this chapter), they should again be reviewed position by position, looking at all responses for a given position for outliers or sore thumbs.

Generate a list of questions, if any, for each respondent, so you can make just one follow-up call during which you verify responses, review matches, and discuss reasons for particularly high or low rates of pay. Sometimes the respondents made an error; other times there are legitimate reasons for what appear to be inconsistencies. An example comes from a public library in Maryland. In reviewing its data, the consultant noticed that the actual and average salaries paid to many incumbents were close to, at, or over the maximum of their reported pay range. A conversation with the library's contact revealed that ranges were particularly narrow (e.g., 35 percent for senior-level positions) and that many employees were long-service and were receiving longevity payments. These facts explained what appeared at the outset to be inconsistencies.

STEP 8: ANALYZE AND ADJUST DATA

Figure 7.1 is a sample Excel spreadsheet for entering and analyzing the data, and figure 7.2 is a summary of one position (librarian) that could be used to look for sore thumbs.

Regardless of what method you choose to input your data, keep it fairly simple and focus on a few meaningful figures such as the following:

> *Mean*—the average of all the data points. It treats each respondent's data the same, regardless of number of incumbents.
>
> *Weighted mean*—each respondent's data are weighted by the number of incumbents in the position; therefore, salary data from respondents with many incumbents in the position will have a greater influence on the weighted mean than will data from respondents with few incumbents.
>
> *Median*—the value at which half the data is higher and half is lower. This measure minimizes the influence of extreme highs and lows and is generally considered one of the most useful measures in compensation unless there is a specific reason not to use it.
>
> *Data range*—shows the salary data from high to low. This gives an indication of how dispersed the data are.

Figure 7.1
Sample Spreadsheet for Analyzing Data—Position: Public Librarian

Respondent Agency	Minimum Education	Degree of Match	Rationale	Number of Employees in Position	Number of Hours/ Week	Raw Data	
						Average/ Actual Pay ($)	Minimum of Pay Range ($)
Your library	MLS			13		33,072	25,526
Library 1	MLS	equal		18	37.5	40,619	30,401
Community college 1	MA/S/L	+20% scope	Broader	4	40.0	49,920	30,700
Library 2	BA/BS	10%	Education	5	37.5	28,490	27,008
Library 3	MLS	equal		29	40.0	28,413	24,960
Local school board	MLS	equal					31,721
Library 4	MLS	equal				42,768	32,243
Average (excluding your library)						38,042	29,506
Variance % over/under average						13%	13%
Median (excluding your library)						$40,619	$30,551
Variance % over/under median						−19%	−16%

Figure 7.2
Sample Spreadsheet for Capturing Data—Position: Librarian

Respondent	Average/ Actual Salary ($)	Number of Incumbents
Your Library	**44,820**	**2**
Library E	45,000	5
Library F	41,515	1
Library B	37,869	10
Library I	37,800	50
Library D	37,000	4
Library H	36,705	2
Library A	33,300	8
Company G	30,000	4
Company C	29,200	14
Total		100

Unweighted mean	$37,321
Weighted mean	$36,289
Median	$37,400
Data range	$29,200 to $45,000 (or $15,800)
Rank (your library)	2 of 10
25th percentile	$32,475
75th percentile	$42,341

| Midpoint of Pay Range ($) | Maximum of Pay Range ($) | Longevity | Adjusted Data | | | | |
			Degree of Match	Average/ Actual Pay ($)	Minimum of Pay Range ($)	Midpoint of Pay Range ($)	Maximum of Pay Range ($)
32,955	39,195		1.00	33,072	25,526	32,955	39,195
35,139	39,878	45,864	1.00	40,619	30,401	35,139	39,878
52,958	75,216		0.80	39,936	24,560	42,366	60,173
33,755	40,502		1.10	31,339	29,709	37,131	44,552
28,891	31,866	38,730	1.00	28,413	24,960	28,891	31,866
38,861	46,000		1.00		31,721	38,861	46,000
42,768	53,293		1.00		32,243	42,768	53,293
38,729	47,793	42,297		35,077	28,932	37,526	45,960
15%	18%	100%		6%	12%	12%	15%
$37,000	$43,251	$42,297		$35,638	$30,055	$37,996	$45,276
−11%	−9%	−100%		−7%	−15%	−13%	−13%

Do *not* include your own organization's data with others in the analysis. As in figure 7.1, your data should be shown for comparative purposes separately, by placing it in the first or last line. The spreadsheet shown in figure 7.1 can easily be adapted for your needs. You may want to change requested data or column headings to suit your needs. You may also want to include a column where you apply an aging factor—essentially adding a set percentage to each salary figure—to reflect the current point in time if the data are known to be a year or a fiscal year behind. This could be the degree of match column (see the following explanation of columns) or an additional column if *all* data are to be aged rather than only certain participants.

The columns in figure 7.1 provide places to record the following information:

Column 1—name of respondent

Column 2—minimum education required for the position by the employer; this may differ widely within the same position

Column 3—degree of match. Remember, all who were surveyed were asked the degree, from 20 percent less to 20 percent more, to which their position matched your library's job.

Column 4—rationale to substantiate the degree of match. You want to know the basis on which the respondent's position was deemed bigger or smaller than your own. Often the discrepancies are based on different educational requirements, years of experience, or supervisory status.

Column 5—number of employees in each position

Column 6—hours in the participant's workweek for the position

Column 7—actual (if single incumbent) or average (for positions with multiple incumbents) pay in each job surveyed

Columns 8–10—minimum, midpoint, and maximum of the pay range to which the job is assigned

Column 11—amount of longevity pay, if any, awarded to employees with specified amounts of seniority or tenure with the library

The next section of columns (adjusted data) provides the same information, as adjusted. Data would be adjusted to

ensure that all data are as of or effective to the same date

allow for a differential such as education, supervisory responsibility, scope of work

provide a geographic differential, if appropriate

Excel makes it quite easy to develop formulas that will do the remainder of your work. Even for relative novices, the median and mean formulas are very intuitive. For each position, you can ask the spreadsheet to calculate the average (mean) and median of each position (average/actual, minimum, hiring rate, midpoint, maximum or longevity pay) as well as the percentage of variance from your library's data. This activity will give you excellent information about the relationship of your library's compensation to what is offered by those in your market.

Adjustments to Survey Data

As mentioned previously, you will have asked your survey participants to provide a degree of match for their positions. This percentage will adjust the survey data to more closely match your benchmark positions. In addition, you may further adjust survey data to reflect differences between your library's job and respondents' jobs that you believe are appropriate. Survey participants often either don't have the time to conduct this level of analysis or might miss key components of the position that may affect the match. This is a perfectly legitimate compensation practice. Some reasons for doing so include the following:

Scope of the job—your organization or job covers more or less than the scope reported by respondent

Level—respondent's job is at a higher or lower level in the organization than your job (e.g., your job reports to a branch manager and the respondent's job reports to the assistant library director)

Required knowledge—your job requires more or less education or knowledge to do the job (knowledge and experience are generally strongly correlated with market pay levels)

Breadth of responsibility—the job in your library has different responsibilities than respondent's (e.g., the job for which you surveyed also supervises staff and respondent's job does not)

Impact on organization outcomes—the job for which you surveyed has more or less impact on the library than that of the respondent. For example, the position of marketing director in your library system might include responsibilities for public relations, marketing, fund-raising, Friends of the Library, and working with the library's foundation, while in another library system, the incumbent is responsible only for public information.

Figure 7.3
Framework for Adjusting the Data

±5 to 10 percent (just noticeably different)

One level movement in career path or job family (i.e., Library Associate I versus Library Associate II)

Added responsibility is less valuable than the core job

Education level—Typically add or subtract 10 percent for MS versus BS and 5 percent for BS versus AA, although this also depends on accompanying years of experience (e.g., AA with 4 years' experience might equal a BS)

Supervisory responsibility—Adjustments could be made for differences in numbers of people supervised (e.g., 15 versus 5)

Levels of experience—Position requires more or less previous or related experience than benchmark job

±10 to 15 percent

Nonexempt position versus supervisory level

Supervisory or lower management jobs—Double or half of scope measures or level of responsibility (e.g., number of employees supervised, number of branches)

Supervisor versus manager or director versus manager

Supervises professional-level positions

Upper management jobs—Double or half of scope measures (e.g., revenues, large differences in budget, number of branches, collections)

Significant difference in levels of experience—Position requires much more or much less previous experience than benchmark job

Manages systemwide program or service versus branch or main-library located program/service

±15 to 20 percent (significantly different)

Director versus executive

For senior managers—Double or half of scope measures (e.g., budget, number of branches, collections)

For senior managers—Added responsibility is less valuable than the core job

---

Market demands—new technology or hot skills (e.g., fund development, children's librarian) have made the position more highly valued

In general, you would not make an adjustment to market data of more than ±20 percent. You should make very few adjustments, if any, at this level. Most of the adjustments you make should not exceed 10 percent. (A framework for adjustments is provided in figure 7.3.) In addition, adjusting data is part of the art-versus-science aspect of compensation, as it can be subjective. However, once the percentage of adjustment is identified, it should be kept consistent throughout data analysis. For example, if you choose to adjust data by 10 percent for a position for which you require a master's degree but the minimum qualification for some respondents is a bachelor's degree, then maintain the 10 percent education differential throughout.

An important note: although it often seems counterintuitive, the adjustment of data is designed to bring the survey data more closely in line with the reality of your positions. Therefore, if your cataloger position requires an MLS and a respondent's position requires a BA/BS, the respondent's job is "smaller" than yours. To adjust the data, you need to *increase* the respondent position by effectively adding 10 or 15 percent to the reported salary.

Hybrid Jobs

In the past, jobs were created using a homogenized hierarchy—jobs devoted to one functional area and expertise were organized from department head down to clerical or blue-collar jobs. Whether because of the unique needs of each library, the specific capabilities of certain employees, or the desire to capitalize on interests and provide new challenges, many jobs are now designed in a nontraditional way. In today's world, the hybrid job—

one that *regularly* consists of work in more than one functional area—is becoming more the rule than the exception. Recent client positions include a librarian/web developer, an audiovisual materials selector/library associate, and an accounting technician/benefits specialist. We're sure that you can name a few in your library as well. As you will typically not find matches for these hybrids that have evolved out of the need of the library system or the particular skills and talents of the incumbents, there are three possible approaches for market pricing hybrid jobs:

Majority approach—Where more than 50 percent of the job is an identifiable function, price the job based on the major portion of the job. This is especially appropriate if the other portions of the job are of equivalent degree of difficulty or have about the same market value.

Weighting approach—This approach is appropriate when you prefer to acknowledge the different aspects of a job by pricing and weighting its component parts. (See worksheet 8 in chapter 6.) For example, if a job is 70 percent financial analyst and 30 percent accountant, take 70 percent of the average actual salary data for a financial analyst and add to it 30 percent of the average actual salary data for an accountant to determine the going rate for your hybrid job.

Highest value approach—Where you are competing for technical talent or other in-demand expertise, market price the entire job based on the portion attributable to the highest market rate. Do this regardless of the percentage of time spent on that task. For example, for a financial analyst/accountant, you would market price the job as that of a financial analyst, which is the higher paying job in the market.

Note that the value of the job is not cumulative. Don't simply add up the market value of both jobs to get the combined value of the job. In addition, minor add-on functions with market values less than the highest market value don't increase the value of the job being priced. It is important to note that the best way to slot these unique hybrid positions may be to rely on the internal equity of the position, whether that is determined quantitatively using a point factor system or qualitatively using whole-job evaluation. The approaches just listed may often be too rigid to successfully meet your needs and identify the correct fit for the position.

STEP 9: PREPARE AND SEND REPORTS

The final report of your findings and results should conform to your library's style for its other reports (e.g., summarized versus fully detailed). Attempt to present only the most useful and descriptive data, which will be different depending on the audience. Are you presenting this information to the library board of directors, the academic vice president, or the county commissioners? On the one hand, the more information included in your final report, the more questions that may arise about what data are more valuable. In addition, each constituency will view what is valuable differently. On the other hand, you want to provide enough information so that informed, intelligent decisions can be made. It is perhaps best not to give anyone but the project manager the line-by-line data, but do provide summaries by category of position (e.g., nonexempt, exempt, management). See chapter 10, "Implementation," for more important information about communicating findings and results. As discussed in chapter 2, get input and buy-in during the initial stages of the project on what the report should contain, including whether participants will be coded or identified. Generally, your report should

- include an executive summary
- be consistent
- be well documented
- be attractive and easy to read (perhaps with bar or line graphs)

This report should include summarized results of the survey and be brief but meaningful. After your final report has been presented to the board, an additional report should be promptly sent to all participants who responded to your survey. You most likely do not want to send participants the level of detail you share with library leadership, the board, or your funding source, but you do want the information to be helpful to participants who took the time to complete your survey. We often include a summary of the range of data for each position—for instance, the lowest and highest range minimum for the position and the lowest and highest range maximum for the position, giving participants an idea of the boundaries of market levels for each job. Also include a summary of any additional questions you may have included in the survey. For instance, include information about the low, high, and average number of branches of each system responding or the variety of ways participants move employees through salary ranges. Include a list of participants as well as your name and telephone number in case there are any questions. When preparing the participants' reports, don't give specifics or break confidentiality. In other words, provide summary data, not individual data points identifying what respondents are paying. Use averages or means, highs and lows, and so on. Make sure that you've provided enough information to be useful to those who took the time to provide you with their salary and other data.

Chapter 8 provides an in-depth review of executive compensation in libraries, and Chapter 9 will provide you with helpful information on how to take all the data you have gathered—internal and external—and make something useful from it!

eight | **Executive Compensation**

I t's easy to think that executive compensation in libraries is an oxymoron. When we read about the inflated compensation packages of corporate executives, it's hard to relate. After all, most library executives don't receive huge bonuses on top of their base pay, not to mention stock options, deferred salary, incentive pay, or lavish perks. But even in the public sector and higher education there are more options than you might think, and, as competition for top library executives increases, both employers and employees need to be aware of the alternatives available to them.

WHAT AND WHOM ARE WE TALKING ABOUT?

Typically, *executive compensation* refers to the salary, benefits, perquisites, and anything else of value that constitutes the agreed remuneration package for the top administrative position in an organization, or in this case, the director or executive officer of the library. The compensation package for this position is usually more detailed and is negotiated to a greater degree than are compensation agreements for other positions in the library. In fact, most other library employees typically do not negotiate at all, and the compensation agreement is simply the hiring rate, with an explanation of how an employee can progress in the future. In the public sector and at many universities, all other positions are usually covered by a pay schedule (a system of predetermined pay grades and salary ranges) that provides much less latitude to both the employer and the prospective employee in negotiating salary or benefits. In hiring or retaining a library director, however, the library board often has much more flexibility in designing a pay package that can attract a star candidate or retain an excellent incumbent director. This is increasingly important as library executives are often willing to move across the country for the right job. Boards that are not open to working with candidates or incumbents to design a package that fits may find themselves losing their first-tier choice, often over reasonable requests on the part of the employee or candidate.

Executive compensation in libraries is more of an issue today than ever before. The forces of demography are being felt not just in the library or academic worlds but throughout the world at large. The American Library Association's Office for Research and Statistics reports that 58 percent of professional librarians will be eligible to retire by 2015.[1] One in five *Fortune* 500 executives are eligible for retirement right now, and corporations are scrambling to find replacements. About 80 percent of the senior and middle managers in the U.S. federal government are also eligible for retirement now, as

Much of this chapter is adapted and updated from Jeanne Goodrich and Paula M. Singer, "Executive Compensation in Libraries: An Oxymoron?" *The Bottom Line: Managing Library Finances* 7, no. 4 (2004): 132–36.

are huge percentages in state, local, and municipal governments. One million college professors, one million public school teachers, and 50 percent of all community college presidents are also eligible for retirement.[2] Many may only be holding on for health insurance coverage offered by the employer and may leave as soon as they become Medicare-eligible.

All these statistics add up to one conclusion: every library, every organization, every university, every public jurisdiction, and every nonprofit will be competing for top administrative/leadership talent in the coming years. There will be far fewer candidates with the experience, skills, and breadth of competencies than will be needed to fill the available, more complex jobs. Competition for seasoned library executives will be fierce, and although there can and should be many inducements to lure a candidate to a position, compensation is still a major factor, especially when the competition is so strong.

COMPENSATION PHILOSOPHY

As discussed in chapter 3, a compensation philosophy is a brief statement of your library's goals for what compensation will accomplish in your organization. Remember, as noted in the same chapter, you may have a different compensation philosophy for your executive-level staff, particularly for your director. The compensation philosophy should specify whether you will include bonus, incentive, or other pay-at-risk elements as well as state who has responsibility for reviewing the performance of the director and how often that review will take place. An example compensation philosophy for an executive appears in the accompanying text box.

ANYTOWN PUBLIC LIBRARY: EXECUTIVE COMPENSATION PHILOSOPHY

- Anytown Library strives to be a market leader in providing a total compensation pay package for an experienced, talented library director.

- To facilitate its ability to recruit and retain a superior executive director, the library will pay a high-caliber director at the 75th to 90th percentile of the market.

- Anytown Library is willing to negotiate a total compensation package that reflects the needs of the library and the individual hired as director.

- Anytown Library's market for the position of director is Anytown, USA, as well as the Mid-Atlantic region, but also considers the national marketplace and Bigtown, USA. It consists of a mix of library systems of similar and slightly larger size (budget and employees) with a national scope.

- To stress the importance of achieving the library's important strategic goals and to support its focus on performance, the pay/pay increases of the director are tied to meeting measurable long- and short-term strategic objectives.

 Anytown Library may reward its director with a performance-based bonus. This bonus will not be attached to base pay.

- Performance reviews are integrated into Anytown Library's approach to compensation and provide accountability, learning, and development experiences for the director and the board.

- The executive committee of the board is responsible for developing and recommending a compensation plan to the full board and maintaining the director's compensation plan.

- A market review will be conducted regularly by the executive committee, generally every three to four years.

Make sure to refer to your document and/or to update it if you uncover differing parameters for the market or level of competitiveness when reviewing executive compensation. Finally, some boards place "reasonableness" boundaries around compensation for the director. The compensation philosophy shown in the text box mentions compensation at the 75th to 90th percentile of the market. This is fine unless for some reason the 75th percentile of the market is found to be $250,000 for a smaller, non-metro-area library. The board may wish to have certain caveats in place to allow for the reasonableness of the compensation package offered to a director.

THE MARKET

A library wanting to attract and hire an executive or a library executive wanting a new position or wanting to renegotiate a compensation package needs to think about the labor market within which both will operate. Although the labor market for library clerks is very much a local one (because there are many potential employees available in the immediate area with the experience and skills needed for such a position), the labor market for a library executive is statewide, regional, and, very often, national.

Some libraries are also considering the labor market beyond the library profession. Find out what others with comparable responsibilities, job scope, and job requirements are being paid and how they are being recruited. Look beyond the library world. Look at executives of local and regional nonprofit agencies and organizations, association executives, and community college deans and presidents. Look at the department heads of equivalent scope in the local city or county government. What compensation is offered to the finance director, public works director, city engineer, or director of public health or corrections? If the library is part of a university, what is the salary range for other vice presidents and directors? What do the chief technology officer, facilities director, controller, director of security, and dean of admissions earn? If you are conducting a study of executive compensation, your board should definitely have input into the discussion of what organizations and even what comparable positions make up the labor market for this position.

Comparisons with these other positions should provide a sense of the scope, size, and responsibilities of the job by analyzing the size of the budget administered, the number of staff people in the organization, the organizational structures, number and scale of facilities managed, and the governance structure. Find out if the position reports to a board or a council. Is there an advisory board or committee also? Does the position report to an executive manager, such as a city manager, county executive, provost, or academic vice president? What will the fund-raising requirements be? For many executives, a primary responsibility is to interface with donors, foundations, and grant-making bodies in order to raise significant amounts of money.

A final point of comparison comes down to an ineffable factor: some institutions and some positions just seem more worthy than others. As a hiring body or as a candidate, you might find yourself in the position of challenging a long-held value system. One state has legislated salary caps on all public positions that preclude the placement of salaries at levels higher than a certain percentage of the governor's salary. In other cases, county commissioners, the local press, and many citizens may be astounded that a library director would be the highest-paid county department head. If you know what others who are leaders of comparable organizations are earning, you've got the potential to make a strong case for the library.

You can collect data about executive pay during a regular compensation study of other library positions; however, because of the different level of detail required to make an accurate assessment of a total compensation package, we recommend that a separate study be conducted, particularly if you have a recruitment or retention issue where the director is concerned. A very effective way of gathering this information is to design and conduct a telephone survey. The survey should include questions about the organization's demographics (budget, population served, number of employees, number of facilities, etc.) as well as questions about the responsibilities and scope of the executive director or CEO's position (fund-raising responsibilities, level of community and political interaction, reporting structure, etc.). Finally, the survey should contain a series of questions designed to gather information about the salary and benefits of the director of the organization. You will want to speak directly with the director or CEO and should plan at least one-half hour for each conversation. In some cases, the director may refer you to the library's director or human resources manager—as long as the discussion is sanctioned by the director, this is fine as well. Send an introductory e-mail or letter to the director on behalf of the library board or the consultant you may be using or both, explaining the purpose of your research. Assure participants that their individual data will be kept confidential. You may think that other directors or CEOs would never participate in such a study and provide this type of information, but we have had incredible success with these types of surveys on behalf of library systems and nonprofit organizations. We often hear participants speak of their own wishes to conduct such a study, and these individuals are happy to participate once they are told that they will receive a summary of findings (provided by you or the consultant). Promise the confidentiality of individual responses and make sure that the summary document does not include identifying features of the organization so that you can uphold your promise of confidentiality. Using slightly modified questions, you can use the same survey to gather information from organizations other than libraries—boards of education, nonprofit organizations, or local government. You can, by the way, use the same or a slightly modified survey to gather compensation data on the assistant director or other top-level management positions. Figure 8.1 is an example of a survey that could be used to gather information from library directors.

The "What else should I have asked?" question may seem extraneous after all the other questions included in the survey, but we are constantly surprised by the responses to this question. To reward employees who had more than one year's employment with the library, one organization provided a $500 "quality of life" bonus to be used for anything to make the workplace more user-friendly (i.e., noise reduction headphones or in-the-workplace massages). Another nonprofit employer paid for a speech coach for its executive director. One director received an extra week of vacation at the fabulous resort home of a trustee. Yet another had her pension time bought out as part of the agreement to take the job. Others negotiated extra vacation or personal time off. Each library and organization offers unique benefits, and it wouldn't make sense to include every possible option on the survey. Just include this question and you'll allow the participant to reveal any other compensation or benefits he or she receives.

Another source of executive compensation data is the Guidestar website (www.guidestar.org). This site provides the Form 990s that all nonprofit organizations must submit to the IRS each year. For a small fee, you can access a multitude of data, including the salary, benefits, and expense account figures for the highest-paid employees of the organization. The database is sortable by geographic region, budget size, type of organization, and other categories. In addition to the 990 you can access organizational information such as the mission, number of employees, and the organization's website. Keep in mind that you will not be able to get meaningful detail on benefits from the IRS forms, only the total dollars paid in benefits to the executive. In addition, these forms can be out of date by two to three years; the year will be listed at the top of each 990.

Figure 8.1
Sample Executive Compensation Survey

LIBRARY DIRECTOR TOTAL COMPENSATION STUDY
on behalf of Anytown Public Library

Date: _____

Name: _____ Name of library: _____

How long in position? _____ Prior position/library: _____

1. What is the base pay of the library director? $_____

   On what data or circumstances is it based? Is the salary determined by negotiations with trustees, market survey, city/county mandate, etc.? How often is the salary reviewed?

   _____

   _____

2. Is there a salary range for this position? _____ If so, what is it? _____

3. Do you (does the library director) receive an annual increase? _____

   A. If so, what is the basis of the increase? (step, performance evaluation, same as staff, etc.) _____

   B. What percentage of pay/dollar amount did you (the library director) last receive? _____

   C. When? _____

4. If you are (the library director is) eligible for any type of bonus or additional incentives, please describe:

   A. Percentage of pay or dollar amount: _____

   B. Basis of award: _____

   C. Is this additional pay/bonus "all or nothing" or can it be partially awarded? _____

      How is this determined? _____

5. Are other employees eligible for bonus or incentive awards or performance evaluation–based increases?

   A. Percentage of pay or dollar amount: _____

   B. Basis of award: _____

6. To what extent, if any, do you think that your (the library director's) compensation is influenced by the compensation of

   A. Library directors of other local, regional, or national libraries? (specify) _____

   B. Other CEOs/directors of nonprofits? _____

   C. Department heads or other public employees in your local jurisdiction? (specify) _____

   D. Other employees? (specify) _____

7. Are you (is the library director) a participant in the library's pension program (if applicable)?

   If so, what percentage of your (the library director's) salary is contributed by the library? _____

   Could it contribute more? _____

8. Which of the following additional benefits and perks are included in your (the library director's) total compensation package (beyond what is offered to employees as part of the library's benefits package)? Please note the approximate dollar value and describe each benefit.

	Approximate Dollar Value	Description/Negotiated?
Health Benefits Same as/different than staff? If different, please list.		
Additional Life Insurance Benefits "Key man"?		Terms:

	Approximate Dollar Value	Description/Negotiated?
Leave (paid time off—vacation, holidays, personal days) Any in addition to F/T staff?		Number of days vacation holidays personal leave
Long-Term Care Insurance Same as/different than staff?		Terms:
Legal Insurance Same as/different than staff?		Terms:
Supplemental Executive Retirement Benefits (SERP or other) Same as /different than staff?		Terms:
Deferred Compensation Same as/different than staff?		Terms:
Tax Shelter Annuities Same as/different than staff?		Terms:
Vehicle/Vehicle Allowance Same as/different than staff?		Terms:
Free Parking Same as/different than staff?		
Home Computer/Laptop/Blackberry/etc. Cable/DSL/Telephone line at home/Fax		Could have if wanted?
Cell Phone Same as/different than staff?		Work only?
Conference Attendance/Fees Same as/different than staff?		
Executive Physicals/Health Exams Same as/different than staff?		How often?
Club Memberships/Dues Same as/different than staff?		

(Cont.)

Figure 8.1
Sample Executive Compensation Survey (Cont.)

	Approximate Dollar Value	Description/Negotiated?
Professional Association Memberships/Dues Same as/different than staff?		
Professional Development Conferences/ Workshops Same as/different than staff?		
Coaching Expenses Same as/different than staff?		
Relocation Expenses (if applicable) Same as/different than staff?		
Tuition Assistance (reimbursement/time) Same as/different than staff?		
Flextime/Telecommuting? Same as/different than staff?		
Sabbatical Same as/different than staff?		How long? What conditions?
Other sources of income/expenses, etc. (e.g., trustees, foundation, Friends)? For what?		
Other:		

What else should I have asked? _____

_____

Demographics

Operating budget: _____

Number of employees: Full-time _____   Part-time _____

Main library?   ☐ Yes   ☐ No   Number of branches: _____

Is there a union?   ☐ Yes   ☐ No

Does the director have fund-raising responsibilities?   ☐ Yes   ☐ No

Library circulation: _____

Library population area: _____

You can easily adapt the survey in figure 8.1 to fit nonprofit agencies as well and gather additional information in that way. Be cautioned, however, that some nonprofit executives' salaries are artificially low. The position could be a volunteer job with a nominal salary assigned to it. The salary could also be affected by the constituency of the group; for instance, salaries for organizations involved in the arts are often much lower than those for health-care organizations. Be sure to do thorough research and make appropriate comparisons.

Finally, you can obtain salary information on local government officials through locally compiled salary surveys. Many public universities often conduct annual or biannual salary surveys of local governments and jurisdictions and include salary data on a variety of positions. Again, you will not have access to the type of detail on benefits or other perks that you will obtain through a salary survey, but in the case of local government, having salary information alone is often a helpful comparison if your local government's human resources department is hesitant to share these data. Of course all these data are public information and can be requested through the Freedom of Information Act. However, this is not the best way to keep your good contacts in your local city or county government.

The following positions in local government match the position of library director:

- finance director
- public health director
- county engineer
- police chief
- head administrative officer
- director of public works

Above all, make sure that you as the employee or hiring body are familiar with the market for an executive-level position in your area. Library employees and boards must move past the mind-set that all employees (especially directors!) work for the love of the job. Though this intangible certainly plays a part for the successful employee, it doesn't pay the mortgage.

COMPENSATION OPTIONS FOR EXECUTIVES

In most libraries, setting the salary and benefits of the director has been straightforward: a beginning salary is negotiated, annual increases are provided up to a predetermined top level or maximum, benefits and leave provisions are basically the same as those received by other managers or for that matter the same as all other employees, the pension is whatever the institution provides for all its employees, and so on. This is particularly true in public libraries where the director does not report to an independent board but, rather, is a department head in the local government. In the current compensation environment, particularly in support of recruitment and retention efforts in a competitive market, new options for executives are beginning to appear.

Base Pay Alternatives

The traditional pay system in most libraries—for executives and other employees alike—has been one of a base salary with known steps or annual increase percentages, continually provided so long as performance is deemed satisfactory. This salary progression usually tops out after a period of time at a predetermined maximum. Cost-of-living increases might also be given in an attempt to keep the salary's buying power more or less current with the state of the surrounding economy. This type of pay system was traditionally used, particularly in government or public sector organizations, to provide a known pay environment for employees. Many employees appreciate or are simply used to being able to see, literally, how their pay will progress on a grade-and-step system. Meaningful performance evaluations were often not a real part of the process, and most, if not all, employees, including library executives, got their annual increases year after year, without fail. The only variable may have been the cost-of-living increase, or COLA, that could fluctuate with the economy.

Many of you know this type of compensation system as a "merit system." As discussed in chapter 11, even though performance management plays little if any part in this type of system, many governments and libraries continue to call this a merit-based pay plan. As libraries and their parent jurisdictions, school districts, and universities begin to experiment with various alternatives to a merit- or step-based pay plan, job performance becomes more clearly linked with the opportunity to achieve greater compensation. Such incentive systems are common in the private sector but are still quite rare in the public sector. For library directors, many of whom have contracts with their boards or institutions, extending or renewing contracts is often more closely linked with job performance. For library boards, this is by far the most effective way to make sure that library directors are earning their salaries and that the library is reaping the highest possible reward from the work of the director. Chapter 11 details how effective performance management systems can be developed and implemented. Briefly, an effective performance management system should include the following:

> goals set and potential rewards identified *before* the evaluation period begins; ideally, in the case of the director, set jointly between the director and the board

> decisions made specifying the most important accomplishments in any year as well as within one to three or more years to achieve both short- and longer-term planning

> goals linked to the strategic priorities of the library; ideally, linked to the initiatives generated by the strategic plan

> quantifiable and outcome-related measures identified for each goal

In a system that truly rewards high-quality performance, the most common method for delivering this reward is an annual increase to base pay. Many libraries believe that their compensation system does this, but ask yourself, "Do virtually all employees get the same increase every year, even though some may have 'outstanding' or '5' ratings and others have 'satisfactory' or '3' ratings?" If the answer is yes, your system is performance-based in name only. Much less common is the system that provides that annual increase to base pay but differentiates in a meaningful way the increase to the most outstanding performers. Perhaps all "fully successful" performers receive a 3.5 percent increase; in this scenario the "exceeds expectations" performer receives a 6 percent increase. Again, see chapter 11 for more detail on performance management as well as the pros and cons of pay-for-performance reward systems.

Additional forms of pay are available to the library executive and board, beyond the traditional addition to base pay.

Bonus programs. A portion of the executive's pay is at risk, meaning it is linked to the achievement of specific, measurable results. The bonus is paid only if the quantifiable, outcome-related goals are achieved. School superintendents, for example, are often given a pay bonus if achievement levels on standardized tests increase by a certain percentage in their district. The bonus is a one-time payment and does not affect the base salary. Libraries have given bonuses tied to meeting fund-raising goals, completing major construction projects on time and on budget, and acquiring and implementing new computer systems. Alternatively, if a bonus is not a viable option in your system, these same types of goals can be incorporated into the overall performance management program for the director (see the following paragraph). If you are adding a bonus component to the director's pay, make sure to consider why you are doing so. What will you reward? What are the implications for other staff? When should the bonus be triggered? Only after a special project is completed? Only after all aspects of the day-to-day job have been performed in an above-average manner?

Pay-for-performance. As discussed, salary increases—percentage increases to the base salary rather than one-time bonuses that don't affect base pay—are linked directly to the achievement of goals or to an overall performance rating during the rating period. Increases are often a percentage range, from 1 to 15 percent, for example. The differences between this and a typical grade-and-step progression plan are that the yearly increases are not predetermined and that they are tied to a very specific set of goals and objectives.

Skill-based pay. Another variant on the traditional base pay system, this approach recognizes up front that a salary higher than the going market rate for a library executive will be paid for the special skills brought to the position. These skills could include fund-raising, dealing with difficult employee issues, special abilities in the area of board and community relations, highly specialized technical expertise, the ability to turn around troubled libraries, and so on.

These approaches can be mixed and matched. A library might desire, for instance, to hire a new executive at or below the market rate initially, with the opportunity, through a bonus or performance pay, for that level to be surpassed. Some compensation systems include a base pay level, pay-for-performance, and a bonus on top of that if all goals are met or surpassed. The key feature of all these alternatives and their variants is that job performance and meeting major targets and goals are tied together in a very tangible way.

In addition, linking pay to performance requires developing outcome-based performance measures, so that everyone knows what is expected. It's not enough to say, "Improve fund-raising." To set a goal that can be attempted and reached requires specificity and a time frame: "Increase outside fund-raising by 20 percent during the next fiscal year" or "Raise $50,000 more in FY2010 than was raised in FY2009." The bonus or salary portion tied to achieving the agreed goals and objectives must be significant enough to truly be an incentive for the executive and a measure of the importance of the goal to the organization. If the bonus or salary portion is tied to overall performance, then a full performance plan must be drawn up and discussed (see chapter 11) so that everyone knows what is expected and the weight that the expectations carry. Absent a full plan and discussion of it, a bonus or salary award can seem (and may well be) simply subjective capriciousness.

Why Look at Options?

Why would an organization wishing to hire a new library executive want to consider alternatives to the traditional base pay system? What should a library executive considering a new position or negotiating her compensation package know about possible options?

A hiring board or organization may wish to consider alternative forms of pay as a way to more clearly link performance (meeting the organization's strategic goals and objectives) with compensation received. The variable part of the compensation can be adjusted to reflect the degree of impact the executive has had, which calibrates performance with compensation much more closely than does the traditional all-or-nothing (meaning full salary or full increase or loss of the job) system. Clearly identifying performance indicators and the increase, improvements, or accomplishments desired is an important process for the hiring body to go through and is an important message to convey to the library executive. The same holds true for boards trying to set performance measures for incumbents.

From the library executive's viewpoint, it's critical to know that some libraries are using variable pay systems for executive and, in some cases, senior managers. She will then know how to react if offered compensation under such a system. Or, she may be able to suggest such an approach as a way to provide more options during the compensation negotiation process each year.

Other Financial Inducements

In addition to considerations about pay approaches, the library executive or library employer might want to consider inducements that are appearing in other fields to attract and retain employees. These can include

> *Signing bonus*—This is a bonus given on completion of the hiring process. It is a one-time bonus that doesn't impact base pay.
>
> *Retention bonus*—This is a bonus given at a set interval or at the completion of a contract renewal process.
>
> *Employment contract*—Both the executive and the library may feel more secure if a three- to five-year contract is in place. The contract will stipulate basic terms of employment and job performance and will usually have language covering termination and procedures if either party wishes to sever the relationship.
>
> *Assistance in acquiring appropriate housing*—In communities with excessively high housing costs, assistance is given in the form of housing loans or housing subsidies. This is still rare, but it has been done.
>
> *Deferred compensation*—An agreed amount is set aside for an agreed amount of time and is then provided to the director at the end of that time (in the form of a lump sum rather than as an addition to base pay).
>
> *Enhanced retirement*—Some libraries are adding up to $20,000 per year to a deferred compensation or 457 plan for their library director.

MORE THAN MONEY

Compensation is much more than salary. It includes everything that the employee perceives to be of value resulting from the employment relationship. It's a mix of salary, bonus, benefits, various perquisites, and the work environment.

Benefits and Perquisites

Benefits are usually determined by the library's parent organization or by the library system's board of trustees if a stand-alone district, regional system, special library, or independent taxing authority. There are often differences in benefits offered to management and line employees, and there may be some opportunity to offer or ask for additional benefits for the library executive. For example, the employer could provide expanded long-term disability coverage, enhanced life insurance coverage, or an enlarged contribution to the pension or deferred compensation plan.

Perquisites can include a number of (not uncommon) sweeteners for the library executive:

- a car or car allowance
- payment of moving or relocation expenses (including a house-hunting trip)
- equipping of a home office so the executive can stay in touch or telecommute (should be a given)
- provision of personal electronic devices such as personal digital assistants (PDAs), cell phones, pagers, laptops (should be a given)
- parking space
- club memberships or dues, such as membership dues to professional associations, local chamber of commerce, Rotary, city clubs, and the like
- professional development, such as conference attendance and support for study visits to other libraries
- tuition assistance and time to attend classes or to work on class assignments
- extra leave after a significant event, such as completion of a major building project
- management leave to compensate for attendance at after-hours meetings, community events, and so forth
- sabbatical opportunities
- additional life or "key person" insurance
- provision of funds to pay for executive coaching
- additional days of paid time off

Depending on the library, this list might contain several familiar extras or provide new ideas for ways to enhance the compensation package offered to or requested by a library executive.

Intrinsic Rewards

In education, social service, and government service, intrinsic rewards play a key role in attracting and retaining employees. Most library employees, at all levels, value the purpose and mission of the library. They enjoy providing a worthwhile service to their library users, and they enjoy working in an environment dedicated to learning, knowledge, and personal fulfillment. They know that libraries make a real difference in people's lives.

Intrinsic rewards are more than just personal satisfaction. For the library executive, they can include

- feedback on the job you do from your administrator, dean, or board
- public recognition for doing well
- coaching or mentoring to do even better
- attendance by board members, administrators, or deans at public and community events

- a pleasant work group and organizational values that support people working well together
- a work environment that supports a balance between home life and work life
- the opportunity to learn new skills
- possibilities for advancement
- a culture that believes in and cultivates continuous improvement

Library executives are attracted to a position for these reasons as well as for financial reasons. Maybe one is looking for a way to build on the experiences he's had and stretch himself further by taking on a larger or financially troubled library system. Maybe another is interested in working in a library that is challenging but in a less frenetic environment than the urban system she's been working in. A third might find a position attractive because there is domestic partner insurance coverage and an organizational value that everyone, including executives, should have a reasonable number of evening and weekend hours to spend with family or alone.

THE TOTAL PACKAGE

Pay, benefits, perquisites, and the work environment and the intrinsic rewards that it offers should all be used to attract the executive the library needs and wants. It is rare that any one element will be the deciding factor. It's usually a combination of these elements that makes an employment offer attractive or encourages the retention of the current executive. By having a larger view of the possible components of a complete executive compensation package, hiring libraries and executive candidates can both come to the table with a larger number of options.

WHAT WOULD YOU DO IF . . .

It's important to remember that the subject of executive compensation applies not only to hiring a new director but to retaining your current director as well. Having said that, think about what you would seek in a new director were yours to suddenly announce his or her retirement. If your executive were to leave, what would you be looking for?

- Someone with experience managing professional staff? If so, how many years?
- Someone with library experience? If so, how many years?
- Someone with a master's degree in library science? Or not? Perhaps an MBA or a master's degree in public administration?
- Someone with prior experience as a library director? Or not?

Having these criteria in mind not only will help you in your search for a new director but can also be useful when conducting compensation research for the executive position, as it can ensure that you are comparing like jobs, levels of responsibility, and so forth. In short, executive compensation in libraries is *not* an oxymoron and, more often than not, should be approached differently than compensation for other staff in order to recruit and retain the most highly qualified and successful incumbents and candidates.

HOW DOES IT LOOK TO EVERYONE ELSE?

Libraries are typically funded with tax dollars. Just as you would be concerned about the appearance of giving all staff members an increase of 15 percent in one year, any adjustments to executive compensation must also be considered in this light. Are you comfortable with the results of any study being published on the front page of your local newspaper? Will it pass the "smell" test? Even with the blessing of your governing board and funding authority, is it the right thing to do? It is also very important to consider how the results will look to the library's employees. A lot of employees will hear about an increase for the director and think, "What have they done for me lately?" It's critical to balance the needs of all parties—staff, the director, and the library as a whole—when implementing any changes to pay. Particularly when dealing with executive compensation, it may be wise to engage the services of a consultant to ensure the integrity and objectivity of findings and recommendations. Think about all these questions and implications as you study and implement changes to executive pay. Perhaps the solution is as simple as a two- to three-year implementation plan. Appropriate executive compensation is critical to recruiting, retaining, and motivating the most highly qualified and high-performing leadership. Putting your research and data in the context of your organization's environment will help guide you in developing recommendations for fair and equitable compensation for your library's executive.

NOTES

1. M. J. Lynch, "Reaching 65: Lots of Librarians Will Be There Soon," *American Libraries*, March 2002, 55–56.
2. W. J. Rothwell, "Beyond Succession Management," *Link&Learn* [e-newsletter], no. 1 (September 1, 2003), www.linkageinc.com.

nine | **Salary Structure Design**

Now that you have gathered external market data and have created an internal hierarchical ordering of positions, it's time to make this information work for you and use it to design your salary structure. Salary structures consist of jobs of roughly equal value or worth that are grouped into grades with competitive salary ranges. Pay (or salary) ranges express rates from the bottom to top or from minimum to maximum of each grade. The pay range represents a group of jobs. The intent of having salary ranges is to put limits on the lowest and highest rates your library will pay for any given job. Positions are assigned to grades, and pay ranges are based on job content, market value, internal equity, or a combination of these factors (*not* on employee value or individual performance).

Each salary range includes a minimum, midpoint, and maximum, with the midpoint typically representing the market or going rate for the job. The minimum is the least amount, and the maximum is the most an employee should be earning for the job. Figures 9.1 and 9.2 show two examples of salary structures. The first is the set of salary ranges developed for a university that has two major libraries—law and medicine. The second shows ranges developed for an urban city/county public library system.

The pay structure is a tool for management and employees. Within policies that provide flexibility for making pay-related decisions, managers need guidelines to ensure organizational consistency, and employees need to know that pay will be equitable and competitive. By having a pay structure, employees are also able to see how jobs are grouped in the library, what possibilities may exist for career development, and what possibilities exist for pay increases. Although the pay structure is a tool, adherence to it should not be so rigid that responses to a changing environment and opportunities to reward, recruit, or retain your most highly productive employees are difficult to make or are ignored. It is also not a contract. A pay range does not automatically guarantee that an employee will reach the maximum of that pay range or that the maximum will stay the same over time. Pay ranges and pay structures can change in relation to market and internal equity, and funding issues may prevent employees from moving through pay ranges as quickly as they (or you) had anticipated. Nonetheless, a pay structure is an excellent and necessary framework for defining pay in your library.

You now have all the data you need to prepare your salary structure—information obtained through job analysis, job evaluation, and market review and analysis. Armed with this information, you can follow several steps to develop your salary structure. This chapter discusses these steps and provides additional information on

- clustering jobs to create pay ranges
- calculating range spreads
- determining range progressions

Figure 9.1
Salary Ranges for a University

Grade	Minimum ($)	Midpoint ($)	Maximum ($)
1	70,000	105,000	140,000
2	64,000	91,000	118,000
3	55,000	79,000	103,000
4	48,000	69,000	90,000
5	42,000	60,000	78,000
6	36,000	52,000	68,000
7	32,000	45,000	59,000
8	27,000	39,000	51,000
9	24,000	34,000	44,000
10	21,000	30,000	39,000

Figure 9.2
Salary Ranges for a Medium-Sized Public Library

Grade	Minimum ($)	Midpoint ($)	Maximum ($)
1	16,452	20,400	24,348
2	17,940	22,254	26,568
3	19,272	23,886	28,500
4	21,240	26,352	31,464
5	22,980	28,506	34,032
6	25,272	31,350	37,428
7	27,132	33,648	40,164
8	30,516	37,848	45,180
9	33,936	42,576	51,216
10	36,552	45,864	55,176
11	39,420	49,482	59,544
12	43,704	54,846	65,988
13	48,816	61,962	75,108
14	54,492	69,156	83,820
15	55,644	70,614	85,584
16	59,784	75,864	91,944
17	65,796	85,470	105,144

- identifying the number of grades
- costing the salary structure

This chapter also contains examples of salary structures and compensation plans as well as sample spreadsheets to help you design your salary ranges and calculate the costs to implement your new program.

DEVELOPING PAY RANGES

The first step in developing pay ranges is to compile all the salary data into one chart, allowing you to look at the big picture. First, group together jobs with similar value to the library based on points (chapter 6), similar market data (chapter 7), or a combination of the two to determine salary grades.

Determine Variance

The variance, or difference, between the market data and your library's data is best expressed as a percentage. This number will show the relationship of each of your positions to the market (for those positions for which you were able to collect data), either as a positive number (above the market) or a negative number (below the market). To calculate a variance, divide your salary data for a given position by the average or median salary data for the same position in the market, then subtract 1 from the total. For example:

(your data/market average or market median) – 1 = % variance

The following example is from ABC Library for an entry-level librarian position:

ABC average/actual salary = $40,851

Market average salary = $41,080

$40,851/$41,080 = 0.99

0.99 – 1 = –0.01 or –1%

ABC's job is 1 percent behind the market's average/actual salary for the same position.

Why subtract 1? It may seem odd, but adding this extra step allows you to clearly see the variance (–1 percent in the example) versus having to do the calculation in your head (0.99 minus 1 is 0.01, or 1 percent less than 100 percent—the market value for the job). This formula is easily entered into an Excel spreadsheet such as the one shown in figure 9.3. Figure 9.3 is a market analysis, showing all positions and salary data collected for ABC Library. The spreadsheet shows major data points—market hourly average/actual, market minimum, market hiring rate, and market maximum—and compares them with the same points for ABC Library. Note, however, that the cells showing the variance will need to be formatted to express their result as a percentage. Another important note: this calculation will work for any of the salary data comparison points—average/actual, minimum, midpoint, and maximum. Just be sure to compare apples to apples—that is, compare the same data point in your library to that of the market.

Set Up the Spreadsheet

When setting up the spreadsheet in Excel (figure 9.3), it is very helpful to take the time to link the market analysis to the salary data spreadsheets (see chapter 7) for each position. Linking is an Excel function that automatically updates data in all linked sheets when changes are made to the source sheet. In other words, if you link the market analysis sheet to the individual salary sheets, any changes made to the salary data sheets (adding an additional participant's data, for instance) will automatically be reflected in the market analysis, eliminating the need to duplicate efforts and eliminating the need to constantly check to make sure all changes have been captured.

You will notice that the salaries in figure 9.3 are given as hourly figures. Many libraries find this a more useful comparison than annual salaries, while some use a combination of both. This decision is entirely up to you; however, if you use an hourly figure, be sure you know how many hours per week each position works (a question usually asked in a market survey—see chapter 7). Many full-time library positions represent a 35-hour workweek, some a 37.5-hour workweek, and others a 40-hour workweek. If you gather this information, you can translate the hourly figure to an accurate annual one if necessary and ensure a valid comparison to your annual figures. An easy way to do this follows:

Your workweek = 40 hours × 52 weeks = 2,080 hours/year

Participant A's workweek = 35 hours × 52 weeks = 1,820 hours/year

Figure 9.3

Sample Library Market Analysis

Job Title	ABC FLSA	Average/Actual			Range Minimum			Hiring Rate			Range Maximum			Market Spread (%)	ABC Spread (%)
		Market	ABC	Variance (%)	Market Min.	ABC	Variance (%)	Market	ABC Min.	Variance (%)	Market	ABC	Variance (%)		
Shelver	NE	8.10	7.55	-7	8.64	7.31	-15		7.31		12.20	10.41	-15	41	42
Mailroom Technician	NE	11.10	12.58	13	8.34	10.21	22		10.21		13.94	14.68	5	67	44
Circulation Clerk	NE	11.87	11.95	1	9.66	10.21	6	10.76	10.21	-5	13.93	14.54	4	44	42
Physical Processing Clerk	E	12.83	14.79	15	9.78	10.21	4	11.95	10.21	-15	15.16	14.54	-4	55	42
Purchasing Specialist	NE	14.00	21.13	51	11.25	14.60	30		14.60		21.08	21.13	0	87	45
Security Guard	NE	14.38	13.86	-4	11.34	12.06	6		12.06		18.02	17.16	-5	59	42
Library Associate I	NE	15.41	17.47	13	14.38	14.60	2		14.60		19.99	21.13	6	39	45
Help Desk Technician	NE	17.38	15.40	-11	13.98	14.60	4		14.60		23.17	21.13	-9	66	45
Librarian I	E	19.75	19.64	-1	15.88	16.67	5	17.26	16.67	-3	26.81	24.13	-10	69	45
Librarian II	E	19.88	26.67	34	15.58	19.35	24	19.24	19.35	1	24.34	28.02	15	56	45
Electrician	NE	20.66	23.44	13	15.44	16.18	5		16.18		24.25	23.44	-3	57	45
Maintenance Supervisor	NE	21.82	27.88	28	17.26	13.01	-25		13.01		29.89	18.84	-37	73	45
Accountant	E	22.12	21.70	-2	17.16	19.35	13		19.35		31.51	28.00	-11	84	45
Circulation Manager	E	25.08	29.11	16	18.62	20.63	11		20.63		30.50	30.39	0	64	47
Branch Manager II	E	27.53	33.11	20	20.21	20.63	2		20.63		31.20	30.39	-3	54	47
Technical Services Manager	E	28.66	23.47	-18	24.04	20.63	-14	28.33	20.63	-27	36.06	30.39	-16	50	47
IT Manager	E	38.15	24.50	-36	30.51	20.63	-32	23.47	20.63	-12	45.94	30.39	-34	51	47
Division Director	E	42.01	37.66	-10	29.87	27.80	-7	26.41	27.80	5	45.46	40.96	-10	52	47

If Participant A has given you an annual salary for a library associate position of $29,800, follow this example to get the annual rate for a 40-hour workweek:

$$\$29,800/1,820 \text{ (35-hour workweek)} = \$16.37/\text{hour}$$

$$\$16.37/\text{hour} \times 2,080 \text{ (40-hour workweek)} = \$34,057$$

Similar calculations can be performed for part-time workweeks as well (e.g., a position only working 20 hours per week).

Review Results

After you have determined the variance from the market for each position, review the results. For example, the first job shown in figure 9.3 is shelver. Reading across, you can see that ABC's actual or average salary is 7 percent behind the market average. The minimum of ABC's salary range is 15 percent behind the market minimum, and ABC's range maximum is also 15 percent behind that of the market. Where employees top out, or hit range maximum, is often as important if not more important, depending on the makeup of your workforce, than the entry-level salaries can be.

In some cases, as with the maintenance supervisor position, the average or actual pay is ahead of the market but the range is below it. How can this occur? Several hypotheses can be formed. Because average/actual pay is the actual (if only one incumbent in this position) or average (if multiple incumbents hold this position) pay received by employees in the position, high average/actual pay could indicate that the individuals in the position are long-term employees. Although the salary range may not have been adjusted in quite a few years, actual employee salaries could have increased year after year, moving them toward range maximum. Along these same lines, remember that the data collected from other libraries and organizations does not typically account for years of experience. Thus, this data point could represent a group of circulation clerks that (on the whole) are new or newer employees and are therefore receiving pay at the beginning of their salary range. Although it is important (depending on your philosophy) that average/actual pay be competitive with the market, the range minimums and maximums are also important because they affect recruitment and retention as well as implementation costs.

The market analysis data should then be sorted by whatever data point is most useful to you or on which you would like to focus. For purposes of this example, we have sorted the data by the median market average/actual pay from lowest to highest. However, it is again important to look at the big picture—at all data points—as well as to consider the source of each to make a proper assessment of market competitiveness.

You will notice two other important data points in figure 9.3. The second column shows the exempt or nonexempt status of each of ABC's surveyed positions. The exempt or nonexempt status of positions (according to the Fair Labor Standards Act, or FLSA) can change periodically as positions change and grow or as processes and jobs are streamlined. We often ask survey participants to include the classification of their positions, and we can then make surface-level comparisons about FLSA status. For instance, if ten or eleven survey participants have a circulation clerk position classified as nonexempt, but the client library has the position classified as exempt, we may recommend that the client review that classification. Of course, libraries and all employers need to be careful in making changes to FLSA classifications and should always check these decisions with a labor attorney or library counsel.

On the far right of figure 9.3 you will see two columns referring to range spread. These data points are discussed in detail later in this chapter.

Cluster Jobs

Figure 9.4 shows the beginning of the formulation of data clusters, which will ultimately become salary ranges. Reviewing the market analysis, begin to group the positions into clusters. A cluster is a natural grouping of jobs based on job evaluation points (if used) or market data or a combination of both. These groupings will represent the first draft of your salary grades. You may eventually shift jobs in and out of these clusters based on internal equity issues, office politics, or other reasons, but for now, consider this the starting point for your salary structure.

It is difficult to say which data point is the most important for this clustering process. Because the range midpoint theoretically represents the market (where fully competent employees in the various positions should be paid), your midpoint should reflect salaries actually paid. Yet range design is important too. If recruitment is a major issue facing your library, pay attention to the minimum of the range and hiring salaries. If many staff members are at or near the range maximum, survey findings about maximum pay should be highlighted. Again, job evaluation data and many other factors can affect these decisions. Rarely does, or should, a library system end up with all employees being paid at range midpoint. This will be discussed further in the section on Costing the Salary Structure.

The columns in figure 9.4 show the following:

> *Proposed range*—a number assigned to put the clusters in context; these numbers may change as you develop final salary ranges
>
> *Job title*—you may also include a space for a new or proposed job title if any titles have changed or been consolidated during the project. Be sure to think about whether your titles will be understood in the marketplace. As a client recently learned, even with the job descriptions included, survey participants are sometimes swayed by the position title. This client included in its survey a position called administrative services manager. This position manages the finance, budget, and accounting functions for the library. Almost every library has a finance director, right? Right, except the library received very few responses for this position because people weren't familiar with the administrative services title. Think about using common, generic titles for your survey. You aren't changing the content of the position, just titling it so others will recognize it.
>
> *Current grade*—a helpful data point to review, although it should not drive the placement of jobs into clusters unless one of your goals is to not stray too far from the status quo
>
> *Salary data* (columns 3–8)—data points brought over from the market analysis sheet, again, to provide context
>
> *Cluster data* (columns 9–11)—after these jobs have been grouped into clusters, determine the average of each salary data point per cluster (This sheet does not limit the analysis to only one data point but shows several that may be useful in ultimately designing ranges.)

Looking at cluster (or proposed range) 11, you can see that the average minimum for this cluster is $11.24 per hour, the average/actual salary for the cluster is $13.95, and the average maximum is $17.37. These data represent only market data and do not include ABC's salary information. Once jobs have been grouped into clusters, rank the groups from high to low or vice versa based on whichever data point or points you've decided to

Figure 9.4
Sample Library Structure Design

Proposed Range	Job Title (1)	Current Grade (2)	Median Market Avg./Actual (3)	ABC Avg./Actual (4)	Median Market Minimum (5)	ABC Minimum (6)	Median Market Maximum (7)	ABC Maximum (8)	Average Avg./Actual Per Cluster (9)	Average Minimum per Cluster (10)	Average Maximum per Cluster (11)
5	Shelver	4	8.10	7.55	8.64	7.31	12.20	10.41	8.10	8.64	12.20
6											
7	Mailroom Technician	7	11.10	12.58	8.34	10.21	13.94	14.68	11.10	8.34	13.94
8	Circulation Clerk	7	11.87	11.95	9.66	10.21	13.93	14.54	11.87	9.66	13.93
9	Physical Processing Clerk	7	12.83	14.79	9.78	10.21	15.16	14.54	12.83	9.78	15.16
10	Bookmobile Driver	7									
11	Security Guard	8	14.38	13.86	11.34	12.06	18.02	17.16	13.95	11.24	17.37
	Purchasing Specialist	11	13.51	24.63	11.15	16.21	16.72	36.25			
12	Library Associate I	11	15.41	17.47	14.38	14.60	19.99	21.13	16.40	14.18	21.58
	Help Desk Technician	11	17.38	15.40	13.98	14.60	23.17	21.13			
13	Librarian I	12	19.75	19.64	15.88	16.67	26.81	24.13	19.82	15.73	25.58
	Librarian II	14	19.88	26.67	15.58	19.35	24.34	28.02			
14	Electrician	12	20.66	23.44	15.44	16.18	24.25	23.44	20.66	15.44	24.25
15	Maintenance Supervisor	10	21.82	27.88	17.26	14.60	29.89	18.84	23.01	17.68	30.63
	Accountant	14	22.12	21.70	17.16	13.01	31.51	28.00			
	Circulation Manager	15	25.08	29.11	18.62	20.63	30.50	30.39			
16	Branch Manager I	16									
17	Branch Manager II	15	27.53	33.11	20.21	20.63	31.20	30.39	28.10	22.12	33.63
	Technical Services Manager	15	28.66	23.47	24.04	20.63	36.06	30.39			
18	Branch Manager III	16									
19	IT Manager	15	38.15	24.50	30.51	20.63	45.94	30.39	38.15	30.51	45.94
20	Communications Director	15									
21	Division Director	18	42.01	37.66	29.87	27.80	45.46	40.96	42.01	29.87	45.46

146

focus on. In this case, we've used the average/actual data point. Don't forget that you will have job evaluation data as well and that this will need to be factored into your decision-making process about pay ranges (more on this later in this chapter).

Your data cluster spreadsheet may not exactly follow the order of positions in your market analysis. This is perfectly acceptable and actually preferable. It is rare that a salary survey of current market data mirrors the library's values for internal equity, recruitment and retention issues, and financial abilities. Differences in placement could be based on internal equity, recruitment or retention issues, political considerations, or all of these. Remember, compensation is both an art and a science!

It is clear that figure 9.4 is by no means a final product. There are differences that need to be smoothed. Look, for example, at proposed grades 7 and 8. The difference in the market maximums for the mailroom technician and the circulation clerk is only one cent; however, the positions are separated by a grade in this version. When looking at the same clusters' market minimums, it becomes apparent that an adjustment has been made, as the difference in minimums is quite significant. These and other issues will have to be addressed as you move forward, taking into account internal equity, external competitiveness, and what fits in your library.

Calculate Range Spreads

You are now ready to calculate a pay range for each grade. Assuming that the market rate for the job cluster is placed in the middle of the range (midpoint), establish a range spread. The spread should fit with the type of positions and the number of grades.

Range spreads are expressed as the percentage difference from the minimum to the maximum of a grade and can be derived from the minimum, midpoint, or maximum market rate for a group of jobs. Following is an example calculation using a range spread of 50 percent and a range midpoint of $25,000.

To find the minimum, divide the midpoint by 1.25. Why 1.25? A range spread of 50 percent means that there will be a 50 percent difference between the minimum and maximum of the grade. Because the range spread in this example is calculated from the midpoint, it follows that—since the midpoint is one-half the distance between the minimum and the maximum—there would be a 25 percent difference between the minimum and the midpoint.

$$\text{range midpoint}/1.25 = \text{range minimum}$$

$$\$25,000/1.25 = \$20,000$$

To find the maximum of the same pay grade, multiply the minimum (which you found previously) by 1.5. The desired difference between the minimum and maximum is 50 percent. Once you have calculated the minimum, you can find the maximum of the pay grade by adding 50 percent to the minimum:

$$\text{range minimum} \times 1.5 = \text{range maximum}$$

$$\$20,000 \times 1.5 = \$30,000$$

Remember, the 50 percent range spread is just an example. You need to determine the most appropriate spread for your library system because it will affect hiring and retention costs. Therefore, you need to consider economic projections and the number of employees whose actual pay rates will fall below the minimum or above the maximum of their new salary range. If, for example, the salaries of many of your employees will fall below the minimum or above the maximum of their new pay grade, one conclusion might be that the range spreads are too small or narrow.

Range spread can also be calculated from the minimum you have identified for a group of jobs (using the market data). For example, you have identified $36,000 as the appropriate starting salary for a librarian in your market. If you want the librarian pay range to be 55 percent wide, simply add 55 percent to $36,000:

$$\text{Range minimum} \times 1.55 = \text{range maximum}$$

$$\$36,000 \times 1.55 = \$55,800$$

Range midpoint could then be calculated by adding the minimum and maximum and dividing by 2:

$$\text{Range minimum} + \text{range maximum} = \text{range midpoint}$$

$$\$36,000 + \$55,800 = \$91,800/2 = \$45,900 \text{ (midpoint)}$$

For help in determining appropriate range spreads, in addition to the suggestions given in figure 9.5, review the information received in your market survey data to see what spreads were reported by other organizations. To determine the spreads used by respondents, divide the market range maximum by the minimum—for example, an answer of 1.25 means a spread of 25 percent. Don't forget that because you are working with averages as well as ranges, and because every organization has a potentially different structure, the spreads reported may be scattered from wide to narrow. However, you will be able to note trends and understand what other organizations are doing simply by analyzing the individual data reported.

Typically range spreads are narrower at the lower pay grades of the library's structure and wider at the higher grades. This reflects several considerations: lower-level jobs are typically in grades with narrower spreads to avoid overpaying for what are usually more-defined, fairly stable, entry-level, nonprofessional positions. Senior-level jobs normally have wider range spreads to allow for professional development and job growth in managerial or other professional positions that may change and grow over time. It also takes a longer time—often several years—to learn jobs and achieve competency at senior levels; thus, it is expected that it will take longer to reach the midpoint or market rate for the job. Furthermore, jobs at the senior level are frequently evolving, allowing for job growth in a wider salary range without the need for frequent reclassification. In other words, if a physical processing clerk begins supervising staff, chances are this position would be reclassified to a physical processing supervisor or lead worker in a higher pay grade. If an MLS-degreed senior librarian is asked to supervise a library associate in her work with a special collection on African American resources, chances are this position would not be reclassified, as there would be sufficient room in the pay range to allow for the additional responsibility (and other jobs in the same pay grade are most likely already assigned supervisory responsibility). Finally, additional responsibilities, technologies, and so on may make these positions worth more to the library and, therefore, result in more dollars to the incumbent.

Determine Range Progression

After calculating your range spreads, determine the progression from grade to grade. While the range spread indicates the width of a grade from minimum to maximum, the range progression indicates the difference, or jump, from one grade to the next. Just as

Figure 9.5
Typical Range Spreads by Employee Category

Employee Category	Range Spread (Minimum to Maximum)	Range Progression (% from One Minimum, Midpoint, or Maximum to the Next)
Nonexempt entry-level	Narrow ranges	8–10
Custodial and maintenance job families Pages Entry-level circulation, physical processing staff	35%–40%	
Nonexempt technical	Relatively narrow ranges	10–12
Circulation staff Clerical Library assistants First-level supervisors	40%–45%	
Paraprofessional	Wider ranges	12–15
Library associates First-level supervisors	45–50	
Professional	Wider ranges (50%–60%)	12–15
Librarians Administrative Department heads Branch managers		
Management	Widest ranges (60% and wider)	15–25
Senior managers Director of finance Director of human resources Associate directors Deputy directors Library directors		

with range spreads, the progression of grades can be calculated from whichever data point is most useful to you. Just make sure to use the same data point for both calculations. In other words, if you use range minimum to calculate range spread, also use range minimum to calculate range progression.

When designing a salary structure, it's important to keep in mind the anticipated increase from one grade to the next. This increment shouldn't be so small as to be inconsequential when an employee receives a promotion or takes a new job; however, it shouldn't be so large as to be financially impractical in advancing employees. It should also reflect an appropriate difference between supervisory and subordinate positions. Range progressions typically vary from 8 percent to 10 percent between grades at the lower end of the structure to more than 15 percent at the higher levels. The increment does *not* have to be consistent. That is, you do not need to design a structure with evenly spaced increases from one grade to another (e.g., 10 percent or *x* percent between all grades) or evenly progressing midpoints or minimums (10 percent, 10 percent, 11 percent, 11 percent, 12 percent, etc.) between each grade. Your range progression, as always, will be a function of the market data and your compensation philosophy.

Typical range spreads and range progressions by employee category (nonexempt entry level, nonexempt technical and paraprofessional, professional, and management) are shown in figure 9.5. The figure shows the typical range spreads and range progressions for groups of jobs that usually cluster together in the same pay grades of a salary structure. For instance, the second category (nonexempt technical/paraprofessional) shows a fairly narrow range spread for circulation and clerical jobs because these jobs are normally well defined and relatively routine and would not grow or develop significantly in terms of responsibilities; rather, an individual who has grown out of this position would be reclassified or promoted. Therefore, a narrow range spread is appropriate. The last two categories, however, show a much wider range spread. This wider spread takes into consideration that these professional and managerial jobs may grow or develop, more responsibilities are likely to be added, or new skills could be learned and included in the positions without having to reclassify them. The room for growth and flexibility is built into the wider range.

The larger range progressions at higher levels of the organization follow the same logic. A promotion from an entry-level circulation assistant to a senior circulation assistant may be an 8 percent increment, reflecting that the incumbent is performing basically the same duties and responsibilities in the senior position but has more experience or perhaps some lead-worker responsibilities. A promotion from librarian I to branch manager, on the other hand, may represent a significant increase in responsibility and, therefore, is differentiated by a wider progression between these grades. Finally, it's important to note that the jobs grouped together in each row are presented not in hierarchical order but, rather, as groups of jobs that share similar characteristics and would fall into similar grades in the salary structure.

Identify the Number of Grades

You may wonder how many grades the structure should have. The answer is simple: there is no right answer. The number of grades in your system depends on two major factors: the market data (salary data of competitors) findings and your organizational structure. If you have a flat structure (see figure 9.6, part A), with fewer rather than more levels of management and middle management, you will need fewer grades. In addition, if your pay ranges are wider and employees move through them based on acquired skills and competencies, or if you promote cross training so that the level of responsibility remains the same but employees are trained in other departments or functions at the same grade, you will design a structure with fewer grades. If you currently have more levels of management and staff positions and your culture dictates the only way to increase base salary requires a move up in job family (a common practice in academic libraries and higher education in general) and a new title and grade are necessary (e.g., a system with three levels of library associate in three separate grades), you will need to have more rather than fewer grades. See figure 9.6, part B, for a graphic example of this concept. It shows a deeper system with differentiation made among different levels in the same job title—library associate and librarian, for example. This type of structure would usually be appropriate for a larger system that by its nature would have more staff, provide more services, and necessitate more positions. However, it could also work in a smaller system that wants to provide more opportunities for advancement and career progression for its employees.

Other considerations when determining the number of grades your structure will have include

Figure 9.6
Flat and Multilevel Organization Structures

A. Flat Organization Structure with Few Grades		B. Multilevel Organization Structure with Many Grades	
Grade	**Title**	**Grade**	**Title**
1	Page	1	Page
2	Circulation clerk	2	Circulation clerk I (entry-level)
3	Library assistant	3	Circulation clerk II (3 years' experience)
4	Circulation supervisor	4	Circulation supervisor Library associate I (entry-level with bachelor's degree)
5	Librarian	5	Library associate II (bachelor's degree with state certification)
6	Manager (materials, cataloging, processing)	6	Library associate II (bachelor's degree, state certification, and 4 years' experience)
7	Branch manager (large branch), department heads	7	Librarian I (entry-level, MLS)
8	Assistant director	8	Librarian II (MLS and 3 years' experience)
9	Library director	9	Branch manager I (small branch)
		10	Manager (materials, cataloging, processing)
		11	Branch manager II (larger branch)
		12	Department head
		13	Assistant director
		14	Library director

the number of skill or responsibility distinctions in your library system (Your job evaluation/point factor plan will indicate natural breaks by points, as will your own assessment of internal value.)

the number of jobs in different job families (i.e., branch manager I, II, and III)

room for appropriate differentiation in pay between supervisors and those they supervise

administrative and political considerations

Experience with academic and public libraries has shown that—excluding the director's position—you will have no fewer than eight and should if possible have no more than seventeen grades. The number of grades has to fit the organization and its structure, size, culture, and management philosophy—which differ from system to system. Generally, if your library hasn't conducted a study for a while, the possibility of eliminating or combining/collapsing some grades and having fewer grades with wider ranges is possible.

DRAFTING THE STRUCTURE

By now you will have reviewed and analyzed market data, grouped jobs into like clusters, calculated draft pay ranges and range spreads for each new grade, and developed progressions from grade to grade. Figure 9.7 shows the development of the structure incorporating all previous activities to this point. The figure provides the following data:

> *Grade number*—new grade numbers assigned to each cluster
>
> *Title*—the position titles that are included in each salary grade
>
> *Salary range*—the minimum, midpoint, and maximum salary for the range (shown both hourly and annually)
>
> *Range spread*—the percentage spread between minimum and maximum
>
> *Range progression*—the percentage difference between ranges; in this case, at range midpoint

In figure 9.7 the ordering of positions and the associated salary data have been further refined from the structure design (figure 9.4) to allow for a variety of factors, including internal equity, culture, the market, and so on. You will also note that there are two empty or open grades at the beginning of the structure. ABC Library determined that the lowest possible salary it will pay for the positions it currently has is $8.00 an hour for the shelver position. However, what happens if this system decides in the future to add other lower-level positions that may have more responsibility than the shelver but are not at the same level as the grade 7 positions? The structure has been designed with some built-in flexibility that will allow ABC Library to place lower-level jobs on the salary structure in grades 6 and 8 without conducting another study. You'll also notice that the circulation clerk position is placed in grade 9 with the processing clerk. A review of market data showed that this position was actually paid lower in the market; however, for political and internal equity reasons, having the circulation clerk in a lower grade than the processing clerk would not fly in this organization. Remember that after a pay plan is designed, approved, and implemented, you and everyone else in the library will have to live with it. In some instances, it may not be worth sticking strictly to the hierarchy the data show if it goes too far against the grain of your culture or organization structure.

You may also design open or vacant grades higher in the structure. From salary data and current position descriptions, it may be determined that no current positions fit into a particular grade. However, the grade is left in the structure because the increment to move from one grade to the next may be too high of a percentage jump—say, 25 percent or more. In most cases this is too large an increment from one grade to another, except at the highest levels of the system. In the future, your library may have another level of manager or may expand a current position into a larger, more responsible position worthy of a different level of pay. On the other hand, the potential exists for employees to assume they can move into the next grade simply because it is vacant, so employers need to be mindful about communicating the meaning and intent of salary ranges with no positions assigned to them. Just as with job family or career ladder positions, there is no promise of automatic movement from one position to another—the incumbent must have the necessary skills, experience, and educational degrees or certifications; the library must need for the position to be filled; and, hopefully, the employee must have documented outstanding performance in order to move into a new position.

Take your time reviewing this information and designing the ranges. You probably will need several drafts before getting all the pieces to fit appropriately.

Non-benchmark Jobs

Because not all jobs were market-priced during your salary survey, the remaining jobs need to be slotted into the salary scale. This can be done in one of two ways or a combination

Figure 9.7

Sample Public Library Salary Ranges

Grade	Title	Hourly/Annual ($)			% Range Spread	% Minimum Progression
		Minimum	*Midpoint*	*Maximum*		
5	Shelver	8.00 16,640	9.80 20,384	11.60 24,128	45	
6	Vacant	8.75 18,200	10.75 22,360	12.75 26,520	46	9
7	Mailroom Technician ILL Technician	9.25 19,240	11.43 23,764	13.60 28,288	47	6
8	Vacant	10.25 21,320	12.73 26,468	15.20 31,616	48	11
9	Physical Processing Clerk Circulation Clerk	11.00 22,880	13.63 28,340	16.25 33,800	48	7
10	Bookmobile Driver Maintenance Technician Literacy Assistant	12.25 25,480	15.18 31,564	18.10 37,648	48	11
11	Security Guard Circulation Team Leader	13.00 27,040	16.13 33,540	19.25 40,040	48	6
12	Library Associate I Help Desk Technician Youth Services Specialist HR Specialist	14.75 30,680	18.28 38,012	21.80 45,344	48	13
13	Librarian Cataloger Accounting Specialist	16.25 33,800	20.38 42,380	24.50 50,960	51	10
14	Electrician Purchasing Specialist Executive Assistant Physical Processing Supervisor Volunteer Coordinator	17.50 36,400	22.00 45,760	26.50 55,120	51	8
15	Maintenance Supervisor Accountant Circulation Manager	19.00 39,520	23.88 49,660	28.75 59,800	51	9
16	Branch Manager I Main Library Department Manager Senior Engineer Database Programmer	21.00 43,680	26.38 54,860	31.75 66,040	51	11
17	Branch Manager II Technical Services Manager	23.50 48,880	29.75 61,880	36.00 74,880	53	12
18	Branch Manager III IT Manager Facilities Director	26.25 54,600	33.25 69,160	40.25 83,720	53	12
19	Communications Director	28.75 59,800	36.50 75,920	44.25 92,040	54	10
20	Division Director	31.50 65,520	41.00 85,280	50.50 105,040	60	10

of both. First, if you established a hierarchical ordering of positions via the point factor process (chapter 6), you will have a database of points indicating the number of levels and the number of points within each level. Simply slot each job into the appropriate salary grade with other jobs having a similar number of points. For example:

Number of Points	Salary Grade
0–100	1
101–200	2
201–300	3

The second method of slotting is just that: jobs are slotted into the system without point totals, often by the committee. This method is based on the value of each job compared with other jobs in the job family (e.g., if you placed a senior circulation assistant in a salary grade 4, you might slot a circulation supervisor into a salary grade 5 or 6 depending on the verifiable differences between both jobs) and/or the value of the job in relation to other jobs within the same grade (e.g., accounting clerk might be slotted in the same grade as circulation assistant because of the similar level and types of skill, effort, and responsibilities).

While going through the slotting process, remember to keep a differential of 10 to 20 percent between an individual contributor and that job's supervisor or manager. The size of this gap will differ if your organizational structure is flat or hierarchical or has few or many levels of supervision. The nature of the position (circulation supervisor in a branch or department head) and the type of work being performed (highly skilled or technical or more routine in nature) will also determine the differential.

Sample Salary Structures

Examples of salary structures that show the assignment of all library positions to a salary grade are in figures 9.8 and 9.9. Keep in mind that these structures were custom designed to meet the specific needs and internal and external conditions facing the library systems at the time. Each was designed in consideration of the value of certain positions to the system in meeting institutional goals, fiscal constraints, staffing needs, training opportunities, the difficulty attracting and retaining employees, and so forth.

The structure presented in figure 9.8 has at its foundation a large, custom market study and the creation of an internal job-worth hierarchy developed with a whole-job ranking system. Senior management was quite involved in providing input and review at the appropriate times. This structure shows the job titles in alphabetical order that were grouped into each grade and the associated salary range. The structure was presented to this library's board in this simplified format; you could certainly modify the format to suit your needs by adding the midpoint of each range, showing hourly rates, and so forth. In this example, the director is contractual and does not have a salary range; the salary for this position is determined by the board and is not included in the salary structure.

The library in figure 9.8 is financially sound and in a fund-raising, construction, and renovation mode. Included in its constituency are many sophisticated library users and researchers. The system stays up to date with new technology and trains staff appropriately and often. Individuals with MLS degrees, including those with a specialized focus, are highly valued in this system, and they are paid accordingly, as is reflected in the salary structure.

The salary structure for a smaller library (shown in figure 9.9), with four small branches and two storefront locations, was developed using a combination of point factor

Figure 9.8
Salary Structure for a Public Library Using Market Study and Whole-Job Evaluation

Grade 1 / $8.00/hour (flat rate)

Shelver

Grade 2 / $18,075–$25,616

Book seller

Business office cashier

Physical processing assistant

Reserves assistant

Grade 3 / $19,906–$28,210

Adult coordinator assistant

Assistant, business and technology

Assistant, outreach services

Assistant, readers' services

Interlibrary loan assistant

Grade 4 / $19,760–$28,003

Acquisitions clerk

Bookmobile/delivery driver

Branch/central circulation assistant

Catalog clerk

Database assistant

Maintenance technician I

Media clerk

Serials control clerk

Grade 5 / $23,452–$33,235

Library assistant

Mail assistant

Maintenance technician II

Personnel assistant

Reference library assistant

Secretary

Grade 6 / $26,312–$37,289

Community information database editor

PC help desk assistant

PC technician trainee

Security officer

Senior circulation assistant

Grade 7 / $29,968–$42,469

Branch library associate

Materials selection associate

Outreach services library associate

Public services library associate (floater)

Reference library associate

Senior security officer

Grade 8 / $32,318–$45,800

Administrative assistant

African American resource center coordinator

Branch circulation supervisor

Catalog support supervisor

Cataloger

Children's specialist

Communications specialist

Events coordinator

Graphic artist

Interlibrary loan supervisor

Literacy specialist

Media specialist

PC technician

Personnel specialist

Purchasing agent

Grade 9 / $33,844–$47,900

Reference librarian

Carpenter

Catalog librarian

Children's librarian

Grade 10 / $35,844–$50,796

Branch supervising librarian I

Database supervisor

Literacy coordinator

Volunteer coordinator

Grade 11 / $38,200–$54,624

Accountant

Acquisitions supervisor

Computer training librarian

First-class stationary engineer

Genealogy librarian

Government documents librarian

Subject specialist librarian

Web manager

Grade 12 / $42,636–$60,422

Assistant facilities manager

Branch supervising librarian II/III

Managing librarian, outreach services

Supervising librarian, children's services

Supervisor, central circulation

Grade 13 / $46,773–$66,285

Branch supervising librarian III/IV

Managing librarian, readers' services

Managing librarian, reference

Supervising librarian, catalog

Coordinating librarian, young adult and training services

Grade 14 / $51,474–$70,247

Coordinating librarian, adult services

Coordinating librarian, children's services

Facilities manager

Manager, microcomputer and networks

Manager, human resources

Manager, public relations

Grade 15 / $57,585–$81,607

Manager, automation and technology

Manager, central library

Managing librarian, branch services

Grade 16 / $68,350–$90,125

Assistant director

Figure 9.9

Salary Structure for a Small Public Library Using Point Factor and Market Data

Grade and Points	Current Title	Proposed Title	Proposed Salary Range ($)
Grade 1 <500 points	Custodian/Delivery clerk Processing assistant III	Facilities and delivery Technical processor I	15,600–20,280
Grade 2 501–650 points	Library technical assistant I Library assistant I Circulation assistant I	Technical processor I Library assistant I Library assistant I	22,360–32,422
Grade 3 651–825 points	Circulation assistant II	Library assistant II	27,040–41,912
Grade 4 826–1,075 points	Processing assistant III Secretary Branch library assistant IV Library associate I Library associate I, training Library associate I, children's Library associate I, reference/children's Library associate I, bookmobile Branch library associate Library assistant IV	Library associate I Administrative assistant to the library director Library associate I Library associate I Library associate I Library associate I Library associate I Library associate I Library associate I Circulation supervisor	30,576–47,393
Grade 5 1,076–1,400 points	Branch library associate II Library associate II, children's Library associate II Library associate II, reference Library associate II, bookmobile Financial secretary	Library associate II Library associate II Library associate II Library associate II Library associate II Finance and facilities manager	35,880–55,614
Grade 6 1,401–1,800 points	Library associate III, special services Library associate III, borrower services	Library associate III Library associate III	40,560–62,868
Grade 7 1,801–2,250 points	Librarian Branch services librarian	Librarian Librarian	45,240–68,122
Grade 8 2,251+ points	Assistant director	Assistant administrator	58,240–90,272
Grade 9 (Typically contractual and not on salary scale)	Director		70,720–116,688

and market data. In this example you can see that the emphasis is on library assistants (with a high school diploma plus experience) who perform circulation duties and the day-to-day functions of customer service. Branches are managed by library associates (with a bachelor's degree plus experience). The assistant director and library director are the only library personnel who hold MLS degrees. The director of this system supervises approximately thirty-seven employees and is responsible for many of the external and policy-making functions, and the assistant director handles the day-to-day running of the library. Figure 9.9 shows not only the positions grouped into grades and the associated salary ranges but also the point factor results for each grade (shown in a range, e.g., 501–650 points for grade 2). This library decided to streamline its titling system while conducting its compensation study, and the example structure shows the proposed new titles as well.

These structures are only *examples*. Again, your structure must reflect *your* library's needs, structure, culture, financial abilities, and goals.

COSTING THE SALARY STRUCTURE

Undoubtedly, there will be a cost to implement your new salary structure because some employees' pay will fall below the minimum of their new grade. Figure 9.10 shows an example spreadsheet for calculating adjustments.

Note that this spreadsheet is for only a portion of the positions you may have. However, it shows the same layout and process you would use for a much larger system. Individual salary data for each employee involved in the study should be included on the spreadsheet. Often, this information will already be in a spreadsheet format available from your payroll or human resources department. You will then enter the proposed grade and minimum salary for each person. If part-time employees are involved, you will need to include hourly salaries as well because adjustments to these salaries will be made on an hourly versus annual basis. This spreadsheet uses a formula to calculate the annual difference (if any) between the current salary and the proposed minimum of the new salary grade. The initial total cost impact will be the sum of all the increases to minimum necessary for your system. We also find it helpful to calculate the proposed increases as a percentage of payroll; this is a figure that boards of directors often like to see.

Although it does not carry a cost implication, you will also need to be prepared to address how you will handle those employees' salaries that may fall above the range maximum. In addition, moving some employees' salaries to the new range minimum may create a compression problem with other employees whose salaries are close to the minimum but who will not receive an adjustment. Considering an employee's experience, performance history, and capabilities, an adjustment to move that person's salary toward, though not necessarily to, the midpoint (or market rate) may be appropriate. The issues surrounding implementation, salary compression, and salary administration will be discussed in greater detail in the next chapter. The following two sections deal with salaries below and above the range.

Salaries below the Range Minimum

It is quite common that the salaries of some employees will fall below the minimum of the new pay range to which their jobs are assigned. Assuming satisfactory performance, each employee's salary should be adjusted at least to the minimum of the range, immediately if possible or by a targeted or phased-in approach if the fiscal impact is severe. A policy of immediately adjusting the salaries of those employees protects the integrity

Figure 9.10

Sample Spreadsheet for Calculating Adjustments to Minimum of the Salary Range

Title	Current Salary ($)		Proposed Grade	Proposed Minimum ($)		Hourly Difference to Minimum ($)	Annual Difference to Minimum ($)
	Annual	Hourly		Annual	Hourly		
Circulation Clerk	22,880	11.00	2	24,232	11.65	0.65	1,352.00
Circulation Clerk	23,400	11.25	2	24,232	11.65	0.40	832.00
Circulation Clerk	23,920	11.50	2	24,232	11.65	0.15	312.00
Delivery Driver	22,360	10.75	2	24,232	11.65	0.90	1,872.00
Maintenance Technician	22,006	10.58	2	24,232	11.65	1.07	2,225.60
ILL Assistant	31,637	15.21	3	27,040	13.00		0.00
Tech Processing Clerk	25,189	12.11	3	27,040	13.00	0.89	1,851.20
Tech Processing Clerk	28,101	13.51	3	27,040	13.00		0.00
ILL Manager	37,565	18.06	4	30,160	14.50		0.00
Secretary	28,371	13.64	4	30,160	14.50	0.86	1,788.80
Tech Processing Supervisor	37,565	18.06	4	30,160	14.50		0.00
Head, Circulation	34,528	16.60	5	34,320	16.50		
HR Specialist	31,158	14.98	5	34,320	16.50	1.52	3,161.60
Bookmobile Associate	33,738	16.22	6	36,920	17.75	1.53	3,182.40
Programming Associate	34,133	16.41	6	36,920	17.75	1.34	2,787.20
Programming Associate	37,898	18.22	6	36,920	17.75		0.00
Children's Associate	35,838	17.23	6	36,920	17.75	0.52	1,081.60
Reference Associate	36,774	17.68	6	36,920	17.75	0.07	145.60
Branch Manager A	44,637	21.46	7	42,640	20.50		0.00
Branch Manager B	39,458	18.97	7	42,640	20.50	1.53	3,182.40
Branch Manager C	40,851	19.64	7	42,640	20.50	0.86	1,788.80
Branch Manager D	33,509	16.11	7	42,640	20.50	4.39	9,131.20
Children's Librarian	43,139	20.74	7	42,640	20.50		0.00
Head, Maintenance	58,240	28.00	7	42,640	20.50		0.00
Reference Librarian	50,170	24.12	7	42,640	20.50		0.00
Reference Librarian	55,702	26.78	7	42,640	20.50		0.00
Reference Librarian	41,330	19.87	7	42,640	20.50	0.63	1,310.40
Web Developer	62,005	29.81	7	42,640	20.50		0.00
Head, Adult Services	46,883	22.54	8	53,248	25.60	3.06	6,364.80
Head, Children's	51,459	24.74	8	53,248	25.60	0.86	1,788.80
Head, IT	50,107	24.09	8	53,248	25.60	1.51	3,140.80
Head, Tech Processing	60,965	29.31	8	53,248	25.60		0.00
Assistant Director	73,507	35.34	9	72,800	35.00		0.00
Director	100,006	48.08	Ungraded				0.00
Total Current Payroll	1,399,029					Total to Bring to Minimum	$47,299.00
						Increase as a % of Payroll	3.38%

of the new pay system in that all employees' salaries are at least *on* the new pay scale. However, if many employees fall below the minimum, a careful review is required: not only may the costs of adjustments be high but also equity issues between the employees receiving minimum adjustments and other employees who may be near the range minimum but not eligible for an increase may require further analysis and a phasing-in of compression increases (see the next chapter).

If it is not possible to make immediate adjustments to new salary minimums because of the fiscal impact, following are several options you may want to consider:

- At the employee's next review date, or when salary increases (cost-of-living adjustments or step adjustments) are awarded, implement the new increases *or* bring the employee's salary to the new minimum of the salary range, whichever is greater.

- At the employee's anniversary or review date, add the amount of the minimum adjustment to the planned increase.

- Target the positions most significantly below the new range minimum and increase those salaries first, with the others being addressed within the next six to twelve months.

- The option with the highest fiscal impact, and one not often chosen in academia or the public sector, is to immediately adjust the salaries of all employees to the same relationship to midpoint they had before the implementation of the new pay plan. Thus, employees paid at midpoint in the prior pay plan would have their salaries adjusted to the midpoint of the new pay plan. In a step system, the employee at step 2 would be placed at step 2 in the new system. This can be prohibitively expensive but also does not necessarily reflect the data, as you may end up overpaying employees relative to the new pay range.

Salaries above the Range Maximum

When implementing a new pay program, particularly in systems with many long-term employees, it is common to have some salaries that are above the new maximum for the range. In the order of relative cost impact, alternatives to bring the salaries of those employees who are above the maximum into the new range include the following:

- Immediately reduce the employee's salary to the new range maximum (not recommended).

- Freeze any pay adjustments until future *salary range* increases catch up with the employee's salary.

- Red-circle or freeze the employee's salary, but grant lump-sum increases at review time or whenever increases are generally granted (preferably based on performance rather than simply longevity).

- Continue to grant a salary increase, but grant less than the amount of the annual structure adjustment.

- Red-circle or freeze the employee's salary but grant COLA increases only, rather than COLA and merit, step, or other annual increases.

The next chapter will provide valuable information on how to successfully implement, roll out, and communicate to employees the salary structure you have developed.

ten | **Implementation**

This chapter focuses on the implementation of your new compensation plan. Its two main topics are each critical components of implementation: making salary administration decisions and communicating the plan. These are not linear processes; both are activities in which you will be engaged throughout the life of the project and well beyond.

SALARY ADMINISTRATION

Implementation and administration are the next set of decisions needing to be made. This section deals with "what happens next." It covers compression issues and potential solutions; the salary budgeting process for hiring and for moving employees through the salary ranges; step (or automatic) and merit pay systems; cost-of-living adjustments; new-hire salaries; promotions; temporary/acting pay; and policies.

Compression

Salary compression, if not inevitable, is certainly quite likely to come up as an issue during the implementation of a new program. When implementing a new salary structure, one of the key changes in most programs is an increase to range minimums. As the new plan is rolled out, minimum adjustments are typically funded immediately. However, some employees with salaries close to or at the new minimum generally do not receive an automatic adjustment, as their salaries are already within the new pay ranges. Look at the following example to see why compression can have such a financial impact on organizations as well as a psychological and emotional impact on employees.

> The new pay range for librarians in Anytown Public Library has a minimum salary of $36,700.
>
> Librarian A was hired by Anytown last year at the former range minimum for librarians and has received one merit increase. Her current salary is $32,900. She will receive a $3,800 implementation increase to bring her salary to the new range minimum of $36,700.
>
> Librarian B has worked for Anytown Library for four years as a librarian. He has received three annual merit increases, and his current salary is $37,000. He will not receive an increase for study implementation because his current salary is above (though only by $300) the new range minimum.
>
> Librarian C will be hired next month. She is fresh out of library school and has no previous experience. She will be hired at the new range minimum of $36,700.

As you can see from this example, there are many potential problems to deal with. Librarian A is probably quite content with her $3,800 increase, until she realizes that

Librarian C will be making exactly the same salary with one year less of experience. Librarian B is probably quite annoyed to discover (and employees always do discover these things) that Librarian A, with three years less of experience, and Librarian C with *no* experience (!) are now making essentially the same salary as he is. Compression is one of the hardest challenges to address when implementing any changes to your organization's salary structure or classification plan. We find that employees are often not nearly as concerned about their own salaries as they are with how other employees' salaries compare to theirs.

Although there is no magic solution to compression (save for an unlimited implementation budget), one option to alleviate salary compression is to review each employee's salary and position in the new range, making recommendations for an appropriate equity adjustment, if warranted. Equity adjustments may be made in consideration of performance, education, experience, length of time on the job, relation of pay to the market, relation of pay to that of others in the same position, or any combination of these that support your library's values. This may be an expensive alternative, but it may be necessary if you are experiencing turnover and equity is an issue. Experience shows that if you uncover a compression problem during the lead-up to study implementation, employees will rest much easier and anxiety will lessen if you at least acknowledge the problem in project communications. Even if you do not have the funds to begin to rectify this issue, saying that you know a compression problem exists (in certain areas or across the board) and that plans are in place to address this issue over time (the next six, twelve, or eighteen months, preferably) goes a long way in helping employees realize that you are not pushing this issue under the rug.

Another possibility for addressing compression builds on the previous solution — using a phased-in approach to grant salary adjustments due to the implementation of a new structure. Using this method, you would identify the adjustments required and design a plan to bring each identified employee's salary up to the target salary over a predetermined period. The time frame should not exceed two years. Other step or merit increases or equity adjustments should not be withheld during this period or the employee's salary will drop even farther behind the market or the salary of other recent hires.

Figures 10.1 and 10.2 show two examples of matrices we have used in previous projects to help address compression issues. Figure 10.1 uses as a basis the position of the employee's salary in the new range as well as his or her years of experience in the current position. We stress that the years of experience be those in the current position, since the pay range in question relates to the current position. As you can see, employees with the fewest years of experience who are the farthest in the pay range receive the lowest increase (or no increase), while long-term employees at low points in the new pay range receive higher increases.

Figure 10.2 adds a third component — performance — but does not have criteria for years of experience. This example is a bit more streamlined, but the concept is the same: employees farther into the range receive an increase less than those in the first one-third of the salary range. In this option, the difference reflects performance.

Following are tips about using a matrix such as one of these examples. In all cases, the matrix should be applied *after* the employees' salaries are brought into the new pay range. All things being equal, you want to make sure employees are on a level playing field before applying the matrix increases. If you start with old salaries (below minimum), you may not be assessing the employees at the appropriate position in the new range. Also, these figures are purely for illustrative purposes. Your percentages may be smaller or bigger, depending on financial feasibility.

Figure 10.1

Salary-Experience Matrix

This matrix is a method of applying equity adjustments consistently to the salaries of all employees using the same set of criteria. The percentages are suggestions; the matrix may need to be modified in accordance with fiscal considerations.

Note: All increases assume satisfactory performance.

Years of Experience (in position)	Position of Salary in New Range			
	1st quartile (%)	2nd quartile (%)	3rd quartile (%)	4th quartile (%)
1–2	2	1	0.5	0
3–5	3	2	1	0
6–8	5	4	2	0
9–12	6	5	3	1
13+	7	6	4	2

Figure 10.2

Salary-Performance Matrix

Current Position in Range	Performance	
	Satisfactory	*Outstanding*
First 1/3	5%	7%
Second 1/3	3%	5%

Notes:

Finally, it is virtually impossible to place each employee at a separate point on the salary range. If you have steps, for instance, you may think about placing employees with five years of experience at step 5, those with eight years at step 8, and so on. Not only is this cost prohibitive, it often places many employees over range maximum, especially if you only have ten or twelve steps in your system. If your system does not have steps, you have more flexibility in placing salaries within the pay ranges, but it is still appropriate to group employees into categories—that is, one to three years of experience, three to five years of experience, and so on. Look at your employee data to see where natural breaks occur. Do many employees have less than three years of experience and many others have ten or more years? Those may be appropriate breaks for determining how to place employees within the pay range. No matter how much work or analysis you do, however, there will always be one or two vocal employees who complain that because they have four years of experience they should in no way be grouped into a category with employees who only have three years of experience. Since writing the first edition of this book, we have conducted many projects, and compression seems to be a growing issue. In a recent study, many employees received large implementation increases. At a final communications session where we explained project findings and recommendations, one employee who received a $7,500 increase told us that the amount was a "slap in the face" because it did not bring her up to par with her coworkers in the same position. As you can see from this drastic example, even a large implementation budget does not solve all problems. In such cases, communication and education are more important than ever so that employees understand how they are placed in the salary ranges and why their salary is what it is after implementation.

Although it is not wise to ignore these problems, you don't have to recommend and fund compression adjustments. You could raise the salary of employees to the minimum of their new ranges if they fall below without giving other employees an equity adjustment. Employees would then move through the salary range based on performance, across-the-board increases, or step increases. Some public, special, and academic libraries facing fiscal constraints in the implementation of their new pay programs must choose this option, at least for the short term.

The Salary Budgeting Process

Whether you are conducting a compensation study or not, the library's annual budget should include an allocation for salary adjustments for presentation to the board of trustees for approval. This allocation can be segmented into two pools: one for merit increases and the second for other adjustments (such as equity, promotions, within-range adjustment, and so on).

During the fiscal year, the library director or designee (often the human resources director or deputy director) should determine each employee's merit, reclassification, or promotional salary increase. The library director should also annually review and approve recommended changes to the salary ranges as determined through periodic market analysis. We recommend that salary ranges, not just employee's pay, be adjusted each year. This ensures that your range minimums and maximums do not fall behind, even as employees move through pay ranges with step, merit, or other adjustments. Though there is no exact percentage or amount to use in adjusting pay ranges, many libraries, governments, academic institutions, and other public sector organizations often follow (as closely as is financially feasible), the CPI (Consumer Price Index) figure set by the Department of Labor for their particular area. Others follow what their county or city government or academic institution is doing, in order to remain consistent and to make the increases to salary ranges palatable to the local funding body. In any case, keep an eye on the increase to the salary range so that it does not equal or eclipse the salary increase for employees in a given year. For instance, let's use the example of a new library employee, hired in the past year, who is currently at range minimum. If the library increases employee pay by 3.5 percent and also increases the entire range structure by 3.5 percent, that employee, even though he is receiving more income, is at the same place in the pay range—in this case, at range minimum. Even though employees receive additional pay, this is psychologically a difficult concept for them to get past. In addition to pay increases, employees want to feel that they are moving forward or through their pay ranges. In addition, moving pay ranges and employee pay by the same amount can create salary compression; now that employee who has worked for you for one year is at the same place in the pay range as the new candidate you may hire tomorrow—again, a difficult situation for current employees who may feel that they are not being valued.

Hiring and Moving Employees through Their Ranges

All progression methods specify how a person moves from the bottom to the top (minimum to maximum) of the salary range. The major difference among them is the criteria for movement. The major methods are

- automatic increase
- merit increase
- combination of automatic and merit increases

It is important to note that in many organizations, merit increases *are* automatic increases, for all intents and purposes. Though there may be verbiage about increases being based on performance, it is actually often more difficult to *not* receive a merit increase than it is to receive one! Additionally, there are no differentiations in the amount of merit increases between the fully competent performer and the outstanding performer. True merit pay reward systems are discussed in more detail later in this chapter.

Whatever systems are chosen or available, the library does not have to restrict itself to only one progression method. It may use different methods for different jobs or even different methods for a single job when the employee's salary is at different parts (minimum or maximum) of the range.

Step (or Automatic) Pay System (Time-Based)

Many (too many) academic and public libraries divide their entire salary range system into steps. The number of steps is a function of the breadth of the range, the time required to achieve proficiency in the job, whether there are to be steps beyond the market rate, and a determination of the size of a meaningful pay increase.

Step rates facilitate the planning and granting of pay increases by determining the amount of any increase. Of course, it is possible to move a person two steps, but this usually requires a special approval process.

In a time-based system, time in place or time on the job is the basis for the amount and timing of pay increases. An employee is generally hired at or near the minimum of the salary range. Sometimes the practice is extended to hiring slightly within the pay range, perhaps up to step 3, though this varies depending on the number of steps within the grade.

Generally, step increases are granted annually. However, as the employee moves closer to the range maximum, there may be a two- or three-year wait between step increases, or the step increments may be lower than the typical salary increase.

Most libraries with such plans have a structure with many steps (eight to fifteen per salary range; see figure 10.3). They usually move employees to the next step once a year at the beginning of the fiscal year or on the employee's anniversary date. In these situations, longevity on the job (theoretically) leads to higher proficiency, and the library wants to reward continuity of employment.

A major source of variation in automatic plans is the nature of the maximum rate—that is, whether it is the market rate or an above-market rate. Libraries that move only to the market rate tend to have salary ranges with a small number of steps and a short time frame for progression. Libraries that move beyond the market rate are specifically rewarding longevity on the job and tend to spread out the progression to the top of the grade over a longer period. This latter variation is common among both public and academic libraries.

Automatic progression does not have to be totally automatic. A fully automatic progression plan is actually a variation of the single-rate or flat-rate system. If all employees can expect to reach the maximum of the rate range after a given period on the job, the assumption is that the maximum is the real rate for the job. Public organizations use

Figure 10.3

Sample Steps in a Salary Range

Proposed Grade	Steps ($)									
	Minimum 1	2	3	4	5	6	7	8	9	Maximum 10
4	11.14	11.70	12.26	12.81	13.37	13.93	14.49	15.04	15.60	16.16
3	10.61	11.14	11.67	12.20	12.73	13.27	13.80	14.33	14.86	15.39
2	9.80	10.29	10.78	11.27	11.76	12.24	12.73	13.22	13.71	14.20
1	8.54	8.92	9.30	9.68	10.06	10.44	10.82	11.20	11.58	11.96

automatic progression via steps more than their counterparts in private industry, but this is changing. The emphasis on productivity and flexibility in reinventing products, processes, or services is translating itself into a search for ways to make employees more productive and adaptive. Focusing on performance instead of longevity is part of this trend.

Merit Pay or Pay-for-Performance

Simply put, pay-for-performance is a rewards system that links a salary action directly to an employee's performance during the rating period. A pure merit pay system uses an open salary range with only the minimum, midpoint, and maximum defined. Performance is the basis for movement within the range, and there are no adjustments for cost-of-living or other across-the-board increases. This pay-for-performance system requires an integration of performance appraisal with pay determination. The rationale for merit increases is that the movement to proficiency is actually an improvement in performance and should be treated as such. It should be taken into account that employees differ in their rate of improvement to proficiency, and it is higher performance that the organization wants and should reward.

In step systems, most employees (good, excellent, or poor performers) eventually get to the top of the pay range. In a merit pay system, the excellent performer should get there faster than the good performer, and the poor performer would generally not receive any salary increases (or not move toward maximum at all). Figure 10.4 shows a pay-for-performance matrix. Figure 10.5 accounts for another variable: this matrix provides for larger (percentage) increases for employees whose salary is in the lower half of their ranges. The percentage of merit pay decreases as employee salaries move past the market rate (midpoint) for the job. One college was adamant that no employee rated less than outstanding would be awarded a salary increase above midpoint. Needless to say, a rule like that requires careful attention when updating salary ranges to ensure that the ranges are, in fact, in line with the market. It also requires clear and accessible communications to employees so that they fully understand the system and the logic behind it.

As mentioned earlier, many employers, libraries included, claim that they use a merit progression system. However, some studies show that as many as 80 percent of employees are at the top of their rate range, belying the use of a true merit system. The problem is compounded when management mixes automatic increases with merit pay. Granting all employees the same pay increase and announcing it as a merit increase destroys the concept of merit.

Figure 10.4
Typical Merit Increase

Performance Rating	Merit Increase
Outstanding	6%–8%
Fully Competent	4%–6%
Needs Improvement	0

Figure 10.5
Matrix of Salary to Market and to Performance

Evaluation Category	Below Midpoint (%)	At Midpoint (%)	Above Midpoint (%)
1. Results exceeded overall expectations	7.5	5.0	4.0
2. Results fully met basic expectations	5.5	4.0	3.0
3. Results met objectives at a minimal level	3.5	2.5	1.5
4. Performance needs improvement	0	0	0

Employees should have the opportunity to move toward (or above) the midpoint of their salary ranges or market band based on performance contributions to their immediate work group, their department or branch, and the library as a whole. Plans using pay-for-performance move the evaluation mind-set from a once-a-year event and entitlement to a continuous process grounded in performance. These plans effectively redistribute the compensation pie available for salary increases in unequal slices.

With a pay-for-performance system, pay becomes a function of two variables:

> the relationship of existing base pay to market
>
> overall performance as measured through the performance evaluation plan

Distinctions in pay through pay-for-performance plans can be more significant than across-the-board adjustments and yet not exceed the merit budget. The eligibility for a merit adjustment should be clearly linked to the employee's performance contributions during the review period.

You should be aware of a few potential problems with performance-based pay before making your final decision regarding this type of system. First, many library managers do not have experience managing performance, coaching, and providing feedback to employees. Pay-for-performance systems cannot and should not be just dropped into place in a library. To be truly successful, they must be designed and rolled out with sufficient time and input from employees so that employees are not only comfortable with but also supportive of the new system. Second, limited salary budgets do not allow for sufficient differentiation of salary increases for employees performing at different levels. For example, if an employee who "meets expectations" is awarded a merit increase of 3 percent and one who "exceeds expectations" is granted an increase to base pay of 4 percent, the extra 1 percent is generally not sufficient to motivate higher performance.

A third drawback is that ratings are often inflated. Very rarely do they approximate a bell-shaped curve of employee performance: more often than not, 80 percent of the employee population is rated "outstanding" or "superior" in a five-category system. Managers do not like to rate someone "satisfactory" or "competent" because most, according to employee focus groups, view this rating as equivalent to a "C" or "average" rating, and nobody thinks his or her performance is just average. Since the first edition of this book, we have helped with the successful design and implementation of many systems that use pay-for-performance. Two important trends have emerged. The first is a moving away from the "satisfactory" or "average" rating to a more positive and realistic "fully competent" or "fully successful." The performance rating system and the individual levels within it should reflect the reality of a true bell curve—with most employees falling within the "fully competent" or "successful" rating category. A few will need improvement, and a few will be outstanding. And, importantly, the same few will not always be outstanding. These will change from rating period to rating period, depending on the individuals and on the work assigned, and that is as it should be. A rating of "outstanding" or "exceeds expectations" one year does not and should not automatically mean the same rating from that point forward. The rating must be earned each year, based on that year's performance.

The other trend is the emergence of systems with few ratings levels, for instance, three instead of five. Such systems not only allow the distinctions between ratings to be more clearly defined (since there is less gray area between levels 1 and 3 than between levels 1 and 5) but also allow for more clear and significant distinctions between the awards percentages assigned to each rating.

Finally, a mentality of entitlement exists in many libraries. It is an unspoken part of the culture. The expectation is that just about everyone will get an increase each year. This expectation is often supported by managers ("makes it easier to manage") and unions ("to ensure fairness and equity") as well, making it difficult to change. Unless a performance appraisal system is tied consistently to merit pay increases, either the system comes to be seen as arbitrary or supervisors tend to grant the same increase to all employees, thus destroying the performance-reward connection.

Combination of Automatic and Merit Pay

In an encouraging compromise, some libraries have been introducing merit pay in automatic progression systems that have historically focused on longevity. It is also possible to design progressions that try to balance merit and longevity. These salary progressions usually focus on different criteria at different places in the pay range.

The usual combination in these instances is automatic progression to the midpoint—usually the market rate for the job—with salary increases beyond the midpoint only on the basis of merit. The rationale for this combination method is that employees can be expected to reach average proficiency within a certain time on the job; this period matches the automatic movement to the midpoint. However, not all employees are expected to exceed average performance on the job, and salary increases above the midpoint should be based on performance that is above average to substantially above average. If your library does a good job of matching time taken to reach the midpoint with time taken to reach proficiency in each job in the salary range, then salary costs are equalized. If these elements are out of balance, then salary costs are higher or lower than is optimum. This combination approach can take one of three forms:

> The first possibility has a series of steps from minimum to maximum with the market rate as the middle step. The distinguishing feature of this system can be how movement is determined after the midpoint has been reached.

> In a second form there is a series of steps up to the midpoint with an open range from that point on with movement of any percentage possible (within published guidelines) decided by merit.

> A third method is to combine longevity and merit at all points in the range. Under this arrangement all employees receive an automatic step increase, but those with above-average performance receive more, such as a two-step jump. In this situation, it is also suggested that you defer increases for those who are not performing well. A variation of this method, used by a metropolitan library system in the Midwest, is a system in which every employee receives a cost-of-living increase (determined by the library board each year and in consideration of the current economic and financial factors facing the library). This increase is awarded at the beginning of the fiscal year. Then, at the employee's anniversary date, she is awarded a step increase based on her performance rating for the year. If performance is lacking, no step is awarded. This system does not, however, take into account the "above and beyond" performance; no extra step or additional pay is awarded for the highest-level rating.

Automatic-progression methods of moving through salary ranges are simple to administer because they are purely mechanical adjustments made by time in grade. Introducing merit complicates pay decisions by adding a judgment about how well the person is doing the job and developing a way to incorporate this judgment into a salary increase. This makes administration more complex and, if the judgments are perceived as arbitrary or subjective, raises concerns about the equity of the system. The advantage is that a connection is made between performance and reward, which has been found to be worth the trouble and has served as a transition to a true merit system in which no increases are automatic.

There are some potential negative effects of integrating merit pay in automatic plans if the system was designed to be automatic and variations are seen as exceptions and not the rule. Often, lack of appropriate funding may not allow for a significant enough differentiation of increases based on merit. In many systems that allow for either movement ahead (e.g., an extra step) or denial of increases, these alternatives are rarely used—the problems they pose for administration are not perceived by supervisors to be worth the advantages they offer. For example, one client's performance evaluation tool rated employees using a scale of 1 to 7 for a variety of factors. A summary score of up to 700 points could be awarded. Employees who received a rating of 600 and above would be eligible for an additional increase—if their manager wrote a letter justifying the increase. Needless to say, too many employees received a rating of 590. This cumbersome system did little to improve morale and is currently being changed.

Cost-of-Living Adjustments

It is not usually preferable to grant across-the-board cost-of-living adjustments (COLAs), especially in performance-based pay systems. This practice perpetuates the entitlement mentality of receiving increases without any linkage to the library's goals or to an individual's performance. It is more effective to combine any COLA amounts with the total merit pool and allocate it to employees on the basis of their contribution to the library. However, bear in mind that the elimination of COLAs would be a major change in many library systems and that it is not an easy one to make. If politically feasible, it is a doable and rewarding transition. In one library system, the increases are divided so that all employees receive a COLA in July, at the beginning of the new fiscal year, then receive a separate merit-based increase on their anniversary date, if performance is satisfactory. Though the COLA is still in place, moving the merit increase to a different date highlights that the entire annual increase is not automatic and that employees must have successful performance ratings to receive the merit portion.

New-Hire Salaries/Recruitment

Hiring a person at or near the range minimum assumes that the library has been hiring people who just meet the minimum requirements and will move them up in the range as they learn the job. However, the new employee who may have years of library or related experience and who can perform all aspects of the job from his or her date of hire with little on-the-job training will need to be hired at or near the market range (plus or minus the range midpoint). Often libraries do not do this, believing that any new hire needs to be placed at or very near the minimum of the salary range, regardless of experience and background. Libraries have lost excellent applicants because of this policy.

In practice, new hires should be brought into your library anywhere up to the midpoint of the range. When recruiting for difficult-to-hire jobs, consider allowing a new hire to earn an even higher rate of pay. Starting salaries for new hires should be approved and offered based on

- degree of past *relevant* experience
- academic credentials or certifications, if required
- level of competency to perform the job (at an entry, intermediate, or advanced level)

Take care when considering offering a starting salary above midpoint; barring a promotion, there is not likely to be ample room for long-term salary growth for the employee.

The salary offer should also take into consideration any pertinent external market conditions that may be hindering your ability to recruit and retain qualified employees in key positions. Often these are not exclusively management jobs, but those that carry out the core business of any organization (without whom the organization would not be able to satisfy customer requests and demands).

Salary Compression

In addition to limiting room for salary growth for the new employee and creating potential budget problems, offering high starting salaries can create an unintended problem—salary compression—followed by morale issues for incumbents if they learn of the new hire's salary. This is most obvious in the case of new hires brought in at salaries almost the same as or higher than those of employees who have been with a library for some time.

As discussed, compression can also occur during implementation of a new pay program when minimum adjustments are funded immediately but some employees with salaries close to or at the new minimum do not receive an automatic adjustment. It may also occur when first-line supervisors (such as circulation supervisors or branch managers) of employees in nonexempt jobs (such as circulation assistant or library associate) earn overtime pay that narrows the salary gap. Another instance occurs when middle management employees are squeezed between top management and the increases given to lower-level employees. All these examples differ somewhat from the case of new hires in that they involve a hierarchy, and the perception of unfairness is related to an inadequate distance between organizational levels.

Solutions to ongoing compression (not just related to study implementation) depend on what type it is and how serious it appears to management. There are several ways to respond to it. One obvious solution is to ignore it. This is possible if people are moving rapidly and the problem is mostly one of timing. The person feeling the inequity can be told that it will disappear shortly.

A second possible solution is to adjust the internal structure to reflect external realities. Review each employee's salary and position in the pay ranges and make appropriate recommendations for an equity adjustment, if warranted. This may be an expensive but necessary alternative if the organization is experiencing turnover and employee discontent.

Another possibility builds on the previous solution—adopting a phased-in approach to grant salary adjustments to directly address internal compression issues. To implement this solution, identify the total amount of adjustments required and design a plan to bring each identified employee's salary up to the target salary over a predetermined period.

Promotions

A promotion is in order when an employee applies for and receives a higher-level job (internal promotion) or when an employee's job is substantively altered because of significant and substantial changes in the position's primary duties that have evolved over time (job reevaluation or reclassification). In either case, a promotional increase should be authorized of no less than 5 percent and up to 15 to 20 percent of the employee's pay.

Acting Assignment

An acting assignment is generally authorized when an employee is temporarily appointed to a higher-level position—for example, where there is a vacancy that is anticipated to exceed thirty consecutive days. Such appointments may result in a temporary title change and salary adjustment consistent with how other promotions are handled. The amount of the temporary or acting increase, if any, should be based on the following factors:

- level of responsibilities assumed
- assignment of supervisory responsibilities, if applicable
- salary range of the vacant position

The acting pay dollars should not be made a part of the employee's base pay. Rather, a separate check should be issued for the amount of the acting or temporary pay during the approved period. See figure 10.6 for an example of an acting pay policy. This example policy also provides special parameters for acting pay for senior management.

Policies

When you make salary administration decisions, they should be written down and become your policies for salary administration. Begin by including your compensation philosophy and job evaluation method. Add sections on job descriptions, salary range adjustments, and the method by which salaries are adjusted below the minimum of the range and above the maximum of the range. Include guidelines for reclassifications, promotions, demotions, non-base-pay adjustments (incentives) if any, merit pay, and so forth. These salary administration policies should be communicated to employees or, at a minimum, to supervisors.

POSTPROJECT COMMUNICATIONS

The importance of providing ongoing and timely communications to employees throughout the course of the compensation study cannot be overstated. Regardless of the size of your library, it is likely that your new compensation plan will represent a change, perhaps a major change, and a communications plan should be put into place to address it. The goals of your communications plan should include providing

timely, accurate, consistent information

information that relieves anxiety

answers that keep a balance between being overly simplistic and overly technical

an open, honest place for discussion

Following are some possible components of a communications plan. Review them and see what might be appropriate for your library.

senior management overview and feedback

overview for supervisors and employees, facilitated by senior management, the project manager, the review committee, or the consultant and followed by the opportunity for questions and answers

Figure 10.6
Draft Acting Pay Policy

The library establishes temporary or acting pay rates based on new duties performed, usually owing to a long-term absence or vacancy in a job classified in a higher pay grade. All employees are eligible for a temporary pay rate increase. The employee must be qualified (i.e., have the necessary knowledge, skills, abilities, and/or experience) to perform the temporary duties. Department heads will work with human resources (HR) to ensure that the employee is minimally qualified to perform the duties. Minimum qualifications for temporary duties may be different than those required in the position description if not all duties are being performed at the level described in the position description.

A temporary or acting pay rate increase may be authorized when a temporary addition of duties requires an employee to perform *higher-level* duties 50 percent or more of the time for a minimum of thirty (30) days. Departments should not assume that temporary duties are higher-level because they are typically performed by a higher-level position. To receive acting pay, employees who act in a nonsupervisory position must perform most, if not all, of the duties of the position. Employees who act in a supervisory position may not have the opportunity to perform all the duties of the position (e.g., disciplinary actions, performance evaluations, leave request reviews, etc.), but they must satisfactorily perform all the duties that arise. The department head, with HR and library director approval, will determine if the additional duties performed justify a temporary pay rate increase based on the circumstances of each situation. Employees engaged in on-the-job training in a higher position are not eligible for acting pay. In addition, temporary pay rate increases are *not* provided because of an increased volume of the same or a lower level of work.

The pay rate increase will take effect on (or be retroactive to) the first day of the duty if the absence is predetermined and known to be longer than thirty (30) days (e.g., retirement, military leave, extended disability leave) and will equal an increase of 10 percent of the employee's base pay for the first grade beyond the current grade and an additional 5 percent for each grade beyond that. The difference in pay will be provided to the employee performing the acting/temporary duties in the form of a check (not to be added to base pay) included with each regular pay period occurring during the acting assignment. The acting/temporary pay will be discontinued once the position is re-filled by another employee. In addition, employees who use vacation leave will be paid at their regular rate of pay, not the acting rate.

Should the case arise where the length of the absence is not initially known, acting/temporary pay will take effect on the thirty-first (31st) day of the absence and will include retroactive pay to day one of the absence.

Senior Management

In cases where senior management or department head positions are filled in an acting capacity, the salary of the employee performing the acting duties will match the minimum of the pay range of the higher-level job or be increased by 15 percent, whichever is greater. If a job is divided or shared between two employees, the employees will receive one-half the difference between the current salary and the minimum of the acting position or a maximum of 10 percent, whichever is greater.

Special circumstances may warrant exceeding the 15 percent maximum for senior-level positions, as determined and approved by HR and the library director.

discussions of change—why it is necessary and what it means

newsletters

brochures

meetings with staff association/union

meetings with university/college/county/city human resources personnel and officials

letter from library director

frequently asked questions

bulletins (electronic and written)

policies and guidelines

presentations open to all employees such as those conducted at the beginning of the project small-group meetings

web-based tools

To focus your communications plan, you might find it helpful to conduct a force field analysis that will let you know who or what will be the positive and negative forces as you proceed with the implementation of the library's new plan. A force field analysis will reveal all the forces for or against a plan so a decision can be made that takes into account all interests. It helps you plan for or reduce the impact of opposing forces and strengthen or reinforce supporting forces.

Keep in mind that there will be resistance and confusion. Some employees may be unhappy with the outcome of the overall project or process. With the implementation of a compensation program, as with any other program or process involving change, this is normal and to be expected. Your job is to understand that people *will* resist, understand the source of their resistance, and design strategies to minimize it.

On a more positive note, we have found that thorough and clear communications as well as the appropriate level of transparency during and after the project are extraordinarily helpful in ensuring successful implementation and employee satisfaction with the process. Employees may wish their pay were higher, but they will be grateful for the opportunity to hear and ask questions about the findings and recommendations as well as to learn why certain outcomes occurred. If possible, conduct communications at the end of your project with both the library director and human resources manager present to answer questions, showing employees that these recommendations are supported from the top down.

The final chapter of the book addresses current trends in human resources and compensation as well as alternative methods of compensation.

| # Trends

This chapter begins with an updated review of traditional compensation practices used by many libraries and other public organizations and proceeds to a discussion of the challenges that are leading to new compensation and other human resources policies and practices. Trends, including strategies for the recruitment and retention of high-performing employees and alternative methods of compensation that are beginning to gain currency in libraries, higher education, and the public sector, are also reviewed.

As discussed in some detail in previous chapters, traditionally, pay practices in academia and the public sector have focused on

> cost-of-living/across-the-board salary adjustments
>
> automatic step increases
>
> longevity-based pay (salary increases to base pay as a reward for years worked that may extend beyond the maximum of the range)
>
> reclassifications and promotions as the only mechanisms available to provide a decent salary increase or incentive for retention
>
> internal equity
>
> classification studies
>
> market-based equity adjustments (too often limited to moving employees to the minimum of a new salary range)

This chapter focuses on the reasons why some of these common practices are changing as well as on indications of future trends.

THE NEED FOR CHANGE

Public and academic libraries are facing the human resources challenges of their private sector neighbors: keen competition for competent, high-performing employees, and slashed budgets. In the current economy, funding is tighter than ever, as libraries often receive the leftovers from their county or municipality budget, third, fourth, or even farther in line behind public schools, police, EMS, or corrections departments. Libraries also face the same challenges as every other employer in terms of skyrocketing fuel costs for bookmobiles and other library vehicles and never-ending increases in employee health benefit costs. Because of the current economic crisis, many library systems are being forced to reduce operating hours, staff hours, and materials budgets in the face of severe budget cuts and shortfalls. Even as circulation and library visits rise, the same economic conditions causing these increases leave libraries underfunded and understaffed. The response of some library systems to these challenges is to reorganize, leaving the roles or jobs of many employees altered, expanded, enriched, and enlarged. Many companies adjust their compensation philosophies to include pay-for-performance, incentive versus automatic pay increases, and the elimination of costly benefits. The concept of employment for life changes to employment at will. Although aware that change is necessary, library systems, higher education, and many public entities are still finding their way.

In addition to the changes pertaining to funding cuts, five other factors are motivating change. The first factor is the difficulty of attracting, rewarding, and retaining high-performing employees. More and more of the candidates we would like to hire are taking jobs at the local Wal-Mart or McDonald's, and professional librarians are entering the business world as database managers and systems engineers. Even in a flexible labor market, it is imperative to link compensation to recruitment and retention and create a strategic plan and a succession plan to focus on this issue, or the library world will not be able to retain the best and the brightest.

Second, the spectrum of employees is unlike any other and must be recognized and rewarded differently. It is multicultural and multigenerational: retired young seniors are back in the workforce and, just as we have interacted with Gen Xers, we need to learn how to work with—and indeed attract, motivate, and retain—the young members of the Generation Y, or Millennial, workforce. We're also seeing retirees from all walks of life return to work. Many of them, particularly retired law enforcement or military, began their careers as eighteen- or twenty-year-olds, and after twenty or twenty-five years of service, are eligible for a full pension and retirement. Too young at forty-something to retire, they are starting a second career. These employees are working side by side with mentally and physically challenged colleagues. Libraries are truly reflecting the communities and populations they serve.

Third, we're seeing a greater accountability for productivity. Taxpayers want to know how their tax dollars are being spent, students want to know where their tuition is going, and philanthropists want to know what changes are being made by their donations. Organizational outcomes are studied for almost every new program initiative. City and county council members are asking for strategic plans and productivity measures, and academic vice presidents want to know how the library is supporting student and faculty learning, research, and retention. Driving this type of productivity is the goal of many new, custom-designed total compensation programs.

Greater risk-taking by many library leaders to plan and implement major change initiatives is the fourth factor driving change. The library leader of today is more motivated to take risks and even ruffle some feathers to productively and effectively run the organization. Many have to—for survival. There is no choice. Change is coming at us so quickly. Wikis, blogs, and social networking sites are all part of the scene today. Facing each new challenge requires that motivated and competent staff be on board.

Finally, there is the increasing focus on the customer—be it the citizen and taxpayer, a sixth grader with a homework assignment, a PhD student calling on an archivist for obscure research materials, the garden club, freshmen learning online research skills, or a customer yelling, "You can't revoke my card . . . I returned that book six months ago!" A focus on customer service is not only particular to libraries; it's increasingly becoming the norm or the flipside of self-service. Customer service is expected and demanded by the population served by many libraries—even if customers want self-service at times. Library personnel continuously grapple with defining the level of customer service they want (and can afford) to provide, sometimes striving for the Nordstrom model of very high-quality, attentive, personal service. Providing this level of customer service requires that library staff be highly motivated and competent—often a direct correlation to their compensation. We have watched one of our local libraries try to feel out the appropriate level and methods of self-serve—DVDs in this library moved from behind the circulation counter to a self-checkout area to back behind the counter. This same library has introduced a card-scan-driven DVD checkout of the most popular titles in the children's department and is now offering "express books"—the newest and most popular titles featured on shelving right inside the library and available only for seven-day periods, with no holds or reserves. Clearly, it takes a little work and finesse to find the right mix of services for your particular customer base, and these approaches must be continuously reevaluated and updated.

Increasing the level of service provided to customers results in two major organizational design shifts: First, libraries are redesigning bureaucratic structures to be less hierarchical and flatter, with a reduction of management levels. This design change often occurs in conjunction with moving from individualized to team-based problem solving and decision making, empowering individuals and teams to solve problems and make decisions, and broadening job scope. All this needs to be supported, at least in part, by the technology that makes information available and accessible to all library personnel. With information dispersed and available at even the lowest level, there is no need to centralize power and information at the top. Empowered individuals and teams can easily respond to patrons (now customers) clamoring for service. The second shift involves moving from a focus on internal equity of positions to one that rewards performance and pays employees in accordance with the relevant market. This topic has been discussed throughout this book.

Other trends affecting libraries, education institutions, and public and private sector employers alike include increased emphasis on

> green initiatives and buildings
>
> employee health, safety, and security issues, including prevention of identity theft, disaster preparedness plans, e-mail monitoring policies, and the like
>
> ethics issues, including those arising from employee blogs
>
> more emphasis on human capital and talent management, including workforce and succession planning and an emphasis on the importance of organizational culture
>
> staffing management, including increased reliance on technology in recruiting and flexible work arrangements
>
> compensation and benefits practices, including transparency in executive compensation and the impact of an aging workforce
>
> workplace diversity issues, including how demographic shifts affect recruitment efforts[1]

These trends are reflected in the changing and often unarticulated beliefs about compensation shown in figure 11.1. Review these traditional and new beliefs about pay. Where do your beliefs coincide? What are your expectations of employees? What should be the role of middle management in making pay decisions? How should tenure or longevity affect the pay an employee earns? What roles should performance and completion of projects take? By now you probably know a lot and have some strong ideas about these topics, especially if you've drafted a compensation philosophy for your library.

RECRUITMENT AND RETENTION TRENDS

Although a detailed discussion of recruitment and retention trends is beyond the scope of this book, what follows are some approaches to better position your library as an

Figure 11.1
Traditional and Current Compensation Beliefs

Traditional Beliefs	Current Beliefs
We have good relationships with our employees and try to avoid problems.	Every employee is expected to contribute. Our compensation system was designed and is managed as an incentive for employees to use their capabilities to achieve the library's goals.
Compensation is a human resources/county/university function. They manage the program and any salary increases.	Compensation is a management system; human resources/county/university serve as consultants to educate and help managers make pay decisions.
We value consistency in salary management.	Management flexibility is a program goal.
Employees need to know we are paying them fairly, but we do not involve them in redesigning pay programs.	Managers and employees are asked for their input in any pay plan design to ensure that changes are accepted and meet their operational needs.
Pay increases are primarily based on longevity.	Pay increases are primarily based on performance (individual or team) and competence.
We rely on a proven job evaluation system to ensure that pay is equitable.	Pay levels reflect the value and contribution of the employee as dictated by the labor market and individual performance.
Our compensation program is based on internal equity principles.	Our compensation program is aligned with market pay rates.
Our compensation program is consistent with widely used design principles. Many leading employers rely on the same salary management practices.	Our program is based on our needs, our values, and the way our organization is managed. It was designed to fit our library.
Almost all our employees are good people and earn their pay. Salary increases reward them for their continued efforts.	Our managers are expected to identify the best contributors and to make sure their pay reflects those employees' contributions.
Our salary increase budget depends on several factors but primarily on what we can afford.	We rely on variable pay plans to tie rewards to the achievement of our library's goals and to our ability to pay.

Source: Adapted from H. Richer, "Are Public Employers Ready for a New Pay Program?" *Public Personnel Management* 28, 3 (Fall 1999): 323–43.

employer of choice in your community and enhance your ability to attract, motivate, and retain top-flight employees. For the most part, these are nonmonetary strategies that may not cost a cent but will result in change.

Although this book is about compensating employees fairly, research indicates that pay is *not* the primary reason why employees leave jobs. Rather, they leave because of

management's not providing enough freedom or support

current work assignments that are not challenging enough

lack of growth opportunities—the new job is considered a promotion

an opportunity too good (financially) to refuse

the ability to earn more money over their career

quality-of-life issues

It's not all bad news, as there are many innovative methods your library can adopt to retain good employees. The following have proven effective:

Trained, skilled supervisors and managers—Supervisors and managers are held accountable via performance reviews and incentives for keeping good people and are given the tools with which to do so.

Flexible benefits packages—Most libraries offer little choice in benefits options. They seem to be limited to individual, husband/wife, or family health plan coverage and HMO, preferred provider, or traditional insurance. With retirees in the labor force working alongside twenty-two-year-olds who probably will not work in the library for more than three years, it's time to rethink—and to offer—what the *employee* values. We should more accurately align what employees *want* and what they *get*. Beyond a basic level of health-care coverage, must all benefits provided be the same? Should the twenty-year veteran employee with forty-six accrued vacation days earn another twenty this year if she'd rather have sick days that might be counted toward retirement? Or enhanced life insurance? Or an increased contribution to her pension? Maybe the younger employees would prefer a health-care savings account or incentives for promoting the library's green initiatives by taking public transportation or biking to work.

Flexibility in the work environment—To enhance your library's attractiveness as an employer, offer as much flexibility in work scheduling as possible. Library work often allows for part-time jobs, job sharing, and even telecommuting for certain positions. With flexibility prized, your candidate pool will increase, use of sick leave will drop, and productivity will increase.

An environment that is both worker and family friendly—Most of these types of programs are designed to meet the needs of a changing workforce and to support recruitment and retention efforts. However, many employers experience unanticipated benefits: decreased turnover and absenteeism and increased productivity. Examples of programs that are worker and family friendly include well-baby programs, on-site or close-by day care, backup or emergency day care, baby nursing rooms, financial counseling, employee assistance programs, elder-care and child-care referral programs, wellness programs, digital modem lines in the employee's home, and health club memberships.

Opportunities for training and development—Employees want to keep their skills and abilities up to date. It is in your best interest to develop the skills you need internally rather than recruiting the talent. Beyond training, consider providing challenging opportunities for high-potential employees, developing a mentoring program, and structuring opportunities for job enrichment and enlargement. Finally, provide and communicate a policy for tuition reimbursement. The value to both the library and the employee in terms of knowledge, skills, productivity, and loyalty should be obvious, yet education is often the first line item to be cut during a budget crunch. It's time to rethink training and education as an investment instead of an expense.

Support to employees—This should include support through strong leadership and mentoring programs. Quality supervision and leadership are enhancements to retention, as is providing orientation programs that help employees feel welcome. In addition, be conscious and purposeful in getting employees involved in the library and permitting innovation and creativity on the job. Offer and advertise an employee assistance program (EAP) for employees to use as necessary when personal issues come to the forefront.

Competitive compensation—Note that increasing compensation is the last item listed. Although it is important, money is neither the best nor the only way to support retention efforts.

Each of the methods listed is very broad, and each should be evaluated for fit and program design to ensure that it is consistent with your culture and needs. Although these ideas might also sound like givens, some are far more difficult to implement, let alone support, than you'd imagine, especially in a mature organization that is used to the status quo. These methods, however, keep high performers on your staff.

ALTERNATIVE COMPENSATION PLANS

In light of increased financial pressures, organizational redesign, a lagging economy and an extremely competitive labor market, an increasingly diverse workforce, and a desire to focus on the top performers in your workforce, it may be time to consider altering your compensation program or perhaps adding options. Compensation strategies are going beyond market equity and internal fairness. Some recent innovations include cash incentives, noncash incentives, skill- and competency-based pay, gain/success sharing, temporary or supplemental pay, broadbanding, and pay-for-performance plans. Remember, compensation systems are only a tool, but they are a powerful tool to support the behaviors and achievements you want to reward.

Cash Incentives

Incentives are a lump-sum payment or bonus to an employee in recognition of goal achievement. Incentive pay programs help focus employees on the library's goals by rewarding actual contributions toward reaching predefined objectives. The incentive or bonus is typically a one-time payment not added to base salary. Thus, it is also a fiscally responsible way to reward high performers, because the pay raise does not become an annuity. Some believe that incentives are better motivators than pay raises because an employee's pay can be altered (up or down) in different ratings periods, which should happen if pay is to be a motivator of performance.

An incentive program can be designed to include employees at all or a few levels of the library. It should be structured so it is proportionate to the employee's level of responsibility or contribution.

Incentives have become a fairly standard recruitment and retention technique in the private sector. Because of the competitive labor market, incentives are beginning to gain acceptance in the public sector. Incentives can be used effectively in any branch or department to reward individual performance or team or project performance. They can be designed to reward an employee for achieving a project milestone, on project completion, or as a retention device. One potential downside to these types of programs, however, is that while incentives do make use of pay to focus the energies and efforts of employees on desired outcomes, they may also result in creating inequities in total compensation. In library systems where internal equity is a strong value, this may result in a difficult, albeit not impossible, culture change. Incentive programs cannot and should not be designed too quickly—seek input from employees and management about the types of projects or other work that will qualify for a potential incentive. Education and communication about any incentive program are also crucial.

Noncash Incentives

Noncash awards can be given on the spot or as a thank-you for a job well done. They are not expensive and are easy to customize to employee preference. Examples of noncash and low-cash awards that you might offer include

- ice cream sundaes served by project leaders, the library director, or department heads when a team pulls together to complete a project on time
- restaurant gift certificates
- lunch with (and paid for by) the library director or board members
- certificate for a manicure, massage, or haircut
- free parking/metro pass (for a month, quarter, or year, depending on the project/impact)
- spot award—$25 to $50 cash or rewards program gift certificate
- training opportunity
- certificate for casual dress day
- "one day work from home" award
- "afternoon off" award for which the manager does the employee's work and the employee returns to a clean desk and no messages
- award presentation during department meeting/breakfast/luncheon/board meeting/staff day
- small gifts (personalized pens, gourmet coffee sampler, picture frame, gift certificate)
- cookies/donuts/pizza for the department
- movie tickets
- pickup game lunch (Trivial Pursuit, Pictionary, etc.)
- tickets to sporting events
- bowling/shopping party
- free car wash
- 15- to 20-minute seated massage in the office for all project employees
- free health club membership (for a month, quarter, year)
- home cleaning or lawn service voucher for one or more visits
- extra day of vacation

Noncash bonuses are excellent motivators: research indicates that you will receive a three-to-one payback. That is, for each dollar spent on the incentive, the library will receive $3 back in time, energy, or production from the employee. These incentives should be based on what the employee values, not on what you or anyone else might like to have. For example, an opera lover may not appreciate tickets to a rock concert, and a vegetarian is not likely to be motivated by a fancy dinner in a steakhouse.

Skills- or Knowledge-Based Pay

Skills- or knowledge-based pay is a relatively new concept that can be used as an enhancement to a current compensation program or as part of a broadbanded system. This type of system encourages employees to learn as much as they can about their careers by compensating them for learning new skills related to their jobs and the library as a whole. In a skills- or knowledge-based pay plan, the pay of the employee is linked to the number and types of skills the employee is qualified to perform or to the competencies acquired.

Skills-based pay is expensive if used at all levels. It can be cost effective when offset by higher productivity; the need for less staff; and higher-quality, more-productive, and more-flexible employees. It can be designed and implemented for all employees or for certain positions, or to reward skill enrichment of incumbents. If you are having difficulty recruiting employees with certain skills, this type of program can be structured to allow internal recruitment of employees who have a high potential to learn but who may not currently have the minimum qualifications to enter a technical or difficult-to-recruit position. It can also be helpful for retention because as employees learn more and are able to do more, they are often lured away by libraries and other organizations paying higher salaries. For some positions, the market moves much faster than pay plans that reward employees for length of service and merit. For other positions, in today's economy, unfortunately, it is not uncommon to see employees leave for a different position with very little salary increase. Skills-based pay can help shore up your retention plan.

Gain Sharing/Success Sharing

Gain sharing, also known as success sharing, is any organization-wide or unitwide incentive designed to reward all members for improved performance. In these plans, gains, or *measured real dollar savings*, are shared with all employees in the work unit according to a predetermined formula.

Gain-sharing programs focus on improving quality and productivity, increasing the pace of services, reducing costs, and improving employee relations. Employee involvement and information sharing are critical components of gain sharing.

Temporary or Supplemental Pay

Temporary or supplemental pay is compensation that is in addition to, but not part of, base pay and is designated for a specified period for hot skills or special project work. Although an excellent concept, its major shortcomings are twofold: First, it is hard to demarcate and justify the point at which the extra project work goes beyond the employee's regular job. This can be a difficult and disagreeable task if the employee and his or her manager disagree. Second, the add-on to base salary often becomes an expensive, permanent pay raise because management is reluctant to take away salary.

Nonetheless, given the current labor market, temporary pay or a separate salary scale is often given or recommended for positions requiring hot skills. Project pay is rarely as generous as temporary pay for such skills. When ranges are wider and realistically reflect the market, when employees are expected to work flexibly and not stay within the four corners of a narrow job description, working on special projects becomes an important part of many jobs. Having said that, if the assignment the employee is asked to undertake is truly of a higher scope and responsibility level, the employee should be given acting pay while in that role. As mentioned in chapter 10, acting pay should be issued in a separate check that is not attached to the base pay check. One area currently receiving attention through supplemental pay is fluency in a second language.

Broadbanding

Created in the early 1980s by two Navy laboratories, *broadbanding* refers to the combining of existing job classifications and ranges into wider pay bands. Although more commonly adopted in the private sector, several public jurisdictions, parts of the federal government, and a few colleges and libraries have designed their salary structures with much broader salary ranges, or bands, encompassing more diverse jobs with appreciably different pay levels. Although broadbanded ranges in the private sector are often 100 percent or more from minimum to maximum, they are usually quite a bit less in the public sector and in higher education. The ranges are designed this way to encourage lateral transfers instead of promotions, facilitate the ability of employees to enrich and enlarge their jobs without the necessity of a reclassification or promotion, and improve recruitment and retention efforts, especially when competing with the private sector. Broadbanding has also been combined with skills- or knowledge-based pay to provide room for salary growth in a pay range or band after the incumbent has learned the skills required to perform new tasks.

Several universities, libraries, and colleges have customized modified broadbanded systems: pay plans with fewer grades, wider ranges (allowing for recognition without reclassification or promotion), and the ability to develop people via horizontal movement. In one university, a plan for career progression was made available through broader job descriptions that were designed around key activities or results categorized as basic, intermediate, and advanced. In this instance, flexible policies were written and managers were empowered to make pay decisions to move employees through the range based on equity, competency, market, and budget.

As a tool, broadbanding should be implemented to respond to a need. It can be implemented to encompass your entire structure, to support an organization redesign to a multifunctional team-based structure, to use in combination with skills-based pay, or to respond to challenges in recruiting and retaining employees.

There are several drawbacks to broadbanded systems, most of which revolve around the difficulty inherent in their administration. Although jobs are slotted into a target range within the broadband, employees often believe that regardless of their position and its duties, tasks, and responsibilities, they will be eligible to earn up to the maximum of the range. Managers also find these systems difficult to administer because they often are not trained to make these types of pay decisions and find it hard to just say no.

Pay-for-Performance

Although the trend is that some private sector companies are leaving pay-for-performance in favor of incentive pay plans, many public organizations and institutions of higher education are just beginning to take it seriously. While managers in companies are accustomed to holding the accountability that goes with making pay decisions within open ranges or broadbands, most traditional public sector plans are steeped in the traditions of awarding automatic step and cost-of-living or other increases. Although the option of pay-for-performance or merit pay was covered in chapter 10, it bears further discussion, as many library systems are heading in this direction to send the message that performance is important.

Today, more libraries and other public jurisdictions are moving toward performance management by modifying or overhauling their traditional performance evaluation systems. Performance management systems embody the following six key characteristics:

1. Individual performance objectives are tailored to each employee's job.

2. Objectives show appropriate linkage to department or library goals.

3. Interim (not just annual) performance discussions occur between the employee and supervisor.

4. Library-specific competencies are in place that describe the behavioral expectations of all employees.

5. An internal or external customer feedback feature may be included as part of the new performance management system, in addition to a self-evaluation.

6. An employee development plan builds on the employee's career and professional interests.

The linkage (from the results of employee contributions through the performance management plan) to pay is clear and more objectively determined than in traditional compensation systems.

SUCCESSFUL IMPLEMENTATION OF A NEW COMPENSATION SYSTEM

Yes, there is hope if your library wants to move toward a performance-based or other new type of system. Following are some keys to the successful implementation of any new compensation system.

1. Make sure you and your management know why you want to make a change. (Many leaders change their rewards system because their buddy's company/ library did so.) Make sure you clearly understand what you want the new system to accomplish and why. In addition, remember that you want to reinforce and reward behaviors that support your strategic plan. Therefore, design accordingly.

2. Communicate with employees. You cannot overdo communication. Solicit employees' input and involvement, educate them, and keep them informed as progress is made on plan design.

3. Design a performance system that is fair, requires the setting of high-quality short- and long-term goals, is based on objective measures of performance, can provide accurate ratings, and requires meaningful feedback. Note the term *system*, not performance appraisal form. The form is only a small part of an ongoing process that should include coaching, mentoring, regular feedback, development plans, and so forth.

4. Train employees and managers in how to use compensation, classification, and performance systems.

5. Understand that employees must believe that rewards are truly based on their performance and that favoritism, longevity, or other factors will not rule.

6. Know that moving toward performance-based pay or a new compensation system is a culture change that takes time, energy, and effort. It must be seen as a priority of utmost importance: the library director and senior management must spearhead the change. Human resources, other staff members, and even consultants can support the effort, but it must be led by library leadership if it is to be given any life at all.

No longer does the library expect a long-term commitment from employees—such as employment until retirement. Employees work at will and often change jobs as soon as a better offer comes along—one that can use their new skills, will offer training opportunities, and will appreciate and reward their high productivity. Employees will have a shorter career life cycle. An implication for compensation in the library is that many will be entering your library with skills and experience that will warrant their being placed above the minimum of the salary range, and they may, ultimately, earn more money than long-service employees in the same position.

Because of these changes—the requirement for increased productivity, a focus on outcome measures, reductions in funding, the need to do more with less and to do it faster and quicker and cheaper—many libraries have begun to rethink their compensation plans. They are doing so in pursuit of tools that will reward the behaviors, skills, and knowledge that the library needs to reward.

Will human resources and library managers reading this book wholeheartedly adopt these new ways of thinking about compensation? No, not yet anyway. Experience with a variety of clients—even public libraries—indicates that many are seeing a need for reward systems that support goals, mandates, emphasis on outcomes and enhanced customer service, technology changes, and a changed workforce. Both academic and public libraries are beginning to make changes and view some of the new beliefs as a helpful way to manage effectively while recruiting, motivating, and retaining top performers.

Although your library may not yet be ready to implement a new pay program, taking steps, no matter how small, toward implementing new compensation programs can provide important building blocks for future endeavors on a larger scale. In addition, as employees are made aware of these steps to improve and update compensation programs, morale and motivation can increase. These are benefits too significant to overlook.

Keep an open mind and think of some of these new ways of structuring compensation as possibilities—*if* they fit *your* organization—and as something you might want to plan for in the future.

NOTE

1. Adapted from Society for Human Resource Management, *The 2007–2008 Workplace Trends List* (2007), www.shrm.org/research/.

appendix | **Project Work Plan and Time Line**

Step	Week
1. Project Planning and Kickoff	
Meet with project manager and others	1
2. Assessment	
Communications sessions with employees	1
Meet with compensation review committee	2
Interview library director, department heads, trustees, city/county/university/other officials	1–2
Write and send employee communications letter	1–2
Develop communications plan	1–2
3. Develop Compensation Philosophy	3–4
4. Classification/Job Analysis	
Draft job analysis questionnaire	1
Issue job analysis questionnaire	2–3
Copy and sort completed job analysis questionnaires	6
Interview employees	8
5. Classification/Job Evaluation	
Develop job evaluation (point factor) system	4
Hold second meeting with employee committee	6
Form subcommittee to evaluate positions	8–9
Develop database and classification report	9
6. Wage Survey of External Market	
Select organizations to survey	1–2
Draft list of benchmark positions	1–2
Develop survey with brief position descriptions	2
Pilot test survey and contact participants	3
Distribute survey and follow up	4–7
Market price positions using published data	4–7
Compile and analyze salary data	10–12
Prepare participants' report	13–14

Step	*Week*
7. Market Competitiveness Analysis	
Develop summary tables showing market position	10
Prepare assessment of broadbanded and other plans	11
Review	12
8. Salary Structure Design	
Develop new compensation structure plans	13–14
Assess implementation costs, including potential impact of compression	14
Review with compensation review committee	15
9. Draft Report	
Review with library director and others	17
Review with department heads (individually or as a group)	17
10. Analysis of Base Salaries	
Analyze salary adjustments (relationship to minimum, midpoint, and maximum; compression impacts)	18–19
11. Final Report	
Present to library director	20
Present to governing board	21
12. Employee Communications	
Conduct training sessions	to be determined
13. Staff Training	
Provide ongoing education sessions at project completion	to be determined
Develop maintenance procedures	20
14. Develop Administrative Manuals and Maintenance Procedures	to be determined
15. Presentations	
Give other presentations as requested	to be determined
16. Postproject Communication	
Send letter from library director	to be determined
Draft communications plan	18–20

Glossary

Across-the-board increase. Equal pay raises, stated as a flat rate or percentage of salary, given to every eligible (usually satisfactorily performing) employee.

Bonus. Discretionary reward based on individual or team performance.

Broadbanding. Pay strategy that consolidates as many relatively narrow pay grades into fewer broad bands (ranges) with wide salary ranges (typically 50 to 100 percent).

Compensable factors. Attributes selected to provide a basis for comparing job content in a point factor job evaluation system.

Compensation. Cash and noncash provided by the library to an employee for services.

Compensation philosophy. Ensures that a compensation program supports an organization's culture.

Compensation policy. Ensures that a compensation program carries out the compensation strategy while supporting the compensation philosophy.

Compensation strategy. Ensures that a compensation program, consisting of both pay and benefits, supports the library's mission and goals and specifies what programs will be used and how they will be administered.

Competitive pay policy. The strategic decision made by the library regarding which labor markets and organizations to use as comparison groups and how to set pay levels with respect to those groups.

Compression. Pay differentials too small to be considered equitable. The term may apply to differences between the pay of supervisors and subordinates, the pay of experienced and newly hired personnel in the same job, and pay-range midpoints in successive job grades.

Culture. The norms, beliefs, and assumptions adopted by an organization (or that evolve naturally over time in a mature organization) to enable it to adapt to its external environment and to integrate people and units internally. It is strongly influenced by the values of an organization's management team, and it is reflected by actual observed behavioral practices rather than through senior management pronouncements.

Discrimination. Disparate treatment of employees based on factors not related to qualifications, skills, or performance. Under the terms of Title VII of the Civil Rights Act of 1964, the Age Discrimination and Employment Act of 1967 (ADEA), and the Equal Pay Act of 1963 (EPA), discrimination occurs when any compensation decision is made on the basis of a person's age (for those over forty), race, color, national origin, religion, or sex in a way that cannot be justified on the basis of job-relatedness and business necessity.

Employee benefits. Noncash compensation including income protection, health coverage, retirement savings, vacation, and income supplements for employees provided totally or partially by employer payments.

Exempt. Executives, administrators, and professional library employees who are exempt from the overtime provisions of the Fair Labor Standards Act (FLSA).

External equity. A measure of the library's pay structure compared with that of the libraries and other organizations in its labor market. As a fairness criterion, external equity implies that the employer pays wages that correspond to external market rates.

Feedback. Information about the state or outcome of a system that can be used to modify or correct a system's operation. As the term is used with respect to compensation, it relates to the process by which information about the status of performance is given to employees by supervisors: monetary rewards constitute powerful feedback to employees about their performance; nonmonetary feedback (e.g., praise) can provide strong motivation. Performance appraisals are an example of a feedback mechanism.

Flexible benefits. A plan that permits employees to select benefits they want from a menu of choices. Plans commonly include tax-advantaged features and allow employees to select between taxable forms of compensation. Also known as cafeteria plans.

Going rate. Wage rate for any job in the library's labor market.

Hourly rate of pay. The rate of pay per hour for a job being performed. An hourly worker may be assigned to various rated jobs during any pay period and is paid the rate applicable to each job while working on it.

Incentive pay plan. Formula-driven pay plans that are designed to reward the accomplishment of specific results. Awards usually are tied to expected results identified at the beginning of the performance year. The plans can be based on individual or team achievement or project completion. Incentive plans are forward-looking; bonuses are awarded after the fact.

Internal equity. Setting salaries or salary ranges in accordance with each job's relative value to the library.

Job family. A group of jobs with the same nature of work (e.g., librarian) but requiring different levels of skill, effort, or responsibility (e.g., entry-level librarian versus subject specialist).

Job hierarchy. The perceived value of jobs in relationship to each other within an organization. This hierarchy forms the basis for grouping similar jobs together and establishing salary ranges determined by using a point factor or other system.

Job satisfaction. An indication of how well a person likes his or her work, usually determined by a number of factors including pay, promotional opportunities, supervision, coworkers, and the work itself.

Labor market. A place where labor is exchanged for wages. Unique to each library, the labor markets for libraries and other organizations are identified and defined by a combination of geography (i.e., local, regional, national), industry (e.g., libraries), education required and experience, and function or occupation.

Mandated benefits. Noncash compensation elements that employers are required by law to provide to their employees (e.g., Social Security, unemployment, workers' compensation).

Mean. An arithmetic average derived by adding a set of numbers and then dividing the sum by the number of items in the set.

Median. The middle item in a set of hierarchically ordered data points containing an odd number of items or the average of two middle items if there is an even number of data points.

Merit increase. An increase to an employee's base salary based on performance.

Midpoint progression. The percentage difference in wage rates paid between two adjacent grades at the midpoint of the salary range.

Noncash incentives. Incentive payments that are not convertible to cash (e.g., extra vacation time, gift certificates, a reserved parking space, etc.).

Nonexempt employees. Employees subject to the minimum wage and overtime pay provisions of the Fair Labor Standards Act.

Overtime. Under the Fair Labor Standards Act of 1938 (FLSA), nonexempt employees must be paid one-and-a-half times their normal wage rates for all hours worked in excess of 40 in any workweek.

Pay equity. Evaluating and compensating jobs based on their skill, effort, responsibility, and working conditions, not on the people who hold the jobs (men or women). Also known as comparable worth and equal pay for work of equal value; a solution to eliminating wage discrimination and closing the wage gap.

Pay satisfaction. The degree to which an employee perceives little difference in the pay he or she thinks is deserved and the pay actually received. When pay satisfaction is low, the potential for reduced productivity, turnover, grievances, and absenteeism increases.

Rewards system. An organization's choice of cash and noncash motivational elements and the mix of its total compensation program that is used to support its business strategy.

Seniority. Status determined by the length of time an employee has worked for the library; often used as the basis for benefits (e.g., vacation) and longevity pay.

Skills-based pay. A person-based compensation system based on the variety of jobs an employee can perform rather than the specific job that the employee may be doing at a particular time. Pay increases generally are associated with the addition or improvement of the skills of the individual employee as opposed to better performance or seniority within the system.

Step pay plan. Standard progression pay rates established within a pay range. Step increases are generally automatic and a function of satisfactory performance and time in grade.

Total compensation. The reward and recognition package for employees, including all forms of money, benefits, perquisites, and services.

Total remuneration. The sum of the financial and nonfinancial value to the employee of all the elements in the employment package (e.g., salary, incentives, benefits, perquisites, job satisfaction, organizational affiliation, status) and any other intrinsic or extrinsic rewards of the employment exchange that the employee values.

Index

Note: Page numbers in italics refer to entries in the glossary.
Page numbers followed by *f* indicate figures and worksheets.

You may also be interested in

Winning with Library Leadership: This helpful resource offers a road map with strategies and action steps to create shared accountability and responsibility in a customer-focused, fast-paced environment. Library leaders at any level can develop these new skills using the personal leadership assessment in conjunction with the "Leadership Change Cycle" tool to test, practice, and track new behaviors. Current and would-be leaders in public, private, academic, government, or specialized libraries can sharpen leadership skills using this proven toolkit to take action and achieve results.

Human Resources for Results: Expanding the highly effective PLA Results Series, Goodrich and Singer offer a strategic approach to the human resources function in the library. The book focuses on a variety of possible projects and how to staff them, allowing each library to decide where and how to focus their attention. Using this project-based approach, library directors, administrators and human resource managers can identify and motivate the right team members to achieve the library's goals and service priorities as identified in the planning process.

The Quality Library: In an environment of budget cuts and freezes, libraries must keep a tight rein on costs and inefficiencies. Managers, however, often find themselves far enough removed from day-to-day activities in the library that they don't know where inefficiencies, mistakes, and poor customer service may occur. Based on more than 50 years of author expertise in organizational improvement, this book offers a methodology to pinpoint trouble areas and determine areas for improvement that apply directly to the library's goals and missions.

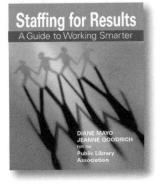

Staffing for Results: Using common public library tasks as the context, this helpful resource walks you through the process of measuring work, identifying best practices, assigning costs to each activity, analyzing resource allocation, and communicating results. With more than 20 customizable figures and workforms, six easy-to-follow chapters provide step-by-step guidance on how to ensure that your library is optimizing its resources. Giving you tools from the experts of PLA to get the job done, this indispensable guide will help you to show and prove results.

Check out these and other great titles at www.alastore.ala.org!